I MUST SAY

Also by Edwin Newman

A Civil Tongue

Strictly Speaking

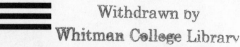
I MUST SAY

...

EDWIN NEWMAN

ON ENGLISH, THE NEWS AND OTHER MATTERS

WARNER BOOKS

A Warner Communications Company

Copyright © 1988 by Edwin Newman

Warner Books, Inc., 666 Fifth Avenue, New York, NY 10103

W A Warner Communications Company

Printed in the United States of America
First printing: November 1988
10 9 8 7 6 5 4 3 2 1

Library of Congress Cataloging-in-Publication Data
Newman, Edwin.
  I must say / Edwin Newman.
    p. cm.
    1. United States—Politics and government—1945– 2. United
  States—Civilization—1970– 3. Newman, Edwin. I. Title.
  E839.5.N43   1988
  973.92—dc19   88-21625
                                                 CIP

ISBN 0-446-51423-3

Book design: H. Roberts

For my wife and daughter

Contents
•••

MUSIC HATHN'T CHARMS

As Only We Can

SECURING THE BLESSINGS OF LIBERTY

ALL OUR OWN WORK

Americans Look Abroad

LOOKING OUTWARD

Live From London

Word Play

Introduction:
Who Let Me In?

It would not be true to say that I became a columnist when I joined King Features Syndicate in 1984. Not quite true. Over the years, I had written hundreds of columns for broadcast on NBC, where most of my working life was spent. For decades, I supplied two or three a week, some for television, most for radio. They were, however, not called columns. The network would not have accepted that term. It preferred "commentary" or "analysis." For a while, the radio pieces were introduced under the name "Emphasis." Sometimes there was no title at all.

Avoidance of the term "column" did not mean that you offered no opinions. It would have been impossible to put forward an analysis of politics or world affairs without your own assessment slipping in. The point was that you could offer assessments; what you were not to do was state your preferences. "Remember," we used to be told before conventions and elections, "NBC has no candidates." We had no causes and no pet issues, either.

This was true even, or especially, when the issue directly affected NBC. On the night of October 10, 1973, Vice President Spiro Agnew (Isn't it amazing that Spiro Agnew was once vice president of the United States?) let go at the network news departments, calling their principal news correspondents "nattering nabobs of negativism," and denouncing the "instant analysis" that followed presidential and other speeches. I had done the lead-in to Agnew and was to close out afterward. As he spoke, instructions from the top level of NBC came to the studio: Get off the air as quickly as possible. There was to be no summary of what Agnew had said, and nothing of what he so vehemently objected to, instant analysis, which is, by the way, nothing more than standard reporting: This is what he said, this is what it appears to mean, these are the possible consequences. As a nattering nabob, there I was with my negativism all but amputated. Soon after, the network, fielding calls from wire services and newspapers, issued a brief statement of its own.

The rules that govern newspaper columnists are different. Columnists are expected to have pet issues and causes, to be free with opinions, to sound off provocatively and stir up controversy, even, in many cases, to be entirely predictable about the side on which they will come down. Most newspaper editors like to know where their columnists fit in. They choose one school or the other—liberal or conservative, Republican or Democrat, thoughtful or volatile, calmly reasonable or angry—or, more often, balance them off.

I like to think that I am not as readily classifiable as some other columnists. I would be uncomfortable if someone were easily able to say, "I know what Newman will write about that." So there isn't any ready or automatic indignation in the pages that follow. There is, I hope, some detachment, accompanied by an attempt to arrive at conclusions rationally.

Of course, columnists all have the same fundamental problem— turning out the required number of pieces, meeting the deadline, finding the subjects to write about. It's tempting to use every subject that occurs to you, so restraint is called for. Not everything is acceptable. As the small print often has it, *Some restrictions apply*. At the time the television networks, because of the spread of AIDS, were deciding whether to carry advertisements for condoms, I thought of offering— with an acknowledgment to Anita "Diamonds Are a Girl's Best Friend" Loos—the slogan "Condoms are a girl's best friend." I thought also of suggesting a title for a popular song that would capture the spirit of the times: "A Condo, a Condom, and You." Cooler heads—more specifically one cooler head, my own—prevailed. I did not play King Leer.

Equally, the phrase "on the Sunni side of the street" has been in my head for years, thanks to an addiction to old songs, including Jimmy McHugh and Dorothy Fields's "On the Sunny Side of the Street." Nothing is funny about the Sunni-Shiite rivalry, however; nothing is funny about the bloodletting in Lebanon or the Iran-Iraq slaughter. Some sense of proportion is required.

Even acceptable ideas do not always work. A brilliant notion hits you: With a suitable nod to Edgar Allan Poe and his poem "The Raven," you will write a column hung on the line "Quoth the Reagan, nevermore." Brilliant, as noted, and with the additional advantage that it demonstrates learning on your part: You are not merely a columnist but an erudite one. So you sit down at your typewriter—and nothing comes out. The idea lies there, limp. Your columns usually run about 600 words. You need another 596.

How, then, are the subjects you write about chosen? You choose subjects that interest you, those that have a proven appeal, those on which you think you write well, and those on which, perhaps arrogantly, you think the nation needs instruction and guidance.

For me, some columns about English were unavoidable. The state of our language meets all the criteria listed above. Indeed, because of my two books on English, *Strictly Speaking* and *A Civil Tongue,* I am fortunate enough to be associated in the minds of many with the cause of preserving American English in reasonable health. (One sunny day, walking along First Avenue in New York, I bumped into Arthur Ashe and his wife. The hands that had held so many tennis trophies now held a baby daughter. "She's eighteen weeks old today," Arthur said, "and so far, her English is excellent.") I am often asked when book three is coming. This, to an extent, is it.

Columns on the news business seemed just as desirable and just as necessary, that is, not merely comments on news events but also some explanation, now and again, of how the news business works. The public is not generally told about that, and the constant use of the term "media" conceals the fact that news is a competitive business. Its habits and usages cannot be understood unless that is understood.

As with those in other lines of work, newspeople usually prefer to keep their workings faintly mysterious. I believe that this is unwise, that we will never get a higher order of popular journalism in the United States unless there is a greater public comprehension of what we do, and what we don't do, and why. So there are columns about that, sprinkled into two subdivisions, one on reporting events in this country, the other reporting from abroad. The reporting from abroad is not an attempt at the day-to-day coverage so many other journalists, often with great skill and courage, supply. It is more nearly an attempt to give the feel and look of a place and of a time, some sense of what they are, and why. Here and there, it amounts almost to travel writing.

There is a related section, Americans Look Abroad. In this section, I have tried to shed some light on issues of foreign policy, sometimes with the advantage of having worked in the countries involved. There was no conscious effort to oppose the conventional wisdom of the moment. Nonetheless, one of the obligations of the columnist is to engage in independent thinking and not to be stampeded. I hope I met the obligation.

So many columns are about British affairs of one kind or another that they have a section of their own. That seems perfectly natural: Britan and the United States do have a "special relationship." More important, Britain and I have a special relationship. My wife is British, and we spend a good deal of time there. In addition, I worked in London from 1949 to 1957, before moving on to Rome and then to Paris. Those were formative years for me as a journalist, and even though they were so long ago, they gave me a lengthy insight into the British. Wherefore the section Live From London.

Most of the book is, of course, about the United States. The United States is a gift to columnists (still more, by the way, to foreign correspondents, who feel freer to write frankly and joshingly about other countries than they do about their own). It is the greatest show on earth, a wonderful, beautiful, inspiring, sometimes heartbreaking country, of astonishing variety and probably unrivaled unpredictability and speed of change, of unrivaled promise, not always realized, and still a place in which to succeed, to get ahead, though there are millions who do not.

Some of these qualities I hope come through in the columns devoted to Americans at home. There is a section devoted to sports, which I find can no longer be taken seriously in their fundamental form—who wins and who loses. They can, in some of their aspects, be taken seriously for what they show about American life. They also offer opportunities for humor.

Music also is set apart. I enjoy many kinds of music, indeed cannot conceive of being without it. Unfortunately, so I believe, the condition of popular music in the United States is deplorable, which led to a column about the Live Aid concerts that I regretted having to write but of which I was rather proud (page 65).

On a few occasions, on New York buses, I have found myself sitting near young people wearing earphones. What they were listening to leaked out. It seemed to be a recording of somebody's tapping of a cymbal. The tapping went on, over and over again, minute after minute, with now a change in volume, and then a slight change in the beat, three taps in a row, perhaps, instead of two. The young people nodded in time and gave every sign of being pleased with what they heard.

The way things are going these days, it is possible that the tapping that so charmed them had been produced mechanically or electronically, that no human being had actually taken a drumstick in hand and produced the sound. What do you suppose the profit margin is?

No less deplorable is the background music everywhere you go. I have sometimes thought that elevators in office buildings should be labeled not only according to the floors they go to but also the kind of music they play. "No Music" stores, restaurants, and airlines might get a surprising amount of business from the grateful not quite dead among us.

The United States, as already noted, is the greatest show on earth. That certainly takes in its government and politics. Something is always boiling up. It is, moreover, never safe to say, about any rumored development, "No, no, that is impossible." Nothing is impossible in the United States. We demonstrate this repeatedly, sometimes on a large scale, as in the Iran-contra affair, sometimes with a kind of pathetic low comedy, as in the marijuana-wrecked nomination of Douglas Ginsburg to the United States Supreme Court.

Any experienced journalist knows something instinctively about stories such as the Iran-contra tangle. That is that they have no foreseeable end. They go on and on and—Watergate was a prime example of this—just when you think you have heard all you are going to, something new and bizarre pops out. The reason is simple: Those involved in these strange schemes get in deeper and deeper; they flail about; in seeking solutions, they become more desperate and their operations become more complex. Follow the path and things become wilder and woollier as you go.

There is another reason, which has to do with the magic powers of the word "intelligence." I have written about this elsewhere (pages 83 and 84), but it is worth saying more than once. The word "intelligence," which in this context is, after all, only another way of saying "information," seems to be thought to give those who gather and analyze it the quality of omniscience, or of second sight. Add the words "covert operations" and all restraints are off. Then too, the more complicated the operation, the more it delights those who run it. It becomes a measure of their intellect and ingenuity. We employ large numbers of people who sit around dreaming up covert things to do. Some of their undertakings no doubt succeed, and as has been pointed out, we normally don't hear anything about those that are successful. The loonier ones are by definition more likely to fail; we hear about them—and write about them—too late.

Back to more mundane matters: Is the columnist of interest himself? How many personal experiences can get by? That's easy to answer when you are moderating a presidential election debate (page 94), not so easy when you are on a private trip and things go, as it seems to you, grossly but amusingly wrong (page 220). There was also the time a television critic on the *Capital Times* in Madison, Wisconsin, reported after interviewing me that my once-black hair was now gray and thinning. Fair enough. Perhaps having hair that is gray and thinning is thought to lend authority to what you write. But should you try to squeeze six hundred rueful words out of it? Maybe it is simply a matter of how accomplished a writer you are.

It isn't much help to say that writing a column is a challenge. It can hardly be otherwise. Do you measure your success by the number of letters you receive, especially letters objecting to what you write and, on occasion, calling you a fool? Do you measure it by the number of papers that carry your stuff? Is there any way you can see whether your ideas have been picked up and whether you have influence? Are you pleased when you find yourself a lone voice, leading inescapably to the conclusion that you are simply more perceptive than the rest?

All of the foregoing have something to be said for them, but in the last analysis, you write for yourself. You write something that you want to be worthy of your own attention, interesting enough to keep you reading. If others find it worth spending time on, so much the better. In other words, King Features or no King Features, contract or no contract, I wrote these columns for myself, and for my wife, whose hand in some of them will be evident to those who know us.

None of this account of a columnist's methods is meant to suggest that those who write columns are among the oppressed of the earth. They do, however, have to be always on the alert for subjects. Your life changes: You are forever asking yourself, "Can I get a column out of that?" Because of this, an essay read in high school came swimming back in memory. It was called "The Old Theme Eye," and although the author's name has slipped away, his point has not. Keep that old theme eye open, was the message. If you are walking along the street and you see a peddler shouting his wares, is there a theme in that? You are awakened in the small hours by a noisy motorcycle. Is there a theme in that? "Noisy motorcycle" is a redundancy. Is there a theme in that?

The term "theme" has gone out of fashion, but a theme is an essay, and a column is an essay. An essay, in turn, is an attempt to say something useful and illuminating on a particular subject. Which is where I started, and where, in the pages that follow, I am going.

I MUST SAY

Americans
at Home

III

In-Flight Movies
III
[2 September 1985]

"Would you mind lowering the shades, please? Other passengers are trying to watch the movie."

For anybody who does much flying and sometimes gets a seat by the window, that may be a request to be dreaded. One complies, of course, most of the time, anyway. Indeed, one usually lowers the shades when the movie is announced and all aboard are asked to do so, so that the issue never arises. Sometimes, however, one rebels, reluctantly, uncomfortably, and feeling selfish about the whole thing. I did, recently, for the first time in a long while and after an hour or so of being cooperative, and a question has nagged at me since: Does the quality of the in-flight movie have anything to do with the case? If it is an obvious piece of junk, does that justify your keeping the shade up, with the light seeping in and the movie less clear for the others? Do you owe it to your fellow passengers to sit in the dark, whatever noisy drivel is being shown and even if—which is often true—most of them are not watching it, either?

Movies nowadays, I readily concede, are not made with me in mind. My interest in watching people beating up one another, shooting one another, stabbing one another, setting fire to one another, and otherwise torturing and mutilating one another, is limited. So is my interest in automobile chases, and in automobiles colliding, automobiles going off roads, into water, off cliffs (usually in majestic slow motion), through walls, through houses, through mud, and over fences and any other obstacles the producers and writers can think of. (By the way, helicopters are beginning to replace automobiles in the chases, but given the rate at which the movies and television have for decades been destroying cars, how did the United States automobile industry ever get into financial trouble? Or were they destroying only imports?)

But even if the movies were to my taste, I might very well mind lowering the shades. If it's a clear day, a marvelous display is going on out there, beyond the shades—mountains, valleys, lakes, rivers, dams, cities, plains, prairies, snowy peaks, deserts, cloud formations, craters, canyons, mists that obscure the passing scene, then pass themselves; quarries, highways, forests, and the farmlands that, their beauty apart, are the food-producing wonder of the world.

All of these, at any rate some of these, are going by outside while,

3

on the screen, actors pummel one another, actresses pummel one another, actors pummel actresses and actresses pummel actors; actresses shrink from rape or possibly commit it; guns blaze; bodies crumble and topple; and screams, groans, gasps, obscenities, and, where appropriate, orgasmic grunts are heard. When all else fails, a new space-age weapon exterminates everyone in sight or recourse is had to the supernatural, so that apparently inexplicable phenomena may be brought in, thereby, so it is believed, heightening the terror.

"Would you mind lowering the shades, please? Other passengers are trying to watch the movie."

Yes, I would. Call it old-fashioned, as graciously argued in a T-shirt message lately spotted: If it's too loud, you're too old. Take it all in all, I'd rather watch it rain.

Wearing Advertising
[15 October 1984]

What is it that makes some people want to wear other people's advertising? Sergio Valente, they proclaim, coming toward you in their Adidases (plural of Adidas), and Yves St. Laurent going away, and Christian Dior, with Jordache and Wrangler signs hugging their bottoms. It isn't easy to know why they do this. They're not being paid for making chunks of their anatomies available in the interests of commerce.

One reason may be that there isn't always a choice. More and more clothes come with the makers' names on them. If you want to wear something by Sergio Valente, you may have to wear Sergio Valente. It is then understood, so you hope, that you haven't accepted whatever may have been shoved across the counter at you. You have good taste and money. That is what these clothes say.

It was eighty-five years ago, in the book *Theory of the Leisure Class,* that the economist Thorstein Veblen came up with his celebrated theory of conspicuous consumption. With respect to clothing, it came, roughly speaking, to this: that the wealthy, giving up comfort, wore clothes and otherwise accoutered themselves—their hair, for example, their nails—to make it plain that they did not have to earn a living as other people did. Indeed, their clothing would have made it impossible for them to do so.

Consumption these days could hardly be more conspicuous, but it doesn't necessarily imply exemption from work. Working clothes carry advertising. Leisure clothes carry advertising. Almost everything carries advertising. Some genius thought about all those surfaces going unused. On the apparently sensible theory that Americans want to be advertised at all the time, clothing manufacturers moved in to fill some of the gaps.

There is a precedent for this. Trucks and automobiles carry their manufacturers' names. So do refrigerators and typewriters, and much more. But these names are placed on the products fairly discreetly. On an automobile, the maker's name occupies a fraction of one percent of the surface. On some pieces of contemporary clothing, it is written in a big round hand and is a claim to glory.

It seems not to have occurred to any of the wearers of the advertising that they ought to be paid. Billboards aren't free. And, after all, the sandwich sign has a well-known place in American history, and the men who walked around in them, unless on a personal crusade involving such signs as "Repent, for the end of the world is nigh," used to be paid something. Not much, no doubt, but something. True, there was not thought to be any social cachet in toting the signs. Now there is this consideration: Is it worth more to you to be wearing Sergio Valente's name than it is worth to Sergio to have you wear it? Who, in short, should pay? Most people evidently think they should.

The kinds of clothes that are popular these days may also have something to do with it. A manufacturer's name could hardly be emblazoned across a suit or a dress now considered conservative and square. But sweatshirts and jeans are a different matter. It used to be thought undignified to wear them to most public places. The manufacturer's name changes that. It makes them a "statement." There may be more statements to come. I fully expect to have someone smile at me one day soon, revealing on his teeth the following: Caps by (here the dentist's name), D.D.S. Similar small signs sticking up out of wigs may also be with us soon.

It is conceivable that people wear advertising out of the same impulse that leads them to put bumper stickers on their cars, and buttons on their lapels, and somebody else's clever, or more or less clever, remarks on their T-shirts. It is a new form of communication. It is a way of identifying yourself and declaring your status, or in the jargon of the day, reaching out. People who are fully clothed seem to feel naked if they're not wearing a slogan.

For myself, I have seen only one message on clothing that I admired. It was on a T-shirt, and it said:
"Ignore previous T-shirt."
Good idea.

Svetlana
[12 November 1984]

Question: Do you think now that it is possible for freedom and communism, or freedom and socialism, to exist together?

Answer: I don't believe that. If I would believe that, I would not leave the Soviet Union. I left it because I found that I couldn't live in that system of life. The main thing is that freedom of the individual, the freedom of the human being, can never go together with communism and socialism.

The question was asked, on September 21, 1969, by Lawrence Spivak on the NBC program *Meet the Press*. The answer was given by Svetlana Alliluyeva, Josef Stalin's daughter, who has now, seventeen years after she left it, and after trying life in the United States and Britain, returned to the Soviet Union. I was the moderator of *Meet the Press* in those days; I remember her asking me, at lunch, what books about the United States she should read; I suggested some history texts. When I mentioned this to another guest, Eugene McCarthy, he suggested de Tocqueville.

With Miss Alliluyeva (her mother's maiden name) back in the Soviet Union, there is some poignancy in looking back at what she said slightly more than fifteen years ago. It was a time of turmoil in the United States, largely because of Vietnam, and in an answer to a question, Miss Alliluyeva said, ". . . people who want to change a democratic system of life for socialism are blind, as blind as were many people in the Soviet Union."

She also said this: "I hope that this life in Russia, which is a nightmare, which goes now for fifty years, has to end sometime, just because the night has to end and morning has to come. That is my only hope." Nonetheless, I had the impression that she was holding back because she did not want to denounce her own father. When asked about "the ultimate judgment of history" on Stalin, she said she had only her own "private, personal opinion and feeling." When the subject came up again, she described Stalin as "an incarnation of communism and the incarnation of communist man and power." Beyond that, she would not go.

Miss Alliluyeva's life included Josef Stalin as her father; her mother's suicide; the deaths of her two brothers; the death of a fiancé; and three marriages and divorces (one of them in this country). She probably could not have found what she was looking for anywhere. In Moscow she will be able to see her two older children and her grandchildren. So it isn't necessarily sad that she has gone back. But her thirteen-year-old daughter, Olga, in addition to coping with being Stalin's granddaughter, will be a transplanted American in Moscow, and the true victim.

One answer Miss Alliluyeva gave is particularly timely now. Lawrence Spivak asked: "Is there anything that the free world can do to help bring freedom to the Russian people?" She replied that the people in the socialist countries "simply don't know how people live outside the socialist countries, as I didn't know much before I came here. They don't know. They don't imagine. If they know more, probably it will help them to realize the truth."

One cannot help wondering what Miss Alliluyeva will tell them, if the Soviet government decides to parade her as someone who returned disillusioned from the West. As it happens, next year marks the fortieth anniversary of Germany's defeat in the Second World War. Stalin will have to be mentioned. His daughter might be useful.

There is another possibility. When Miss Alliluyeva left the Soviet Union seventeen years ago, Prime Minister Aleksei Kosygin called her "morally unstable" and "a sick person." He went on: "We can only pity those who wish to use her for any political aim of discrediting the Soviet Union." Perhaps the men in power will remember that and not use her now.

AFTERTHOUGHT

Those in power in Moscow did not exploit Miss Alliluyeva, though she was quoted from there as saying that she had not had a happy day in the United States. Within eighteen months, she was back in the United States, back in Spring Green, Wisconsin, explaining that she had felt like an exile in her native land. In November 1987, the British Home Office gave her permission to settle in Britain, where she had also briefly lived, and where her daughter was attending school. She then said that she had inquired about working in Britain but had made no formal application, and she was not leaving the United States.

Miss Alliluyeva's plight can probably be summed up in four words: Imagine being Stalin's daughter!

Off They Go
III
[8 April 1985]

Onward, American air cadets, marching as to lunch.

This not inconsiderable operation takes place every day at the Air Force Academy. The cadets form up in squadrons on a great open space called the Courts of Honor. The colors are paraded, the band strikes up, and on they come, advancing on the Mitchell Building, named for General Billy Mitchell, the great advocate of air power between the wars. The day we were there, the sky was blue, only slightly less blue than the cadets' uniforms, the sunshine glinted on the snow-covered Colorado Rockies, and the mind reeled at the thought of the mountains of food it would take to fuel these fit young 4,000, and at the logistics involved.

As they approached the Mitchell Building, each squadron sang out its slogan, and leading the way, two cadets carrying pennant-topped lances dipped them as they went through the open doors. The marching was occasionally ragged, but although visiting officers, American and foreign were present, nobody in authority seemed to mind. In fifteen minutes, barely time enough for a couple of marches—one by Sousa, that military asset no other country has, and the Air Force's own "Off we go into the wild blue yonder"—off they had gone, all 4,000 of them, into the dining hall.

Freshmen at the academy, we were told, are fed "square" meals and are required to eat everything put before them. This had an unforeseen result when the first female cadets were admitted: taking in the same number of calories the men did, many of the women ballooned. Changes had to be made.

The actual eating process we did not see, but it must have gone fast. The cadets looked purposeful as they swung by; besides, food cools quickly at this altitude. These are merely the foothills of the Rampart Range, outside Colorado Springs, but they rise more than 6,000 feet.

That altitude accounts for some dropouts. Not everybody is comfortable with it. Nor is everybody comfortable with what is taught in the four-year course, or with the academy's remoteness, with wild deer roaming around nearby in such numbers that they will soon have to be culled. Freshmen, who draw much of what remains of old-fashioned military school discipline, are hardly allowed out at all during the entire first year.

The dropout rate runs between twenty-five and thirty percent. That sounds wasteful, with the cost of graduating a cadet about $150,000, but it is probably unavoidable. The reality of military life, even in these beautiful surroundings, must come as a shock to many. So, probably, does flying itself. Airsickness knocks out a few.

The flying is compulsory. There is also a compulsory course in philosophy, which turns out to be about the ethics of war and when and whether it is permissible to use military force. The idea is to ensure that when anyone is ordered to drop a bomb, it will be done.

There are also concessions. Male cadets, when wearing open-collar shirts, may hang crosses around their necks. Female cadets may wear gold, silver, and pearl jewelry on fingers, wrists, and ears. They may also put on necklaces, though these must not be visible. Something about psychological value, no doubt, reassuring the women that they are still women without prettying up the uniform.

The cadets were an attractive lot and, as young people preparing to serve their country, perhaps at sizable risk, inspiring. Looking back, one hopes they enjoy their lunches. They deserve to.

The Celebrity Endorsement
[28 May 1985]

Shades of Geraldine Ferraro!

Back in the 1950s, Eleanor Roosevelt was paid $43,000 for a

television commercial in which she smiled for the camera and said, "The new Good Luck margarine really tastes delicious." For those to whom the name is unfamiliar—one must face reality—Mrs. Roosevelt was the widow of Franklin Roosevelt, who was president of the United States from 1933 until 1945. The information about her fee comes from a book called, with notable brevity, *Television*, which is a history of same by Francis Wheen, published in Britain but not yet here. Whether the commercial implied that Mrs. R. served margarine to visiting royalty and other White House guests is not stated; perhaps her mere appearance in connection with Good Luck carried that hint.

Forty-three thousand dollars does not sound like much compared to the $750,000 Geraldine Ferraro is said to have received for endorsing family life on behalf of Pepsi Cola. Still, allowing for the inflation of the last three decades, it wasn't bad. Which raises a question: Why would anyone buy a product because a celebrity endorses it? The public knows, after all, that the celebrities are being paid to say what they do. Nobody is naïve enough to believe that they just happened to be there, raving on about this or that product, when the camera crew, director, lighting man, and set designer chanced to come by.

The public also knows that the celebrities employ agents to get the endorsement contracts for them, and that the celebrities have not compared competing products to determine which is best. They usually don't have any particular expertness about it, anyway.

I myself have occasionally been approached about the possibility of doing commercials, for a carpet, a headache remedy, and a rent-a-car company, among others. Why would anyone buy something I recommended? Because, the generous reply may come, because you have a reputation for reliability. But reliability about what?

Why, then, does the use of the celebrity persist? The explanation is probably fairly complicated. It cannot simply be that someone sees John McEnroe, say, endorse a razor and decides that that is the razor to have. Perhaps people watch the celebrity who does the commercial to see how well he, or she, does it. For the advertiser, that's a start. The message slips in. Then, there may be a liking for, or admiration of, the celebrity. That arouses a friendly feeling toward the product advertised, and since there are some things we must have, that friendly feeling may tip the scales.

Members of the public may also be pleased to think that advertisers go after their business with expensive celebrities. It's flattering, in a way, and those who do the buying may feel that they are conferring a favor on the celebrities by buying the product endorsed. Finally, pick up something associated with a celebrity and you're "in." A tiny bit of fame rubs off on you.

All of that goes into it, and probably more. All the same, the apparent success of endorsement by celebrity remains one of the mysteries of our time. Accept the arguments put forward above. Nod sagely and say, "There's a psychological underpinning." The question remains: If you know that someone is being paid to recommend something, why would you accept that recommendation?

AFTERTHOUGHT

At the time this column ran, I did not know that the book called *Television*, much changed and now written by Michael Winship, would be published in the United States. It was, in early 1988. Not only that, I wrote its foreword, and was the narrator of the PBS series that it accompanied, a series based on the original British version, which went with the original book.

I have also been offered more commercials, including a gasoline.

Have a Good Day
III
[15 July 1985]

Thanks to the fitfully glamorous life I lead, I am occasionally taken here and there by chauffeured limousine. The last time that happened, the driver was a man much impressed by biblical revelation, and who took a dim view of the world's future. Tornadoes, famine, flood, fire, and pestilence, and other grim events, so it seemed to him, were coming together in an unusual way. He didn't quite say that the end of the world was nigh, but he managed a fairly robust implication to that effect. As we arrived at the television studio, he said, with no sense of incongruity, "Have a good day."

Good old "Have a good day." There is no getting away from it. Everybody in sight or hearing is forever wishing you one, including people you don't know, will never see again, and who don't care whether you have a good day or break a leg at the next intersection.

So pervasive is this that even New York City buses, in signs above the windshield, join in the chorus. It would not be surprising to hear that Indian tribes send up smoke signals wishing one another a good day, and that muggers, making off with their loot, say it to their victims.

What seems not to be understood is that the phrase "Good day" itself means "I wish you a good day." It was shortened over the centuries as a matter of convenience. So with "Good morning," "Good afternoon," "Good evening," and "Good night." The "I wish you a" is understood before all of them. The "Have a good day" sayers are simply being long-winded about it.

One can imagine a conversation between vicious criminals:

"Okay, then, so we hijack the truck and leave the driver for dead, and then we dump the stuff on Freddie the Fence. Right?"

"Right. Have a good day."

"Say, I forgot. You remember that cocaine shipment due in next week? It's been held up. Nothing to worry about. Have a good day."

"Yeah, and you. Have a good day."

Bad as the phrase is in person, because you must reply in kind or seem ill-mannered, it is worse on the telephone, especially when you have called to complain about some service or product you paid for but did not receive, and when, having received no satisfaction at all, you are told by the person at the other end to have a good day. You explain that you might if only you could get the toaster or the dry cleaning or the book you ordered. "I understand," says the voice at the other end. "Have a good day."

It is worse still in recorded messages, because it is indiscriminate: "This is Rosanne speaking. I am away just now, but I'd like to know who was calling and why. Just leave your name, telephone number, time and date of calling, and your message, after the tone. Thanks, and have a good day." Rosanne does not know who was calling. It may have been someone who wanted to breathe at her suggestively over the phone, or an extortionist, or somebody using a computerized calling system to conduct a survey (though they are usually heard from when you are in, during a meal), or someone else she devoutly wishes would vanish from the face of the earth. No matter. Have a good day.

There are all kinds of people to whom I do not wish a good day, including whoever it was who got us started saying it. There may be a place here for a citizens' committee to set this right. A Committee of Churlish Americans, perhaps? A Committee of Americans Who Think Only of Themselves? The Limited Goodwill Committee? A Have the Kind of Day You Deserve Committee?

The name doesn't much matter. It's the salutation that counts. Have an appropriate day.

Health and Public Policy
[22 July 1985]

Carl Schramm is director of the Center for Hospital Finance and Management at Johns Hopkins. He is also vice chairman of the commission that reviews the cost of health services for the state of Maryland. He believes that we are in danger of impoverishing ourselves and succeeding generations by indulging in "too much medicine." Gary Strack is chief executive officer of the Orlando Regional Medical Center in Florida, one of the three largest such institutions in the southeastern United States. He believes that if health services continue in the United States as they have been going, they could eat up twenty-five percent of the gross national product.

Schramm and Strack (the interviews were separate) agree about other things. One is that the country is going to have to face the question of how much of our medical resources we want to devote to keeping the dying alive a little longer, rather than spend those resources in other ways. Schramm approaches the question as a medical economist (he is also a lawyer), Strack as a hospital administrator. Neither man enjoys saying this; they regard it as a hard fact that must be dealt with, especially because the technology to prolong life is increasingly available and vastly expensive.

What medicine in the United States is now going through, as Strack sees it, is something like the deregulation of the airlines. The old rules, attitudes, and assumptions are more and more cast aside, competition has burst in, and the result is turmoil. The turmoil is hard on those in the field, says Strack, but in the long run it is necessary and unavoidable.

It appears that great changes lie ahead for American medicine. Smaller hospitals will be under pressure to close. "Hundred-bed hospitals," Strack says, "are doomed." Larger hospitals will be under pressure to merge, to eliminate surplus beds. In Maryland, according to Schramm, 5,300 of 15,000 beds are not needed; Ohio has 9,000 too many; and in New York City, three hospitals now being built "will be dinosaurs as soon as they open." There will be shorter hospital stays, more looking after the sick at home, the use of nursing homes instead of hospitals for the elderly, and more surgery in physicians' offices. All of these are under way now.

Strack points out that thirty-five percent of medical school graduates today are women, and they, he says, are less intent on private practice and more willing to work for a salary. That has its effect on the way medical care is delivered, with more emphasis on group practice, on HMOs, on prepaid plans of all kinds. Schramm points out that medicine has become a way up and a way out for minorities. Again, they are less intent on private practice.

Other prospects: A tighter rein on hospitals and doctors, because of the temptation to them to increase their incomes by using more, and more costly, medical procedures. More payments by patients themselves, because shielding patients from costs, through insurance, offers no incentive to keep expenditures down. That is one reason many corporations are modifying the medical coverage they give their employees, making it less of a blank check.

One large conclusion: Medicine, which will be more often referred to as health care, is going to be a matter of legislation and public policy to a degree not known before. Its place in the national economy, the view that everyone is entitled to proper care, and the necessity of providing that care to those who have no means of their own, make it so.

≡

The Changing Face of Medicine
III
[16 September 1985]

The practice of medicine in the United States—"health care" is a more inclusive and better term for it—is changing before our eyes. Here are some gleanings from recent readings in the field:

There is something like a glut of physicians, and there are no longer enough patients to go around. Competition to get patients is going to be fierce. Physicians may even go where they have not been going, rural America, for example, and hospitals will find it increasingly difficult to survive without a guaranteed "patient pool" to count on. The trend is therefore toward amalgamation, with hospitals, doctors (often in group practice), and health maintenance organizations joining to offer a stream of services ranging from primary care through specialties and hospital care. This goes for nonprofit hospitals as well as the growing number that are out to make money.

Some of the "patient pools" will be supplied by large corporations that have health plans for their employees. These corporations will bargain for the best terms they can get, and they will more and more want to check, through physicians on their own staffs, the medical treatment their employees are advised to have. They may also want those employees to pick up a bigger chunk of the cost themselves.

Many hospitals, especially the smaller ones and those without guaranteed patient pools, will not survive. At the same time, some hospitals will choose to become smaller, because they now have more beds than they need, and their overheads are too high. They may eliminate departments that do not pay for themselves, try to reduce the number of employees per patient, and become known for special expertness in particular fields. If they do manage that last, they will hope to draw patients from outside their immediate areas.

Hospital use probably will continue to decline. More outpatient work will be done, and specialized centers away from hospitals will crop up, diagnostic centers, for example, and "birthing centers" that do nothing but deliver babies. Some of these will result from partnerships between hospitals and physicians, universities, corporations, and other hospitals.

The familiar sources of money—government and philanthropy—will not be as fertile as they used to be. Capital for hospitals will be raised as capital for other ventures is. One result: more for-profit hospitals. Also, a change may come about in the relationship between hospitals and physicians. Hospitals may directly employ considerable numbers of physicians, but even without that, the control that outside doctors have over hospital admissions and treatment will diminish.

There will be more fixed payments, of the kind Medicare is now making, for various services, as a way to keep costs down. Private patient–private doctor "fee for service" treatment will become relatively rare.

Finally—and this is hardly surprising—the pressure to cut costs will continue, pressure from government, corporations, the public. As part of this, attempts will be made to hold down malpractice insurance premiums. Consider: Physicians who pay a premium of $100,000, which is not unheard of, and who put in 2,000 hours a year dealing with patients, are paying $50 an hour for that insurance. If they put in 1,000 hours a year, as some do, they pay $100 an hour. At a guess, the attempts to hold down insurance premiums will not succeed, because the problem lies outside the health field, in the American legal system and in the gigantic damages that some juries hand out.

Can all of this take place without lowering the quality of health care, and while the poor are still being looked after? That is the unanswered question.

===

Living With the Teleprompter
III
[2 January 1986]

Secretary of State George Shultz, who is becoming much more assertive these days—his celebrated remarks on lie detector tests are an example—recently created a small flutter in Washington with a couple of speeches. Not so much because of what he said: speeches by secretaries of state tend, in the nature of things, to be worthy rather than startling or exciting. It was, rather, the way he said it. Instead of reading from a script, as he always had, he used a teleprompter.

This was hardly a revolutionary idea, but it seems that Shultz had not used one until after he consulted his old friend and Princeton roommate, Norman Cook. Norm, after many years of sitting in control rooms and putting programs on the air with style and in good order, had retired as a director for NBC News. Shultz asked him for advice about improving his delivery. Teleprompter use was the result.

The technique is nowadays—no reflection on Shultz—fairly easy to pick up. That was not always the case. In the beginning, when looking down at a script was deemed undesirable, cue cards were employed. They were uncharitably called "idiot cards," and somebody held them just above or just below the camera lens, large cards, perhaps two feet by two, with bits of the script on them, changing them as the reader went along. Somebody else was usually crouched on the floor or the ground, taking away those already read and handing up the next ones. Occasionally, an exceptionally skillful idiot card manipulator could do the job alone.

Next came the prompter. The script would be typed, on a special machine and in large type, on a roll of special paper. This roll was placed below the camera lens and the teleprompter operator kept it moving as you read. For this, you had to learn to read the prompter while somehow casting your eyes up, into the lens. Sometimes, the paper stuck. Don't panic—go to the script in your hand or on the desk in front of you, and wait for a signal from the floor manager to tell you that the prompter is functioning once more.

The next improvement—originated, I believe, by the BBC— was a prompter that used mirrors to get the text over the camera lens. You could read it and appear to be looking right at the viewers, provided you were not so mesmerized by the type rolling in front of you that you developed "prompter stare." How to avoid that? Look down occasionally, pause, speed up here, slow down there, throw in a "well" or a "now" or a shrug not in the script, and make the prompter operator go at your speed, not his or hers. Also, insist that the speech be typed on the prompter roll with paragraphs; otherwise, it all ran together.

Soon, another improvement; no more prompter rolls, but the actual pages of your script appearing over the lens. And another: the electronic prompter, with changes and corrections made almost instantaneously.

One more thing: For politicians—Lyndon Johnson may have been the first—speeches began years ago to be projected onto transparent screens to the left and right of the lectern. The screens were invisible to most watchers, and the speaker appeared to be delivering his remarks from memory. There was one hazard, which was a tendency to read so many, so many, so many words on the left, then so many, so many, so many words on the right, so that it all became predictable and monotonous. Remedy? The same as above: Go at your own speed, and vary it.

Further improvements are no doubt coming along, and teleprompter reading may well become a course in school. An uneasy thought does creep in. Shouldn't public speakers be able to deliver, comfortably and convincingly, a speech from a script? Yes, but it is clearly a dying art.

Martin Luther King
[2 January 1986]

Martin Luther King, Junior, was born on January 15, 1929. The fifty-seventh anniversary of his birth is bringing forth a variety of ceremonies, and newspaper stories and radio and television programs, and not in this country alone. Dr. King was a figure of international stature. The Nobel Peace Prize he was awarded in 1964 did not make him such a figure; it more nearly recognized him as one. Having his birthday as a national holiday is another such ratification.

There is a question that invariably arises when the career of Martin Luther King, Junior, is considered. It is, Why has no one come along to take his place? Why has no other black American approached him in influence? Why has no one turned up as compelling as he was?

There are a number of reasons. One is that great leaders are by definition few and far between. The word "great" itself is used too loosely these days. Greatness is a rare quality, and it is not predictable. It comes as it will. Beyond that, it comes when conditions are right. They were right when Martin Luther King, Junior, burst upon the scene.

The struggle that black Americans waged in the 1950s and 1960s was simpler and starker than the struggle they wage now. The gains they were after then were in the field of civil rights, the right to vote, to use the same shops and restaurants and planes and trains that whites did, not to have to go to the back of the bus. It was the right to be acknowledged as full-fledged citizens and full-fledged human beings. This kind of struggle was peculiarly suited to a religious approach, to exhortation and inspiration, to the display of determination and courage in sitting-in and marching and defying the segregation laws. The concessions demanded were, in a way, easy for whites to grant, for they could be made through large public gestures, through legislation, through manifestations of good intentions and goodwill.

The struggle that has followed is complicated, for it involves jobs, and more. It involves turning the goodwill and the legislation into reality, and doing so when the economy has not always cooperated by expanding. Martin Luther King was only beginning to deal with this second part of the task when he was killed in Memphis in 1968. We cannot know whether his grip on the public imagination would have slipped as the issues and the tactics changed. We do know that there was more than a symbolic significance in his being killed while supporting a strike by black sanitation workers. The front lines had changed.

To say this is to take away nothing of King's extraordinary accomplishments. He was a tremendous speaker and he was brave. He had his vision, or as he liked to say, his dream. He was, in the middle of the twentieth century, a biblical prophet. No wonder no successor has come along.

Like many reporters, I came to know Martin Luther King, Junior. What struck me about him more than anything else was his youth and his smile. The smile was broad, sudden, and infectious. It came seldom, which was to be expected, given the circumstances in which King labored, and it was not used for effect. When the smile did flash on, it was boyish. That was appropriate, for it helped you realize how heavy a burden was being borne by someone so young. Martin Luther King, Junior, was thirty-nine when he was killed. Thirty-nine.

AFTERTHOUGHT

Some might say that King has had a successor in one of his associates, Jesse Jackson. Jackson comes from the same oratorical tradition and he, too, is a clergyman. Yet he is less "civil rights leader," a term virtually synonymous with Martin Luther King, than politician. This is, in part, because of his own personality. It is also because times, and battlefields, change. Jackson recognized the changes and seized the opportunites they offered, opportunities that King, in his life and in his dying, did so much to create.

Alzheimer's
III
[2 January 1986]

A friend of ours has Alzheimer's. He and his wife are old and valued friends; we've known them for more than four decades.

For some years, he has been declining as the disease took its toll. The decline wasn't visible in any physical way: the last few times we saw him, he looked fit and well. Mentally, the effect was sadly evident. He was present, smiling benignly now and then, taking no part in the conversation, neglecting his food until reminded to eat it, occasionally laughing for no apparent reason when spoken to. When I embraced him as we parted, he laughed again.

For some months now, this Air Force veteran and former university professor has been in a center that specializes in the care of victims of Alzheimer's. His wife, a writer, after years of devoted effort, simply could not look after him alone any longer. For all his good nature, it was taxing enough for her during the day; his habit of getting up during the night and wandering around the house provoked more worry and exhaustion than she could bear.

At Christmas, she sent us some details of how he is getting on, and of how she is. With her permission, her letter is reproduced here:

"We are enjoying your cards. _____'s is standing on a shelf above his bed. I said, "You remember your old friend Ed Newman," and he said he did. He is doing so well I have become superstitious. Will not walk under ladders. Will not step on cracks in the sidewalk. He has what he needs: companions, activity, security. And me, of course.

"I am permitted to give him personal care in the morning, so that he is shaved, brushed, combed, washed, and ready for the activity period at nine thirty. About three thirty, I return with fruit and, weather permitting, take him out—to the zoo, to a park or a museum, sometimes to the bank or to shop—getting him back in time to serve his supper tray. Because he now has the 'sundown syndrome' of restlessness, he tends to get up midmeal and gallop about. So I also serve other trays and try to make myself useful while keeping an eye on him.

"At the heart of any nursing home are the aides, and at _____ Health Care Center—the name has been changed, for the better, I think—the aides are trained to work with Alzheimer's people, and they are excellent—firm, kind, and patient. They cannot be expected to care for ＿＿＿ as I do, to floss his teeth, for instance, but they have to do just about everything that would be required of a psychologist and a draft horse.

"The physical plant is unusual in that the wings are small, radiating like the spokes of a wheel around a service core. ＿＿＿'s wing is the smallest, with fifteen residents. It ends in a little sitting room containing a piano and a TV and a number of plastic-cushioned chairs. Just off it, the dining room leads to a large fenced yard with a tree and bushes and interesting corners made by the wings. Last summer, ＿＿＿ spent a lot of time in this yard.

"The wing is locked, but it does not seem at all like a prison. Because they have their own sitting room, the residents become acquainted and communicate—not talking to one another. By now ＿＿ has difficulty forming a sentence. They sit together expressing themselves, and feeling that they are understood.

"＿＿＿ likes the place. He is glad to see me and to go out, but he cheerfully returns and cheerfully sees me go. I tell him I will be back, and he knows I will. Above all, I don't want him to feel abandoned, and he doesn't. Now he can walk around all night, and I can sleep. He can wander away anywhere in the wing and not get lost.

"You said you hoped things were going as well as they can, and this is my lengthy way of saying they are."

Lengthy? Not really. Moving, and instructive. And inspiring.

Spotting the Accent
[27 January 1986]

Although taxi drivers are a varied lot, they have for decades had a particular reputation—rough and ready, but the salt of the earth and full of homely wisdom. The wisdom, so the folklore has it, is delivered with an appropriate accent. In New York, for example, it would be with a dese-and-dose accent—"What's wit' dis Mortimer Gaddafi?"

In London it would be with a cockney flavor—"'E'll come a cropper, sir. Sooner or lyter, 'is kind alwyes do."

This reputation, which is out of date anyway, or wye, is likely to be supplanted soon. For driving a taxi is becoming a refuge and a way up for immigrants. What follows would now be known as merely anecdotal evidence, gathered during a five-day visit to Washington, D.C., but it is persuasive:

January 12—To Woodrow Wilson House for television work for the Foreign Policy Association. Driver from India. Got lost and needed directions, but thoroughly pleasant. Has been driving taxi one year.

January 13—To Kennedy Center. Japanese driver. Spent most of trip grunting in Japanese into his two-way radio. Evidently part of a network of Japanese drivers.

January 13—From Kennedy Center. Driver Iranian. He preferred to say Persian, and on being questioned explained that the language heard on his two-way radio was usually Persian but earlier in our trip had been Ethiopian, because some drivers were Ethiopian.

January 14—To Woodrow Wilson House. Pakistani driver. In country four years.

January 14—To friends in Bethesda, Md. Ethiopian driver. In country six years. English excellent.

January 15—To Woodrow Wilson House. Somali driver. In country four years.

January 16—To National Gallery of Art. Driver from Sierra Leone. Here eight years.

January 16—From National Gallery. Driver from Eritrea. Here five years.

January 16—To National Airport. Driver from Pakistan. Here eighteen years. Studied hotel management in college before dropping out.

This, as noted, is the evidence of only one visit. But earlier trips to Washington led to drivers who were Turks, and some who were Nigerian, and in other cities to Russians, Haitians, Israelis, Rumanians, Sikhs, and a Korean who had mastered English to such an extent that when it was pointed out to him that he was driving in the wrong direction, he replied, "It's no big deal."

As for why so many immigrants drive taxis, one answer is that it's a good job for a student, and many of them are students. They can fix their own hours, and they need not work every day. Some of them are clearly tired of being asked where they came from. One said patronizingly, "A little country you never heard of," which turned out to be Eritrea. Still, eventually all came through. Perhaps they should consider using the device employed in a Las Vegas hotel coffee shop by the female equivalent of a busboy—presumably a busperson. She wore a badge that bore her name and under it: Thailand.

Spotting—or asking about—the driver's accent is a pastime that adds to the piquancy of the trip. I readily concede that most taxi rides are not thought of as piquant. All the same, talking to the driver may be better than counting the potholes and listening to his radio, either the two-way or the other, especially if the latter is tuned to what nowadays passes for popular music. Almost anything short of having your fingernails torn out is better than that.

Concepcion's Demonstration
III
[27 January 1986]

Never let it be said that the United States is not remarkably tolerant and easy-going. Would any other country permit one of the most prominent public places in its capital city to be disfigured in the way that Jackson Square in Washington is?

Jackson Square faces the White House across Pennsylvania Avenue. There is an equestrian statue of Andrew Jackson at its center, and at each of its four corners a statue of a foreigner who helped the thirteen colonies win their independence from the British. One is of Lafayette (the place is also called Lafayette Park); the others of Rochambeau, von Steuben, and Kosciuszko.

It is a pleasant and generally peaceful spot; much was done, beginning in the Kennedy administration, to perk it up and through new buildings and renovation of old ones, restore some of its dignity. It is also a favorite place for public demonstrations, precisely because it is so near the White House, and it now appears to have a permanent and stationary demonstration on its south side. Here, spreading from the Lafayette statue to the middle of the block, is a cluster of signs, perhaps three dozen of them, some ten and fifteen feet high.

They carry such sentiments as these: "A good day to live and let live." "Eliminate all nuclear, chemical, and conventional weapons. Love all people. Share all resources. Open all borders and minds." "Welcome to Peace Park, where creativity counts, and people are free to care." "If genocidal weapons are peacemakers, then Adolf Hitler was a saint." "Money can't buy the talents or time of the moral, sane, and wise." "White House 24 hrs a day anti-nuclear vigil. Since 1981 just two people. Concepcion and Thomas."

Concepcion Picciotto was there the day I stopped by. William Thomas, she said, was away at a law library, preparing for a suit arising from his having been arrested on the site some time earlier. She was sitting, bundled against the cold, on what looked like a folding chair, with her feet propped up on another. I asked where she and Thomas got the money to keep themselves and their display going. "We have no money, only what passersby give us." And the materials from which the signs and their shelter were made? "From garbage. Everything comes from garbage." By this she meant things that others, especially government offices, threw away.

She had, she said, been born in Spain but was a United States citizen who had come here because she believed in this country's ideals. She said that she and Thomas had been harassed and beaten by the Park Police, and that their signs had sometimes been smashed by young people who did not agree with them. She wore one of the world's largest wigs—there is said to be a helmet under it—and she handed me some leaflets that explain what she and Thomas are doing. One explains that she made her first street protest in New York in 1975 because of legal problems that grew out of her divorce.

The presence of Concepcion Picciotto and William Thomas in Lafayette Park results from our legal and constitutional guarantees, and a court ruling against them could still force them out. One of the key legal questions is whether a permanent demonstration is permissible, and involved in that is the question of whether demonstrators may sleep on the demonstration site.

In any case, there the two of them are. Their signs and their vigil disfigure an area with particular meaning for Americans. It is distressing, but maybe, in an odd way, it is also something to be proud of.

AFTERTHOUGHT

Some months after this column appeared, the rules governing demonstrations in Jackson Square were changed. William Thomas and

Concepcion had to go, and their signs with them. The rules that forced them out do not seem unreasonable or oppressive. I wonder what happened to them. Among the homeless, they may now be indistinguishable from all the rest.

Muck in the Mouth
▪▪▪
[27 March 1986]

"It is not macho. It is a disgusting habit with very few benefits."

The Surgeon General of the United States, C. Everett Koop, said that. He was speaking of tobacco chewing. It would be hard to come up with a terser or more accurate description. Perhaps the "with very few benefits" could be dropped, since it is not clear what the benefits are. That would leave "It is not macho. It is a disgusting habit."

Plain talk of this kind is badly needed. Something like 12 million Americans now use smokeless tobacco, that is, snuff and chewing tobacco. Many of them took it up after giving up cigarettes, in the belief that it is safe. Maybe—maybe—it is less damaging than smoking. Maybe. But smokeless tobacco is not safe. Dr. Koop had something to say about that, too: "It is not a safe substitute for smoking cigarettes. It can cause cancer and a number of noncancerous oral conditions and can lead to nicotine addiction and dependence."

The "macho" aspect of using smokeless tobacco may have something to do with the part the frontier played in American life, and of course it particularly appeals to young men. Their view is strengthened when they see athletes using the stuff. Over the years, I have written and broadcast a number of times about the picture presented by tobacco-chewing baseball players, and I don't want to go on excessively about it. But is it not repulsive to see grown men drooling and dribbling tobacco juice, and depositing it over the field? Why, as soon as the camera closes in on someone, batter, fielder, pitcher, base runner, coach, manager, does he feel he has to spit? What do baseball dugouts smell like, with gobs of tobacco-flavored spittle around?

Beyond that, the stuff is dangerous. How can it be otherwise? The trade group the Smokeless Tobacco Council says it has not been shown that smokeless tobacco causes cancer. "We don't know whether it does or whether it doesn't," a council spokesman says. He is entirely within his rights in taking that position, but do we really need proof of a cause-and-effect relationship? Can it help anyone to take this muck into his mouth and into his digestive system? Common sense provides the answer, just as it did before scientific tests and statistical analysis showed what smoking could do.

I once wanted to do a television feature for NBC Sports on spitting in baseball, perhaps using the Handel aria "Where'er You Walk" as a musical background. It would have been necessary to look at and use film controlled by major league baseball, and those in charge there decided not to cooperate. On the whole, they could hardly be blamed. They would have been cooperating in making their own sport look bad, though the feature might have had a useful effect.

I also remember writing a column on the subject some years ago for the New York *Daily News,* which came up with a wonderful title: "Take Two and Spit to Right." That summed up baseball these days very well.

To get back to Dr. Koop, he was asked whether he could estimate the number of deaths caused by smokeless tobacco. He said that he could not, but he thought that among those who use smokeless tobacco, two to three percent develop cancer of the mouth.

Cancer of the mouth. Is that macho?

AFTERTHOUGHT

More recent estimates put the number of those who use smokeless tobacco at 22 million.

The Uses of Charity
▪▪▪
[31 March 1986]

The mail delivery on Good Friday was made up of nine pieces. One was a bill. The other eight were appeals for charity.

Eight appeals for charity in a day—that set a record. Maybe the organizations that sent them timed them for Easter, hoping that the general benevolence loose at that season would help to bring forth contributions. More likely, it was coincidence. After all, days when four or five or six appeals come in are not unusual. A day that brings in eight is, like tacking another half inch onto the pole vault record, different only in degree, not in kind.

There is, however, something self-defeating about that many appeals arriving together. How is anyone to choose among them? The organizations are asking for money for American Indian children; Amerasian children in Thailand, Taiwan, Korea, Okinawa, and the Philippines; abused and needy and homeless children in the United States; handicapped children and adults in the United States; paralyzed American veterans; cancer research and education, and help for cancer victims; medical care and education in poor parts of the world, including some in this country; and helping the hungry and malnourished in various nations to support themselves and grow their own food. How do you decide which needs are the more pressing, and where your money would be most usefully spent?

All of these are worthy causes. The danger, as the torrent of appeals comes through the slot, is that the person at whom they are directed will become annoyed and resistant. The great majority are not even opened; they are simply tossed away. When contributions are made, the chances are that the letters from the charities are not read; instead, a check is put into the return envelope, and the envelope is posted, and that is that.

The reason is that appeals for charity have become part of our lives much as radio and television commercials have. We simply do not hear most commercials. There are those we turn down and even switch off. We may go so far as to avoid buying products whose commercials we find exceptionally obnoxious. In the same way, most of us fix on a number of charities, often for reasons accidental or personal, and give money to them. The rest we ignore. As more and more appeals flow in, we may even come to resent them.

No doubt this sort of reaction is figured in the cost of running a charity. Probably any practiced administrator can tell within a percentage point or two what response a particular mailing will get. Charity has, inevitably, become another field for the professional practitioner, for the expert in the "personalized" letter, in dramatic presentation, and in touching the heart, using, perhaps, a poverty-stricken family in Ecuador, a burn victim in Jamaica, a child with a crippling disease in Swaziland. This is not to say that these pathetic people do not exist, but rather that their sorrows and travail have become part of the system.

Could that system be improved? Unified money-raising drives help, although they seem not to reduce the number of appeals by mail, and so do mergers of charities where they happen to fit together. But at best, the competition for the charity dollar will be costly. The waste involved in sending out appeals that are not even considered must be tremendous. It would be interesting to know whether, as the competition for the charity dollar intensifies, the overhead expenses go up, too. For experience suggests that the number and variety of appeals are increasing all the time.

Graffiti and "Boxes"
▪▪▪
[11 April 1986]

En route, not long ago, to New York's LaGuardia Airport, the taxi went past the building of an organization called The Lighthouse. The Lighthouse works with and for the blind. It helps the blind. That is its only purpose. Somebody had sprayed white paint on one of its doors. The writing, if there was intended to be any, was illegible. The paint had dripped and run. It disfigured the door. That was all.

It is possible that the person who put the paint there did not know that the building housed a charity that helped the blind. Or perhaps he, or she, did. It doesn't matter either way. The message of the paint was clear. It was that the march of technology makes things easier for those who devote themselves to annoying the rest of us. It is a price we pay for the benefits technology brings.

The painting spray-gun demonstrates that. It is invaluable for some purposes, but in the hands of people who think that they are being clever and defiant, it is used to make our surroundings ugly.

There is also the car radio, intended to be a source of pleasure or companionship or information to those who drive. To any number of people, almost all of them young, being in an automobile without having a radio on is inconceivable. More than that, they believe that they are entitled to drive through the public streets with the radio tuned full blast to the din that now passes for popular music and with the car windows wide open. A charitable interpretation would be that they believe they are doing this for the sake of those outside, to brighten the day of those benighted souls who have not made their own arrangements to have their hearing impaired. More likely, they believe that this is their right, like the right to spray graffiti.

A couple of weeks ago, on a busy corner in Manhattan, a young man stood near a bank of telephones. Next to him, on the sidewalk, stood his "box," his portable radio and tape player. It was emitting unmelodious shouting and must have been playing at maximum volume. The young man may have been trying to provoke someone who might have wanted to use a telephone and would have been unable to hear. On the other hand, he may not have cared. Using his "box" anywhere he chose was his right.

There is, it is true, more here than meets the eye. Especially when blacks have the "boxes," there appears to be an element of defiance, of striking back at the establishment that oppressed them for so long, of saying, "If you don't like it, what are you going to do about it?"

There is also this: We have reared a generation, and by now more than a generation, of people to many of whom quiet is unimaginable and unwelcome, to whom privacy is a concept that does not exist, to whom simple courtesy is laughable, to whom brutal and violent sounds are music. The march of technology makes it easier all the time for those people to indulge themselves at the expense of the rest of us, and further technological developments will almost surely make things worse. We are, moreover, rich enough so that people who might be called poor or underprivileged think nothing of squandering what they do have on anonymously defacing the property of others or filling public places with noise.

What is to be done about this? There doesn't seem to be much that can be done. The police have enough on their hands. They can't be called out against "boxes" and blaring radios.

Still, we can at least recognize the problem and talk about it. It's a beginning.

The Johnson Settlement
III
[9 June 1986]

J. Seward Johnson was a Johnson & Johnson Johnson. Last week, after a long legal battle, his estate was shared out. There was one thing wrong with the shareout: the public got nothing. Taxes, yes, but those were due anyway. There should have been more.

Johnson died in 1983 at the age of eighty-seven. He left something like $500,000,000 to his wife. The six children of his first two marriages sued to overturn the will on the ground that he was incompetent when it was drawn up and under improper influence from his wife. That was what led ultimately to the out-of-court settlement last week.

What has this to do with the public, and why should the public get a chunk of the money? Because the family dispute brought on one of those marathon trials that figure so often in the American legal system and was conducted at the expense of the people of New York State. The trial began last February after almost two years of legal comings and goings, such as the taking of depositions. By the time it was over, seventy-five witnesses had been called; the number of pages of testimony reached fifteen thousand.

The cost of the trial is hard to estimate, but nothing comes cheap in the American legal process, except perhaps the jurors, who served for twelve dollars a day for the first two weeks, and twenty-four dollars a day after that. The affair did provide a certain amount of amusement and titillation, in the way a television soap opera does. The Johnsons brought that on themselves, however. Why should the people of New York State pay for these goings-on?

There is of course an answer. It is in the public interest that justice be done and be seen to be done. The rich have as much right to justice and to their day in court as anyone else. Yet consider: Mrs. Johnson, whom the newspapers delight in referring to as a Polish immigrant hired as a chambermaid by Johnson's second wife (she went from chambermaid to mistress of the household days after Johnson divorced his second wife) appears to be left with about $340,000,000. The Johnson children, in addition to the trusts their father set up for them decades ago, get $42,400,000 among them. An oceanographic foundation Johnson helped to found is to get $20,000,000. The fee for the children's lawyers is still to be fixed but will surely be in the millions. A lawyer who was to be executor of the will, which was drawn up six weeks before Johnson died, came out less well. She was to get an annual trustee's fee for as long as Mrs. Johnson, who is now forty-nine, lived. Instead, she is being limited to $1,800,000.

With all those zeros floating around, it does seem that the people of New York State, who pay for the legal system in which this exercise took place, might have been cut in for something more than the $600 fee paid for probating a will of this size, $70 for the filing of a formal objection during the probate proceedings, and $140 more in assorted legal charges. True, the court system has to be there whether the Johnsons use it or not; overhead expenses do continue; and citizens have a duty to serve on juries.

All the same, if there was to be a settlement out of court, why could it not have come sooner? And if ever there were people who could afford to pay for the workings of the legal system, these were such people. The will may have been the largest ever probated in New York State.

It happens that the law does not now provide for an award of costs to the state. Maybe the law should be changed. Or maybe the state could claim a brokerage fee. It did, when all is said and done, broker a settlement.

Your Friendly Bacteria
III
[5 July 1986]

No. You won't have pet bacteria. Dogs, cats, budgerigars, and the rest are safe. You may, however, come to like bacteria very much, and be grateful to them. For the possibility exists that bacteria that live in temperatures of 250 degrees centigrade in deep oceanic vents may be scientifically led to "eat" the kind of industrial waste that causes acid rain. The same bacteria may also be led to ferment some of the primitive living beings of the sea, such as algae, and turn them into fuel. Imagine how we would feel about bacteria then.

This information was picked up in preparation for a symposium on the future of the world's oceans, put on by the University of Rhode Island at its Narragansett Bay campus, with help from the *Providence*

Journal. There were seven experts, from the United States, Britain, and Japan. I was the moderator. Here are some other things I learned:

A higher standard of living, with more consumption, does not necessarily mean more pollution. Some of the underdeveloped countries pollute the ocean more, because they mistreat their agricultural land and let the topsoil run off.

Most pollution of the oceans comes from the land, and it is logical to expect more of it, if only because of the way the world population is growing.

Talk about "floating cities" where some of that growing population might live seems to have faded. If you talk instead about "man-made islands," for airports, perhaps, or for hazardous activities better kept off land, or for "ranches" where fish may be scientifically induced to grow larger and be more plentiful, there may be something in it.

When we speak about sea power, we ought to count in a country's mastery of marine science and technology. The Soviet Union is putting a great deal of time and money into them. China is moving fast, too. The United States is still ahead.

The condition of the United States merchant marine is pathetic. It has shrunk by more than half in the last twenty years. It isn't quite as bad as it looks, however, because so many American-owned ships operate under flags of convenience.

New technology, including satellites, makes it possible to monitor seaborne activity more closely than ever before, illegal fishing, perhaps, or the illegal dumping of waste. The question is, how can the monitoring be turned into regulation?

The oceans are the greatest storers of heat from the sun, heat that might be turned into thermal power. Whether doing that would be economic would depend on what other sources of power existed, and what they cost. Right now, oil is so cheap that the search for alternative sources of power is flagging. Some of the experts thought it would take another oil shortage—which they foresee—to change that.

Wave power has potential, too. By one estimate, the waves that hit the coasts of the United Kingdom could yield five times the electricity Britain currently uses. The question—again—is comparative costs. That applies also to mining the seabed for minerals. Is what is down there—the manganese nodules are much talked about—worth the trouble and expense involved in getting it? The answer depends on what else is available and for how much, which is also the case with increasing the food yield from the sea. We could eat more squid and eat the crustaceans known as krill. Some whales eat krill. Whether we would, or would have to, remains to be seen.

Can the oceans take radioactive waste? They already are taking it, so called low-level waste but not the really hot stuff. They may be able to take that, too, properly sealed in and buried in areas beneath the seabed that are the most stable, geologically, in the world.

The author of the paper used to define the symposium's issues, Miranda Wecker, wrote this: "For the first time in human history, humankind must address the possibility that people are significantly altering the major ecological systems upon which all life depends. At the same time, human welfare demands that we use the available resources." That sums it up. That is also where, a few decades from now, your favorite bacteria may come in.

Surrogate Foolishness
[3 April 1987]

It's been a good week so far. There has been a leveling off in news reports about Baby M and about surrogate motherhood. After last week's wallowing in the story by the press, radio, and television, that comes as a relief.

The wallowing and the excessive coverage were not Baby M's fault. For her, it is possible to feel nothing but pity and to hope that she will have something approaching a normal childhood. Which of course is the point. How can she have something approaching a normal life? How can those who enter into arrangements like the one that produced her—a contract under which the surrogate was paid $10,000 and relinquished rights to the child—be surprised when something goes wrong, when there is anguish? Don't they understand that arrangements of this kind amount to asking for trouble?

What lies at the heart of cases such as that of Baby M is the belief that people are somehow "entitled" to have children, that they are not "fulfilled" without them, and so they are justified in taking extraordinary steps to get them. There is even beginning to be talk of a "constitutional right" to procreate, which will probably be followed by a "constitutional right" to day care centers where the children can be parked.

It goes without saying that some couples are terribly disappointed to find that their marriages (and nowadays their liaisons) will not bring forth offspring. That is, however, a condition that billions of people have faced over the centuries. Millions of Americans face that condition now and find existence acceptable. There are those who prefer it, and those who find consolation in taking care of the children of others.

Chance plays its part in the lives of all of us. Some people seem blessedly lucky; some are handicapped; some are desperately unhappy. It would be nonsense to suggest that things even out; much of the time they don't. Childlessness may be unwelcome to many, but it does not justify creating a child who will be bizarre all its life.

Sometime in the next few years, it will be necessary to begin explaining to Baby M the circumstances of her birth. That will be an interesting exercise. Almost certainly her schoolmates will learn about those circumstances. A pretty prospect.

Technology and medical science have brought us surrogate motherhood and, no doubt, surrogate fatherhood. State legislatures are being called on to enact "guidelines" to settle such questions as who gets the baby; whether contracts such as the one in the Baby M case are legal; whether the costs involved should be paid by health insurance; whether government should bear the costs for those who have no coverage and are too poor to pay themselves; whether homosexuals have the same standing in these matters as heterosexuals; whether children born through surrogacy might old-fashionedly be called "illegitimate"; whether the surrogate mother may elect to have an abortion; whether the insemination of the surrogate mother must always be artificial; and much, much more.

The legislators, who are now pumping out any number of bills in statehouses across the country, are not to be envied. On the other hand, the lawyers have found a new field. In the American system, in which almost everything finds its way into the courts, they cannot lose. As for the rest of us, while not failing to recognize the unhappiness of some who find themselves childless, maybe we can help by calling surrogate motherhood what it is—arrant foolishness.

AFTERTHOUGHT

In November 1987, Baby M's surrogate mother, Mary Beth Whitehead, was divorced. She was thirty years old, had been married for thirteen years, and had a thirteen-year-old son and an eleven-year-old daughter. She was pregnant by a man not her husband, and she intended to marry him "very soon." Her husband's lawyer said that the battle over Baby M had "exhausted their marriage" and was "about ninety-five percent" responsible for the divorce.

Shortly thereafter, the Baby M case was supplying book and television drama material. A happy, commercial ending.

American Incompetence
■■■
[13 April 1987]

An alarming incompetence is at large these days in the United States. So is an alarming lack of realism. Think about them and they scare the daylights out of you. Consider a short list:

There was *Challenger,* when NASA disregarded plain warnings, launched the space shuttle in doubtful weather, and plunged into disaster. That happened last year. This year, again in doubtful weather, NASA launched a $180,000,000 satellite. It was barely out of sight in the overhanging clouds when it was apparently hit by lightning and was lost forever.

There was the Reagan-Gorbachev meeting at Reykjavik, when the United States almost negotiated arms control agreements about which it had not consulted its allies, and when the United States delegation for weeks afterward was uncertain and confused about just what had gone on.

There was the Iran affair, in which a policy it would be generous to call debatable and which was at odds with public pronouncement after public pronouncement was made worse by an almost unbelievable naïveté and ineptness. (The naïveté and ineptness did not begin with the Reagan presidency. The Carter administration had as little grasp as the current White House.) It is tempting to call our conduct in Iran amateurish, but some amateurs are very good at what they do and might sue.

There was, and is, the matter of the contras in Nicaragua, with another questionable policy and one carried through at times by methods that were probably illegal and flouted the intent of Congress. Millions of dollars that flowed through government agencies have not been traced and perhaps cannot be.

Add now the farce of the new Moscow embassy, including its construction at vast expense while the Soviets, so we are told, bugged almost every inch of it. Add the Marines accused of letting Soviet spies into our present embassy at the behest of women with whom they were having affairs. Was there any true supervision, or were the various "administrators" too busy "administering"? The upshot of this triumph was that, with Secretary of State Shultz in Moscow, a specially secure limousine and trailer had to be flown over so that he could chat with his associates in privacy. What did that cost? Was anyone punished for causing it?

Move to private industry. Last September, Thomas Wyman was removed as chairman of the board of CBS. It turns out that when he was removed, he was paid $4,300,000, and is to receive $400,000 a year for life, and the right to exercise stock options, and—this is particularly heartwarming—payments covering his life and health insurance through 1988 and in reduced amounts thereafter.

Another CBS executive, also dumped, is getting more than $300,000 annually for the remainder of his contract, and fifty percent of the bonuses he had been scheduled to receive in those remaining years. Bonuses arranged in advance? Aren't bonuses rewards for work done, not in anticipation of such work? Not, it seems, in today's corporate America.

Maybe CBS should not be singled out. Maybe Wyman should not be. The real question is, How many American corporations burden themselves and their shareholders with obligations of this kind? Can they compete when they carry such loads?

The list is not exhaustive. There are the trade deficit and the budget deficit, and cost overruns on weapons, on nuclear power plants, and on much else. There are expensive weapons that prove to be duds. There was—it is still painful to remember—the murder of 241 Marines in Beirut.

Other countries have problems. Nobody's perfect. We, however, have them in profusion. We would do well to remember that we are not bound to prevail simply because we are Americans. Our resources are tremendous but they are not endless. They cannot be tossed away without consequences. Let's get serious.

Self-improvement
[4 May 1987]

The way it happened was odd. I was preoccupied, trying to decide whether to get a brand-new body in ten weeks through the Nautilus Diet, achieve total weight control through the Champagne Diet, rid my body of excess fat forever through the Underburner's Diet, achieve rapid weight loss through the Good Fat Diet, make my dining healthy and delicious through the Food Lover's Guide to Lower Cholesterol, eat and live like a thin person by being Thin Within, lose up to a pound a day and never gain it back through the Rotation Diet, become fit for life through a New Way of Eating, or turn on to life with No More Cravings, or failing that, No More Snacks.

The indecision was understandable because another possibility was to Eat to Succeed, or to eat for Immune Power, or to lose weight through Self-hypnosis and Subliminal Motivation. Yet another course of action was to balance diet and exercise for lifetime fitness through the Equilibrium Plan, or to acquire A Great Body Through Low-Impact Aerobics, or have a go at Callanetics, or Dianetics, or Non-Impact Aerobics, or do One-Minute Exercises, or to make stress work for me through The Joy of Stress. Alternatively, I could fall back on the Diet Principal or maybe just good old Jane Fonda.

I was still undecided when, as noted above, it happened. Everything became clear. My problems lay elsewhere. I should have been considering Executive Manners, The Persuasive Speaker, Success

Through Self-confidence, How to Remember Names and Faces, How to Tap Into Your Own Genius, How to Manage the Plus Factor in Positive Thinking, How to Manage Time and Set Priorities, and Self-hypnosis and Subliminal Learning.

Here a nagging feeling set in. Maybe it would be better to Play to Win. Or to define objectives and gain leverage through The Art of Negotiation. Or release my business potential through Hyper-Performance. Or perhaps I could find something meant for me in Positively Change Your Life.

I did succeed in deciding against tapping into my own genius. I had been doing that for decades, without much effect. A different course suggested itself. This would be a combination, perhaps remembering names and faces while making stress work for me. Or eating to succeed while following the champagne diet; they did seem to go together. Still another possibility: Could the plus factor in positive thinking be managed at the same time one was learning to eat for immune power?

At this point, something like panic set in. I was still unable to make up my mind. What I needed was a volume called How To Choose Among Self-improvement Books and at the Same Time Stop Torturing Yourself About Your Own Inadequacies Real or Imagined and Accept Yourself for What You Are Without However Being Unduly Self-satisfied and Needlessly Resisting Change When Change May Be Advisable in Your Own Interest—Within Reason.

The bookstore didn't have it. I asked for the manager but he was busy reading How to Run a Bookstore That Has the Titles People Want Without Carrying Excessive Inventories That Clutter the Shelves and Unduly Increase Overheads and So Endanger the Manager's Job and Leave Him or Her Feeling Unfulfilled.

Should I wait for the manager? Gritting my teeth and managing time and setting priorities, I made a decision. I left.

But why? What lay behind that decision? I'll have to go back. Maybe there's a book that can explain it.

The Law's Delay
III
[26 May 1987]

"Help me, God. These people are crazy."

A woman named Milagros Arroyo shouted those words last Friday. As it happened, she shouted them in a courtroom in the Bronx, in New York City, where she was a juror in the fraud and larceny trial of Raymond Donovan, once secretary of labor under President Reagan, and seven codefendants. Result: a bright light shining on the insane excesses of our system of justice.

Ms. Arroyo, who is thirty, also shouted "The Lord is my shepherd," locked herself in a bathroom, and sprinkled water on other jurors and in a ritualistic manner on an apple. On being dragged into court—she would not walk—she told the judge she wanted nothing to do with the trial and wanted to go home. A psychiatrist called in said it might be "incipient psychosis" or "a panic attack."

Ms. Arroyo is now under treatment in a hospital. Yet maybe she had something when she said "These people are crazy." When she said that, the trial was eight months old and had gone to the jury just the day before. The prosecutors had taken seven months to present evidence, including more than nine hundred documents and forty witnesses, in support of a charge of conspiracy to defraud the New York City Transit Authority of $7,400,000 on a subway construction project. The small army of defense lawyers said the government case was so weak they would present no evidence. That took them two minutes. Then came the attorneys' summations. They took a month. The jury deliberated one day with Ms. Arroyo, one day with an alternate juror, and acquitted all the defendants.

The indictments in the Donovan case were handed down in September 1984, from which time the eight defendants, according to one of their lawyers, incurred legal costs of $13,000,000, and their company was precluded from bidding on contracts in New York State. The cost to the taxpayers of New York State is not known but must be colossal. The wonder is that Ms. Arroyo is the only juror who broke down.

Nobody wants summary justice. That, however, need not be the alternative. The alternative should be reasonable dispatch, without dilatory tactics and self-indulgence by lawyers, and with judges who are able—and want to—keep things moving. Why is that too much to ask for? It ought to be taken for granted.

Last month, in Los Angeles, jury selection began in a case in which the proprietors of a school, Raymond Buckey and Peggy McMartin Buckey, are charged with sexually abusing children in their care. The five hundred potential jurors called by the judge were told that the prosecution evidence would take a year, and that the trial could run eighteen months or even two years. Buckey, who is twenty-eight, has been in custody without bail for more than three years. His sixty-year-old mother, the other defendant, was released on bail last year. So far, the case is thought to have cost the taxpayers $5,000,000.

Los Angeles is also the scene of the trial of the film director John Landis and four others accused of involuntary manslaughter. The case arose from the deaths of the actor Vic Morrow and two children during the filming of the movie *Twilight Zone*. The three were killed when a helicopter crashed into the set during a simulated battle scene. That was on July 23, 1982. The trial began on June 24, 1986, and it reached the jury on May 18 of this year. On Tuesday of this week, the jurors were hearing a stenographer read aloud testimony taken eight months ago.

All three cases—Donovan, Buckey, Landis—are extreme examples of what Shakespeare, in *Hamlet,* bitterly called "the law's delay." But they are examples.

We are celebrating the bicentennial of the Constitution. In the Sixth Amendment, the right to "a speedy trial" is guaranteed. You might think that George Mason and the other framers of the Bill of Rights had written satire.

AFTERTHOUGHT

The jury found Landis and his codefendants not guilty. The families of the two children killed still had civil suits pending, and they settled these out of court, it was said for $2,000,000 each. Vic Morrow's family had made a separate settlement earlier.

School Days?
■■■
[8 September 1987]

The school term begins in New York City next Monday. Those in charge have, among a variety of problems, this one: How do you educate homeless children? How do you get them interested in school-work? How do you get them to school at all?

This is not a problem peculiar to New York. All of our cities have it. The New York condition sheds light on the others. Over a period of ten days late in August, school registration teams went to thirty-three of the hotels in the city where homeless people are put up at city expense. (Vast expense, it should be said, as much as $3,000 per family per month, though these are not hotels that most of us would be willing to stay in for fifteen minutes. We would not want to go through the front door.) The teams were preceded by volunteers who handed out leaflets explaining when the teams were coming, and why. During the ten days, 583 children were signed up.

That is not the total number of school-age children living in New York welfare hotels. Something like 6,000 are thought to, and they move frequently. They're hard to keep track of. They're hard to get to school, too. Busing is provided to get them there and in some cases to take them to special after-school programs so that they're not put back in the welfare hotels until six at night. There has also been a proposal to install telephones in their hotel rooms for wakeup calls and to ask parents where their children are when they don't show up for class. The telephone idea has been turned down.

A good deal of information of this kind has been turning up lately, information that hints at the difficulties those in education face. There is, for example, an estimate by the Bureau of the Census that six out of ten children born in this decade will eventually live in a one-parent home. One in five will come from a home where English is not spoken.

Then there is teenage pregnancy. Holyoke, Massachusetts, has opened a pregnancy clinic for adolescents that it is hoped will help to keep the girls in school, even after their babies have come, so that they won't join the 800,000 American boys and girls who drop out of high school every year. This is a mere example. Teenage mothers are everywhere. One estimate is that each day in this country, forty of them give birth to their third child. Not just give birth—give birth to their third child. What is to become of these mothers and children? Who is to support them? How will they live? Do these young women, and the men who fathered their children, have any idea of what they are doing?

There is a related question: Who is to teach them? Who would take on the job? This must be a factor in the shortage of teachers. It is no wonder that some school systems have been driven to recruit teachers abroad. Even colleges and universities are doing that, or using foreign graduate students as instructors, which leads in some cases to complaints that the foreigners don't speak English well enough to make themselves understood in class.

The picture isn't entirely grim. All kinds of programs are under way across the country to improve matters, to reward children for staying in school, to raise standards not only for pupils but for teachers and administrations, and to toughen requirements for graduation at every level. Yet, something larger is needed—an understanding that knowledge and competence are valued, that application and persever-ance are worth the trouble. More than that understanding is required. Society must demonstrate it, as well.

Mountains of Flesh
▪▪▪
[1 October 1987]

This is a thoroughly unscientific observation, based entirely on what the pros call anecdotal evidence. Yet it does appear that something bizarre is taking place in the United States, that bizarre something being that American women in extraordinary numbers are becoming extraordinarily fat. Men also, but not nearly so many.

Americans who might be called ample, or well-upholstered, who weigh ten or twenty percent more than the accepted norm, are increas-ing in numbers, too. The unscientific observation, however, applies not to them but to those who are vastly overweight, lady sumo wrestlers who make you stare in amazement and wonder how they perform the ordinary chores of life, how they get through the day.

Some strain, wobble, and hesitate going up steps a few inches high. Aboard commercial aircraft, they occupy their own seats and, with their flesh jutting over and under the armrests, virtually surrounding the armrests, half of the seats next to them. Passengers in front of them cannot lean back; there is no room. These people must weigh, many of them, three hundred pounds and more, and they are of all kinds and ages. They fill their outsize clothes to the last centimeter.

It is not uncommon to spot children ten or twelve years old who are well on the way to this state. Or young mothers, pushing their children in prams, who are still relatively mobile but who make you gape at their size. Sometimes these huge young women are accompanied by men of normal appearance, which suggests that a new style in beauty—great squishy female mountains—has come into being. Indeed, the clothing industry is making a good thing out of "fashions for the larger woman," or "for the woman with the fuller figure." Less often, the opposite arrangement may be seen—trim woman, grossly fat man.

It must be said that those who carry this gigantic obesity betray no embarrassment about it. They go about their affairs as though their condition was the most natural thing in the world. One woman I saw seemed to have as much flesh on her face below her chin as above. Nonetheless, she had made up her lips and eyelids, though these were all but lost in the great expanse of which they were part. There was another, probably in her midteens, whose thighs did not merely brush each other as she walked along. Each thigh literally had to shove its way past.

The question remains: What is causing this ballooning? (From my observation, the phenomenon also exists in England, but where else I am not in a position to say.) There is, as already noted, apparently a new view of these matters, a let-it-all-hang-out attitude (the phrase is apt) passed along from the sixties. Maybe people who tend to be overweight are deciding that it isn't worth the trouble to deprive themselves of food and drink they enjoy. Once started down that road, they simply grow larger and larger.

Then, too, so-called fast food may be playing its part. It's easy to get and is eaten almost absentmindedly. Television may be involved—all that sitting around, staring at the screen, often munching on something. Add the American addiction to the automobile. There may be another reason. Is something medical at work here? Can birth control methods have anything to do with it?

It is strange that this phenomenon should turn up at the same time that so many Americans are devoted to fitness and cultivation of the body muscular. Maybe the fatness is a defiant reaction. There, in any case, the fatness is, and it is disquieting, as though some sinister force is out to disable a large part of the population.

Look around. What is going on?

Why Do They Do It?

[4 November 1987]

Not long ago, there was a fire in a hotel in New York City. It was one of those hotels the city uses to house people on welfare who have nowhere else to go. Twenty-nine residents were injured, and six of the one hundred twelve families lodging in the hotel were burned out of their rooms.

A resident sounded the alarm. She was thirty-two years old and had five children. Another woman, interviewed as she stood outside the hotel, was twenty-three. She had four children. In neither case was there mention of a husband, or any other man.

The fire, possibly set by yet another resident, showed the danger and degradation in which some people live. It showed also what social workers deal with. Here are a thirty-two-year-old woman with five children and a twenty-three-year-old with four. Why do they have so many children when they have no prospect of supporting them? Knowing the sort of world in which they live, why do they want to bring children into it? Some girls still in high school have more than one. We hear of others who have three or four by the time they are twenty. They surely understand the process by which children are created. What is it all about?

It is, of course, about instinct. Women want to be mothers. There may, however, be something more involved. These mothers may well love their children, and yet they may be using them, perhaps using them unconsciously, to get even with the rest of us. "This is your responsibility," they seem to be saying, "this is your doing." It is no laughing matter, but there is an old number, sung by the fallen woman to the man who wronged her, that sums up this attitude: "You made me what I am today. I hope you're satisfied."

We are told by social workers that many teenagers bear children because doing so "gives them a sense of worth" and makes them the center of attention for the first time in their lives. No doubt this plays its part. Maybe it explains the woman who recently died in an Atlanta public housing project. The cause of death was carbon monoxide poisoning, apparently from a faulty water heater. The woman was nineteen. Her daughter died with her. She was four.

Still, it is probably a mistake to try to work out an entirely coherent explanation of the epidemic of teenage pregnancy in the United States. Some of these young people can barely express themselves verbally. It is unlikely that they reason things through.

What is said about the girls applies also to the boys who fathered their children. What were they thinking about? Is it an act of defiance? They don't expect to pay any bills. Most of them couldn't if they wanted to. They see illegitimate children all around them, and for that matter legitimate children, supported by "the welfare." Why do they condemn others to this grim life?

The two mothers in the hotel fire, and their total of nine children, were, happily, all saved. What is to become of the children? What kind of future can they hope to have? Teenage pregnancy is dangerously out of control in this country. So is the number of unmarried mothers. Something like sixty percent of the single parents in the United States—most of them women, of course—receive no child support from the other parent.

We had better get after these things. They weaken our society, make it sick, threaten—like the carbon monoxide that killed the Atlanta nineteen-year-old—to poison it.

AFTERTHOUGHT

Columnists like to have a "hook" on which to hang their thoughts. Hooks for a column such as this one are easily available, horrifyingly so. A few days before Thanksgiving 1987, a one-year-old girl died of pneumonia and dehydration in a hospital in New York City. She and her two-year-old brother and two sisters, three and five, had been taken from their mother by city authorities and placed with their grandmother. It appeared that the grandmother turned the children back to their mother for a day while she attended a funeral. On that day, the little girl died. The mother of the four children was twenty-two. The police said they were trying to locate the children's father.

Good Sports, Poor Sports

Only Two Hands
###
[2 October 1984]

The Hagler-Hamsho fight is almost on us.

That flat a statement may leave some of my readers gasping, so let me explain. Hagler, more often known as Marvelous Marvin, and Hamsho, whose first name is Mustafa, are to meet in the ring, with the world middleweight championship at stake, in Madison Square Garden on October 19. They have been getting into shape for weeks, and it is necessary for those who will watch the fight on television to be in shape, too. In shape, that is, to listen to the prefight broadcast in which the fighters are analyzed and their chances assessed. In a prefight broadcast, there is always a magic moment. It is the moment at which one of the experts called in for the occasion reveals that each man has two hands.

For as long as there have been fight broadcasts, on radio as well as television, some expert has always come on before the hostilities begin to tell us, "Remember, once they get inside the ring, they both only got two hands." In keeping with the traditions of prefight broadcasts, the two-handedness of the contestants is never revealed early, and it must be built up to. First, comparisons are made based on the fighters' records, their condition, punching power, speed, boxing skill, and the expertness of the cut men in the corners. Speed, by the way, takes in both hand speed and foot speed, the desirable thing being to have what is known as good foot speed and good hand speed. Bad hand speed and bad foot speed are understandably thought to be handicaps. The words "fast" and "slow" are never used.

At this point, the discussion becomes more arcane. What about the size of the ring? A small ring favors the harder hitter and does the opposite for the better boxer. The springiness of the canvas, and the tautness of the ropes—they matter, too. So do the questions of whether one man has more incentive than the other, the wiliness of their respective managers, who takes a punch better, who had the tougher and more highly motivated sparring partners, who did more roadwork, who the officials are, and where the smart money is riding.

Now, at last, the stage is set. The expert being interviewed, preferably grizzled and plainspoken, even somewhat ungrammatical, to demonstrate that he is the genuine article who perhaps used to do some fighting himself, nods in a way that shows an amiable tolerance of what has gone before, and delivers the mighty line: "Remember, once they get inside that ring, they both only got two hands." This information is put forward as though it would otherwise have escaped our attention, as though something hitherto secret was being made known. Accordingly, it is not simply tossed off in a casual manner; it is permitted to hang in the air for a while, so that it can sink in.

The line appears to imply that before climbing into the ring, the fighters may not have had two hands, or that in other bouts, and regardless of the Marquis of Queensberry rules, a one-handed fighter may have been in there, or one with three hands or more. Not tonight. Tonight it's two hands per man, presumably a left and a right, and no exceptions.

And now, as the ring announcer Harry Balogh used to say: "May the superior gladiator emerge victorious." Using no more than two hands.

AFTERTHOUGHT

Hagler, although he possessed only one third of the hands in the ring at any given time (the referee also had two), won.

Baseball and Shakespeare
•••
[9 October 1987]

It isn't easy to broadcast the World Series. There's a lot of time to fill, the situations that arise have all been seen before, and there isn't much that's new to say. Unless, that is, the announcers are willing to look to sources not previously thought to have anything to do with baseball. To be specific, William Shakespeare.

Microphones are never present during arguments with umpires. No need to speculate about what is being said; Shakespeare told us:

Manager, *King Henry VI* in mind, approaches the umpire, who holds up a warning hand and quotes from *Hamlet:* "Give thy thoughts no tongue."

The manager persists. "In thy face," he says, "I see the map of honor, truth, and loyalty."

This is not a bad opening, but the ump can use *The Comedy of Errors:* "These words are razors to my wounded heart," and *King Richard III:* "Harp not upon that string." He chooses the latter.

The manager will not be put off. "I was," he says, using a line from *A Winter's Tale,* "no gentleman born," and goes on accordingly.

This sends the umpire off to confer with his first-base colleague and, with the help of *Love's Labor's Lost,* to make this comment on the manager: "He draweth out the thread of his verbosity finer than the staple of his argument."

Now he returns to the manager with more sarcasm, drawn from *King Richard II:* "Your fair discourse has been as sugar, making the hard way sweet and delectable."

The manager tells the umpire he cannot believe he made the decision against which he is complaining: "If this were played upon a stage now, I should condemn it as an improbable fiction."

To this use of *Twelfth Night,* the umpire, thumbing the manager out, has a rejoinder from *Hamlet:* "Rest, rest, perturbed spirit."

As the manager turns to leave, he mutters a line from *Much Ado About Nothing:* "Oh! What authority and show of truth can cunning sin cover itself withal!"

Let us see what Shakespeare did for the relief pitcher. The manager storms out to the mound to yank his starter. The other team has been bunting successfully on him (*King Henry VI:* "And many strokes,

49

though with a little axe, hew down and fell the hardest-timbered oak''), and now, rattled, he has fumbled a bunt and loaded the bases. The manager asks, thanks to *Two Gentlemen of Verona,* "What is't that you took up so gingerly?" and calls in his best reliever, who is shellacked because he is overworked and, as Shakespeare wrote in one of his sonnets: "The hardest knife ill-used doth lose his edge."

There remains a veteran, once the ace of the staff, who remembering *King Henry IV,* has gone to the bullpen: "I would be well content to entertain the lag-end of my life with quiet hours." Asked now to pitch his team out of a hole, he proclaims, from *As You Like It,* "Though I look old, yet I am strong and lusty." He is hit hard, and the announcer has the last, sad word from *King Richard II:* "Oh, call back yesterday, bid time return!"

Soon the game is over, the stadium empties, and the announcers say good-bye to their viewers (*Love's Labor's Lost* again) "in the posteriors of this day, which the rude multitude call the afternoon."

The Tennis Louts
III
[14 January 1985]

There was a pleasant surprise in the aftermath of the Super Bowl. A few arrests were made during the celebration in the streets, but on the whole, supporters of the San Francisco Forty-niners did not take their team's victory as a license for looting, burning cars, or attacking the police.

Given this example, would it be unreasonable to hope that this restraint might spread to our athletes? I am thinking of some of the top tennis players, whose behavior is worse than that of rampaging fans. It involves no property damage and no overt brutality. But it is worse in this sense—the "celebrating" fans engage in their excesses as though in response to a dare. They take on the psychology of the mob and seem to regard what they do as a form of amusement. They see so much violence in American life and entertainment that they evidently believe they are entitled to some of their own.

The tennis players, on the other hand, are among the privileged of the earth. They earn vast sums on the courts and added sums for product endorsements. They are coddled, travel in high style, put up at the best places, see the world, are idolized, have the honor of representing their countries, and then put on exhibitions of unsportsmanlike conduct and throw tantrums that would disgrace a spoiled seven-year-old in summer camp.

They complain about line calls and other decisions, abuse referees and line judges, make rude gestures at their opponents and sometimes at the spectators—who are often no bargains themselves—sulk, grimace, throw racquets, use foul language, make unkind remarks about one another in public, and generally carry on as though they were persecuted and oppressed. They have turned tennis from a graceful, suspenseful, even thrilling sport into a business, grim and evil-tempered.

They have of course had help in doing this—from the promoters, from the corporate "sponsors" of the tournaments, from the adaptation of tennis to the necessities of television, from sports bureaucrats too timid to take the corrective action they should.

Why has this come about? Technology is one reason. By that, I do not mean television alone. The game has been changed by the use of different materials in the racquets, which are now instruments of execution. The players themselves have tried to become semiautomatic perfectionists. They are not tennis players because they love tennis, which was the case with the leading players not so long ago. They are athletes who have chosen tennis as the pathway to fame and fortune.

Which leads to the next reason—money. Money is the biggest factor in tennis today. The amounts involved are astronomical—or would once have been thought to be so. An incorrect foot fault call may cost a player tens of thousands of dollars, or more. Wherefore the headlines: Tempers Flare as So-and-so and What's-his-name Reach Final, followed by the details, a selection from the list given above, with perhaps a challenge to a fight, an attempt to hit the other man with a ball, and the particularly obnoxious moment when the winner sinks to his knees on the court to give thanks or leaps into the air or goes through the repeated fist-throwing routine.

Yes, there is big money at stake. But that is no excuse. The difference between winning and losing is the difference between extraordinary amounts of money and only slightly less extraordinary amounts of money.

The tennis stars should realize that they are among the blessed and restore some grace and dignity to a wonderful game. But they won't. The temper of the times is against it.

First Four-Minute Mile
III
[11 March 1985]

In the rush of events this year, one has attracted less attention than it should have. It took place in the world of track and field: John Walker of New Zealand became the first man ever to run a mile in under four minutes for the hundredth time. Maybe if someone else, Prime Minister David Lange, hadn't been grabbing New Zealand's meager share of headlines by excluding American nuclear warships, Walker would have come in for more applause. In fact, what he did went by almost as though it were routine. He himself, of course, helped to make it so.

Four-minute miles are now commonplace. Steve Scott of the United States will soon match Walker's century. Walker himself is thirty-three years old and hasn't won a big international race in years. All of which makes it difficult to understand how dramatic an achievement it was when a man ran the first four-minute mile. It was done by a tall, thoughtful Englishman named Roger Bannister, and I have two special reasons for remembering it. I was in NBC's London bureau at the time and knew that Bannister, a medical student at Oxford, had been nearing the four-minute mark and intended, one spring day in 1954, to go all-out to break it on the University track in Oxford. I recommended that I go there, with a camera crew, but something went wrong and the recommendation was not taken up. So we lost one of the great athletic events of all time. (Those were simpler days. All we would have had to do was show up and point the camera.) That was one reason for remembering it. The other was that Bannister came to London that night for a BBC interview and before he got away— which he did as quickly as possible; he was not a gregarious sort—I managed to get him to agree to appear on the *Today* show the following morning.

He was not seen on *Today*. Sitting in a studio below ground—it was a World War II studio—in Broadcasting House in London, he was interviewed from New York by host Dave Garroway on a radio circuit, while stills of Bannister and his record race were thrown on the screen. By the time the interview was over, it was about twelve thirty P.M. in London, so we took Bannister to lunch. We went to a restaurant that gave us a private room upstairs; that meant that nobody else could find Bannister, or come on him by chance.

Then we had a further stroke of luck. We had hired a car to take us around. Bannister, who was gloriously happy but wanted to be alone with his thoughts, asked whether he could borrow the car and go driving in the country. That meant that no other news organization could find him for hours more. This was, on the day Bannister was on the front page of virtually every newspaper in the world, no small coup.

As I say, it may be hard to imagine this now, but there was a time when the four-minute mile seemed flatly impossible. The barrier Bannister broke was as much mental and psychological as it was physical. As a distinctly intellectual athlete—he is now Sir Roger Bannister, a consulting neurologist, and soon to take up a high academic post at Oxford—he was uniquely equipped to break it. He ran that day, by the way, against two friends and teammates, Chris Brasher and Chris Chataway, both world class, but they were not trying to beat him so much as to pace him and pull him to his record time. When he finished, he had nothing left. He crossed the line and collapsed, utterly played out in every way. His time was 3:59.4.

Bannister was realistic enough to say at once that of course his time would be bettered, though he thought by smaller and smaller increments as time went by. That same year, he qualified as a physician and his track career was over. Also that year, John Landy, an Australian, lowered Bannister's record to three fifty-nine flat.

The current world record for the mile, held by another Englishman, Sebastian Coe, is 3:47.33. John Walker, who was the first man to break 3:50, ran his hundredth sub-four-minute mile in 3:54.57. In a way, they were running behind Roger Bannister.

Pity the Poor Ump
iii
[10 April 1985]

Now that the baseball season is under way in the major leagues, and also in earnest, which is a little farther away, a word of tribute to those long-suffering and unappreciated men, the umpires, would not be amiss. They are the truly indispensable men of baseball, and the most abused. There is nothing more unnecessary and more boring than the complaints to the umpires, as the managers flap their arms, throw caps and tantrums, shout, kick the dirt, shove their faces, frequently dribbling tobacco spittle, into those of the umps, and generally carry on in a way that, in a child, would lead any sensible parent to disown it.

The justification put forward for this conduct is that the managers, or coaches, or players, are demonstrating that they have the winning attitude, and that they don't take injustice lying down. With any luck, they will incite some of the sports lovers in the stands, who don't need any incitement, to use foul language, throw things, and if possible do some property damage to show what irrepressibly devoted fans they are.

There is nothing new about abusing umpires, though there is more of it now, and it is more violent. In 1967, an old National League umpire, Jocko Conlan, who had also briefly been an outfielder for the Chicago White Sox, wrote a book about his life. The book contained this passage: "I don't understand why the fans boo an umpire. I know a lot of it is humorous, and it's part of the game, and the American way and all that. But why is it? Who started booing the umpire and calling him a blind bat and saying, 'Kill the ump!'?"

I mentioned this on the air, and along came the New York Public Library with a piece of research that showed that the first unpleasantness on record between an umpire and a ballplayer took place as soon as it was humanly possible, in the first game between organized teams. That was on June 19, 1846, between the New York Knickerbockers and the New York Club, at the Elysian Fields in Hoboken, New Jersey. We have only the last name of the player involved, Davis. He was fined six cents. The umpire's name has not survived.

As baseball is conducted these days, there might be something to be said for giving umpires more authority. The game takes too long, and it has become excessively specialized, with the computer no doubt

54

contributing by revealing everything about opposing players except their charitable contributions and where they stand on Japanese non-tariff trade barriers. This man never bats against left-handed pitchers, and against right-handers only when they are tired. This man pitches only when the wind is from the north quarter and Jupiter aligns with Mars. Fielders' gloves have become as large as lacrosse sticks. Relief pitchers come in with the verve and enthusiasm of a man on his way to the scaffold.

There is a reason, of course. So much money is at stake that it's no wonder everybody is touchy. It would not be surprising to hear that each team carries a staff psychiatrist. Maybe the umpires could be empowered to speed things up, if that wouldn't endanger their lives.

Ah, well, that is probably a dream. Mine is a minority voice. And there is no keeping the season from going on its almost endless way. Play—which doesn't seem quite the right word—ball.

Smiting the Pellet
[29 July 1985]

This column was written when it was still uncertain whether there would be a major league baseball strike. It was conceived of as a public service for baseball addicts who would otherwise, in a strike, have to get along without their daily dose of clichés. If there is no strike— well, it's still a public service. Begin here:

Long Jim Reeperbahn today stilled the hitherto booming bats of the International Falls, Minnesota, Royals. The league leaders were so shackled by the Ponca City, Oklahoma, ace's fast ball and breaking pitches that in seven innings there was a lone base runner, and he strolled, only to be cut down trying to steal by Reeperbahn's iron-armed batterymate, George Smith-Montagu. When the ninth chukka ended, with the series knotted, one apiece, the Royals had just one hit—a double by Marvin Gowanus—and that lone walk to show for an afternoon of almost total frustration.

The lanky right-hander's teammate, centerfielder Earl S. Court, first big leaguer to carry a middle initial onto the field, took apart the Royal hurling almost single-handed. His two circuit blows, both deposited in the distant right field seats, were responsible for four tallies and gave the red-hot Reeperbahn all the edge he needed. With that, the feared Ponca City slugger more than made up for his shortcomings in the first affray, when his failure to connect with men sent the Mudcats down to a narrow defeat.

Ah, yes. Baseballese. Anybody can do it. All it takes is a liking for the overblown and an inability to be embarrassed. So there is the veteran who, though the heady days of glory are behind him, is still patrolling the outer garden with his ancient skill and getting the timely bingle. Here a quote from the manager may be useful: "There's nobody I'd rather see up there in the clutch." So also there is the second baseman who goes gracefully skyward for an errant toss from the backstop, as the runner has the middle station safely pilfered.

This sort of thing can go on forever, and sometimes it seems to, with, for example, the ball being the horsehide, and being not hit but blistered. If it is being blistered, a rookie twirler may be in the bullpen, loosening up under the practiced gaze of veteran pitching coach Adolfo Reposo, who practices gazing even during the off-season.

Baseballese this is, though it is, in our technological age, changing in predictable ways. Players who used to have confidence are now expected to have a high confidence factor. Someone is a good relief pitcher. Try again. He can go out there in a men-on situation. Does someone hit with men on base? Don't put it that way. Is he productive in a potential rbi situation? Don't ask what a team's record is. How is it doing won and lostwise?

At this point, I confess, my own confidence factor is low. I'm losing track of these things. Does a pitcher, pardon, hurler, still get his ears pinned back in the process of being shelled off the mound? Is a first baseman still the guardian of the initial sack? Do fleet-footed outfielders still scamper to the farthermost barrier to haul in arching blasts? Nobody smites the pellet these days, that I know, but it used to be compulsory to unload a double, rather than hit one. Is it still?

That ends this column, which was written slowly and not with good velocity. Now (or, as the case may be, later) on with the game. Or as they put it these days: Organize, bargain collectively, and play ball.

Tiresome Athletes
III
[26 September 1985]

We are now in the third week of a Larry Holmes–less heavyweight boxing division and, no doubt, all much the poorer for that. For Holmes himself has announced (on *Good Morning America*) the following: "I am a great human being," and "I want to be left alone." It seems a shame that the rest of us should be deprived of public manifestations of his greatness.

This Holmes should not be confused with the Holmes who made an ill-tempered exit from boxing after his defeat by Michael Spinks. He had just been paid a reported $3,500,000 for entering the ring out of condition and becoming the first heavyweight champion in history to lose his title to a lightheavyweight champion. One might have expected him to be embarrassed and contrite. Oh, no. Some members of the family of the late Rocky Marciano, whose record for undefeated fights Holmes wanted to surpass, had tastelessly said they hoped he would fail. Holmes was moved to respond that Marciano "couldn't carry my jockstrap." He went on to say that he had been "robbed," to complain of racism in the United States, and to advise Marciano's brother to take Boston, Massachusetts, and the surrounding area and (a euphemism here) insert them in his rear end.

Racism in the United States there undoubtedly is, and Holmes, who says his remarks were "misinterpreted" and that the Marciano family has accepted his apology, has long felt he did not get the esteem and affection he deserved. At the same time, he boasts of having made $65,000,000, and of having two Rolls-Royces paid for, a $6,000,000 hotel, and millions in the bank. Apparently he wants people to fall sobbing with admiration around his neck and to kiss the hem of his garment. He hardly sounds like one of racism's leading victims.

The prevailing spirit in so-called sports these days is unpleasant and graceless. There are the baseball players involved in the recent drug trial in Pittsburgh, and they represent, as everyone knows, only a small part of drug addiction in the big leagues. There are the football and basketball players who have to be suspended and given treatment. There are the track and field athletes, not only Americans who have to be tested for chemicals and illegal blood augmentation. Also the swimmers. In all of these fields, vast amounts of money are involved, either in direct payments or through commercial endorsements or careers in broadcasting.

Among the tennis louts, we have had the inspiring performance by one Kevin Curran, a South African who has found a haven and riches in the United States. Curran complained about the behavior of those attending the national championships in New York. Noisy and inconsiderate, he found them. Added to which was the aircraft traffic overhead. Curran thought it all intolerable, and that for having upset his game, New York could be suitably punished by having an atomic bomb dropped on it. It hardly seems sufficient, for a crime so immense.

What Curran seems not to understand is that there is a connection between the unattractive behavior to which he objects and the amount of money he is paid. Curran is not in a sport but in a commercial enterprise. If some of the fans are crass and noisy, so is the enterprise itself. Nobody forces Curran to compete in public. If he wants to play tennis for sport, that course is open to him. Millions of people do it.

How tiresome and unattractive many of our top athletes are. The professional sportswoman of the year, named by whoever names such things, is a dogsled racer. No wonder.

Quiet, Please
[10 October 1985]

It's World Series time again, wherefore a small suggestion. It is that the broadcasters broadcast less. Not less often. Less. In other words, that they not talk so much.

One of the hardest things to learn in broadcasting is to be quiet. Many of those now in the business have clearly never learned it. What is more, nobody tells them. The ideal now appears to be to be jabbering at every moment. There is no peace for the viewer, so long as the sound is on.

It is understandable. If you are on the air and you don't speak, your colleagues and, more important, your employer may conclude that you don't know what to say. Those at the receiving end may think that something has gone wrong with their set. Still, all of them could get used to an occasional pause. There are pictures that carry themselves and need no description. The pictures may even be enhanced, in the dramatic sense, by silence.

Beyond that, much of what is said may have little or nothing to do with the picture. It may fight the picture. There is endless gabble, about which those who bring it forth have the often mistaken notion that they are being vivacious and entertaining. One reason so many unnecessary and foolish things are said on television is that so much is said. If less were said, more thought might go into what is uttered. True, people who think sometimes get wrong ideas. But the odds are on thought's side.

In the great days of radio, there were sports broadcasters who knew little about sports and others who knew a great deal. Whatever they knew, I believe that all of them, on radio, talked less than the television sports broadcasters do now. One reason was that they usually worked alone. When they stopped to think, or to have a glass of water, nobody was there to fill in the gap. They were also less driven to be amusing and informative, especially about things that did not matter. Nor did they have at their disposal an endless flow of statistics, most of them useless. Technology has made broadcasters more garrulous, because it has supplied more data. In the information age, information comes at you whether you want it or not. During a World Series game, you are told everything about a player except his blood type and his wife's shoe size.

Broadcasters nowadays typically work in teams. For the World Series, it is not uncommon to have four or five going at it, and there is bound to be, though it may not be conscious, a competition among them. Nobody wants to be left out, and each wants to show that he is at least as clever and well-prepared as the others. This is not peculiar to sports broadcasting. Newspeople covering special events feel the same compulsion to talk. Some of them learn that, at times, it is better not to, but that takes willpower and self-control. It also takes somebody in charge who believes that occasional quiet is to be valued. There aren't many of them around.

Broadcasting baseball games isn't easy. There are long dull stretches. Once, during an American League playoff game on NBC, I managed to announce Spiro Agnew's resignation as vice president between the time a pitch landed in the catcher's mitt and the time the next pitch was thrown. It wasn't even necessary to hurry: The pitcher could be counted on to walk off the mound, kick the dirt, take off his cap, put it on again, rub the ball, scratch himself, shrug, sigh, shake off a couple of signs, and if at a loss for anything else to do, spit. Vice presidential resignations don't come along very often, and the broadcasters feel they have to fill the time. Maybe nobody would mind if, once in a while, they didn't. Will we ever find out?

Ach, Tew!

[30 October 1985]

Looking back at the World Series from a safe distance, which is to say out of spitting range, the conclusion is inescapable that in at least one particular, it is not an adornment of American life. That particular, as the phrase "out of spitting range" suggests, is in the drooling, dribbling, slobbering, and expectorating that are a peculiarly unsightly aspect of our national pastime. Indeed, watching bits and pieces of the Series on television, one might have thought that baseball is not the national pastime at all; spitting is. Nobody seemed to be able to be on camera for more than two or three seconds without letting go. Every so often, the camera would pan the dugout, and as it went down the line, the players took turns spitting, one after another, almost as though they were a chorus line.

When I was but a lad, there was a cigar—the name, as I recall, was Certified Cremo, though what the certification was, I do not know—that claimed to be "the good five-cent cigar Vice President Marshall was talking about." (Thomas R. Marshall was Woodrow Wilson's veep. He had once said, "What America needs is a good five-cent cigar.") More to the point, Certified Cremo used the slogan "Spit is a horrid word, but it's worse on the end of your cigar." A Cremo, to explain, was smoked through a holder; no spit.

I bring this up because in those days, the country was acutely conscious of spit. There were campaigns against it. One used the line "SOS! Don't spit on sidewalks." That kind of thing was necessary then. There was even a parody of the toreador song from *Carmen:*

Toreador, don't spit on the floor.
Use the cuspidor.
That's what it's for.

With much effort, and for reasons of hygiene and aesthetics, the nation tried to put spitting behind it. Major league baseball is bringing it back. Sometimes it is hard not to believe that each television camera crew contains a member who signals the coaches and managers and players that they are on camera so that no chance to spit is lost. A search of the credits, however, reveals no spit signaler or expectoration expediter. Another possibility is that the players' union keeps such a person on the payroll, in defense of its members' right to spit in public. That is unlikely also. The chances are that the repellent vision, endlessly repeated, rests on the law of averages: Keep the camera trained long enough on someone in major league baseball and he will come through.

All of this must have something to do with notions of manliness and with the new popularity of chewing tobacco and snuff. Even among the manliest, nonetheless, it is thought not to be a good idea to swallow the slop they produce; it is, therefore, sent on its way, disfiguring the landscape wherever it is dropped. This, by the way, includes college campuses, where, I am informed, growing numbers of the young carry snuffboxes on their hips, plainly a vital part of education.

The baseball season is of course behind us, but devotees of the television spitting scene are not entirely without resources. There is professional football. Spitting by the players is, it is true, limited, because physical contact could easily lead them to swallow any cuds or sachets they happened to have in their mouths. This is not the case among the nonplayers off the field. They are beginning to drool, dribble, and spit in the same virile fashion as the baseball heroes. "SOS! Don't spit on sidewalks" may have to be brought back, slightly changed: "SOS! Don't spit on sidelines."

A final comment: Ugh.

We'll Do Pretty Good
¦¦¦
[21 February 1986]

The baseball spring training season is well under way, and the interviews in which reporters ask managers what they think their prospects
may be are flowing in profusion. To save baseball fans time and trouble,
what follows is an all-purpose interview. There are no teams or managers to whom it does not apply.

The reporter, Buck, is an old hand; the manager, Al, likewise.
Both know the routine. Buck opens with "Well, Al, how do you think
you'll do this year?" Al replies, "Well, Buck, we'll do all right.
Anybody who looks to come in on top of the eastern half of the southern
section of the northern part of the western division is going to have
to beat us. The other teams will know we're here." Buck closes in:
"Well, are you predicting the playoffs, Al?" Al replies that, well, if
his boys can put it all together, they could go that far, and maybe
farther than that. He grins. "We'll do pretty good."

The interview is now two minutes old, and the word "philosophy"
has not been mentioned. Realizing this, Buck asks for Al's baseball
philosophy, and Al says that his philosophy is that the team that scores
more runs than the other wins the game. He is therefore looking forward
to the return of seven-footer Wayne "The Lamppost" Pettengill, with
his good speed and good power, to right field. Pettengill, who began
as a basketball player, has overcome his tendency to pass the ball off
laterally whenever he catches it, but there is another problem: the team
financed courses for him in self-realization and he is no longer sure
that baseball is exactly the way he wants to express himself.

Al also speaks highly of the speedy French Canadian rookie,
Georges "Le Lapin" Cresson, who over the winter showed surprising
power in the New Zealand Instructional League, with one of his longer
drives seriously injuring a sheep. Al plans to platoon Cresson with
first baseman E.W.R. "Whopper" Maxwell, who shows signs of re-
turning to the form he displayed four years ago when he hit sixteen
and three-quarter home runs during a 104-game stretch. The three-
quarters came when he was thrown out at the plate after running through
a coach's sign trying to stretch a triple.

Buck now says that some people regard pitching as the key to
success, and Al agrees that it is and says he thinks his pitchers will

do pretty good. In fact, they have been doing pretty good, though he still needs a left-handed reliever who speaks English and can read the bonus clause. Buck interposes that he had thought that wily veteran Felix Fidel Federico Francisco Gonzales y Arias might be the answer there. Al smiles ruefully. For a while he had thought so, too, but the sore arm that bothered Gonzales y Arias in '85, '84, '83, and '82 has still not cleared up. They just can't count on him.

The interview is approaching its climax. Fielding is described as all-important—"We've got the gloves," Al says—and so is baserunning: "Off what I've seen so far," Al says, "we have good foot speed and good instincts. We run the bases pretty good."

Buck is ready with his most penetrating question. "There's no doubt about it, Al," he acknowledges. "You have the personnel. If anything, you're overloaded with talent. But are they motivated? Do they have that big intangible, pride?"

Al nods. "Pride," he says. "That's what counts. I've always believed in instilling pride in my players. I think I can."

By now, the interview has largely lost its sparkle. There is some compulsory talk about getting the breaks—"We can be hurt by injuries," Al notes—and about adapting to the natural surface, otherwise known as grass, that some clubs still insist on using. Also about getting the necessary support from the fans and the front office. "They support us," Al says, "real good."

With that, Al is out of time, Buck is out of time, and everyone else is out of patience. End of interview.

Music Hathn't Charms

Background Music
III
[2 November 1984]

One of the more profitable lines of work in the United States—it may fairly be described as a growth industry—takes the form of peering into the future and deducing what our lives will be like twenty and forty and a hundred years from now. Futurology, it is called, and it produces books, surveys, reports, conferences, forums, symposiums, hypotheses, and consensuses. Corporations pay large sums for these guesses; so do government agencies; and the academic world gives space, blessings, and respectability to any number of centers, institutes, and foundations turning out learned-sounding forecasts.

Which leads to this question: Among all the high-powered futurologists, was there even one who foresaw the emergence of an occupation devoted to turning out tuneless, monotonous, banal music? In the late 1940s, in a book about Britain called *With Malice Toward Some,* the author Margaret Halsey wrote that British shoes looked as though they had been made by someone who had been told about shoes but had never seen any. Much of the "background music" imposed on us today sounds as though it was composed by someone who had been told about music but had never heard any. The challenge to the "background music" composers is to write something that is unrecognizable and entirely forgettable. Over the centuries, many composers have managed to do this, but only in our time have composers set about it deliberately.

It is, moreover, impossible to believe that anybody responsible for these sounds ever listens to them. In the factories, or whatever they are, where this stuff is turned out, is the "background music" always on? Does the company director have it? In a hotel where it is pumped into the lobby, the elevators, the restaurants, the shops, the swimming pool, does the managing director have it in his office? Does the department store manager who inflicts it on his customers? Does the airport manager or airline president?

Background music has its reasons for being. It is designed to lead people to believe that they are having a good time. It is alleged to be relaxing. It has also been found to make people shop faster. This last is the opposite of relaxing, but no doubt the "background music" entrepreneurs have sounds and rhythms designed to bring about one effect, and sounds and rhythms designed to bring about the other.

Sometimes, when one's mood darkens, the suspicion creeps in that there is a conspiracy here, a conspiracy to soften the brains of the American people, with someone who does not wish this nation well behind it. At the very least, in individual establishments where it comes pounding out of the speakers, there must be torture masters who go about, with whips and chains, making certain that the "background music" is on, that the volume is high, and that no respite is permitted.

Yet another suspicion pops up, that the computer is involved, that the composing process has been put on a mathematical basis, and that so many possible arrangements of notes and instruments and human voice exist that the material for "background music" will never run out. It follows that this nuisance lies ahead of us for all time. Quiet used to be prized. To millions of Americans, that would now seem outlandish.

Live Aid
III
[15 July 1985]

What inspiring events last Saturday's Live Aid rock concerts in Philadelphia and London were—and, though it is painful to say so, how contradictory, and sad.

Inspiring because of the genuine selflessness demonstrated by people to whom time is money, big money, performers, producers, and publicists, and many more. Also because of the outpouring of generosity on the part of those who attended and those who gave money and materials and services. Here were people who saw a need in Africa and set out to meet it. It was a remarkable feat of organization and a chance for decency and goodwill to shine.

Why, then, contradictory? Because of the contrast between precisely that decency and goodwill and the music that brought it forth, music that here and there has some charm and infectiousness but all too often is coarse and violent. Which is also why it is sad. Are these the musical horizons of so many young people, this thin and monotonous stuff, relying as it does on electric amplification and sheer volume? How sad.

At this point, it is easy to see a reply taking shape. The writer is dismissed as out-of-date, an old fogy who wants to impose his taste on others. It is noted that there has always been a clash between generations; these objections are old hat. And what about Bishop Desmond Tutu, Coretta Scott King, Jihan Sadat, and Rajiv Gandhi? They joined in with requests for contributions. In London, even Prince Charles and Lady Diana attended the concert.

There is an answer, given, in the circumstances, almost apologetically and more in sorrow than in anger. Those devoted to rock music, if they think about it at all, probably believe that they are helping to break new ground; that they are defying convention and cocking a snook at their elders; that they are exposing themselves to raw, unbridled passion; that rock is full of vitality and brings people together. See those crowds, after all, swaying to the music, carried along, transported by what they see and hear.

But what is it they are transported by? How do they distinguish one group from another, one song from another? How many young men and women picking at electric guitars and doing a few rudimentary dance steps can anyone want to watch? How many vocalists, grimacing in affected pain and agony, and producing strangulated sounds? Could any of the vocalists perform in a hall of any size without a microphone? If it is possible to pick out words, are any of them worth hearing? When did raucousness and exaggerated percussion become music, and hoarseness a desirable quality for a singer to have?

The excitement in rock music is as nothing compared to the last movement of Beethoven's *Ninth*. Thrills? Try the "March to the Scaffold" in Berlioz's *Symphonie Fantastique*. Tenderness? Try the love duet that closes Act I of Verdi's *Otello*. Sensuality? Rock is kid stuff alongside the opening pages of Richard Strauss's *Der Rosenkavalier*, or Ravel's *Daphnis and Chloé,* the climax of which is, not to put too fine a point on it, a climax.

Nor need it all be so-called classical music, what used to be known as long-hair stuff before long hair became a sign of youthful protest in the sixties and moved on from there. Have these people ever heard real jazz and appreciated the feeling and virtuosity that go into it? Have they ever heard a recording of Louis Armstrong, playing, say, "Potato Head Blues" or "Mahogany Hall Stomp," or singing "Memphis Blues"?

Maybe rock fans do not close themselves off from all of this. One would like to think so. In any case, this is written in gratitude. Call it an appeal to rock fans to open themselves to the musical treasures that are theirs for the taking. They have, in Live Aid, done a splendid thing. Perhaps it would have been wiser to let it go at that. And yet . . . and yet . . .

AFTERTHOUGHT

The classical compositions cited were meant merely as a tiny sample. On the popular side, too, there were many more who could have been mentioned—Scott Joplin, Irving Berlin, George Gershwin, Cole Porter, Victor Herbert for operetta, other composers, other performers. This list would be almost endless.

One of the saddest things about American life today is the way our musical tradition is ignored. The United States has had the best popular music in the world. Nobody doubts that or argues about it. Yet on radio and television, that music barely exists. Jerome Kern, Rodgers and Hammerstein, Rodgers and Hart, where are they, and where are all the rest from Broadway, and Tin Pan Alley, and Hollywood? Where are all the great recording artists? What has happened to Dixieland and Kansas City and Chicago Jazz?

Music must of course push on. There has to be something new, something original. I do remember, however, something the classical guitarist Andres Segovia said to me in the course of a program we made in Spain: "To be original is easy. What is difficult is to be original in continuity."

Semi-Music
■■■
[12 November 1985]

About a year ago, a charmingly ill-tempered column appearing in this space described background music, in airports, for example, as a form of torture and possibly a device used by conspirators seeking to soften the brains of the American people.

Would a change of mind be permitted? Not about the torture part of it, or the brain-softening. Rather about what it is called. Music is not the right word. It is too generous. Non-music isn't quite right, either, though it is tempting. Semi-music is a more nearly correct description. Blap-blap, it goes, strum-strum, twang-twang, burp-burp, never stopping, an endless emission of relentless sounds. When airports interrupt it with announcements that such-and-such an airline is paging so-and-so, the announcement comes as a deliverance; you wish it were longer.

The semi-music fixes you in its grip as soon as you enter the airport building. If the airport is small and in some fairly out-of-the-way place, the assault of the semi-music is likely to begin while you are still outside the building. The walls cannot contain it, and the noise comes out to greet you.

There, then, you are, inside the building, being swatted and harassed by this unmelodious concoction as you check in, go to your gate, wait, shop, converse, read, perhaps close your eyes and try to rest. Go aboard your plane and it is there, too, lying in wait, blaring away, making certain that you do not escape.

Aboard the plane, there may be a refinement. The semi-music may not be purely instrumental, as it is in the airports. Someone may be singing, or more precisely, howling (usually a female voice does this), or if it is a male voice, putting out a meek and sorrowful sound, with overtones of country and western and soul. This is known as boarding music. Come the end of the flight and it also serves as landing music and sends you on your way into the next terminal, where you run the gauntlet of the blapping and burping until you leave the building.

Even that, however, is not the end of it. Your hotel has it, too, pumped into the lobby, and if it is thus blessed, into the atrium, whence it may pursue you into your room. As like as not, when you enter your room, a radio will be playing semi-music, not the same as that in the lobby, said radio having been switched on as a matter of hotel policy to waste energy (the lights are often on, as well) and to make you feel that you are still in the airport. Some hotels with atriums also have live semi-music in the late afternoon or evening. While this is being performed, the background semi-music stays on. (Unlike aircraft, where the cabin crew is frequently happy and relieved to oblige, it evidently takes a coded message from the hotel chain's international headquarters to get it turned off, or even down.) Properly positioned, you may be able to suffer from both the live and the canned semi-music at the same time.

Maybe I am unduly sensitive. Maybe I should be able just to tune this stuff out. Other people evidently do. Maybe I'm old-fashioned and out-of-date, lost in a time not my own. All the same, why can't we be left alone? Why is there a large industry in the United States (and not only in the United States) dedicated to turning out absolutely unmemorable semi-music, engaged in the recording and sale of noise?

What is the objection to quiet?

The Coat-Toters
III
[14 February 1986]

The coat-toters are people who take their coats into opera houses and concert halls, disdaining to check them. Why do they do so? I think there may be reasons buried deep in that well-known receptacle, the human psyche, but let's take the obvious answer first: By not checking, they save time and money on the way out. Simple enough. There is, however, a cost. When acousticians do their work, not always well, they take account of the size of the hall, its shape, its reflecting surfaces, its upholstery, its carpeting, and the number of people likely to be in it. They can hardly be expected to foresee the number of people who will come in with coats. Unfortunately, these garments have an effect on the music, just as an open door would, which is why ushers are required to keep doors closed. The coats deaden the music. There is even a theory that music sounded better in the days when those attending dressed more formally and the men's stiff shirts contributed to volume and resonance. In other words, a heroic tenor was helped to be heroic by what his audience wore.

It isn't only the sound that is interfered with by the coat-toters. There is a visual mood at concerts, and it isn't helped by people who sit on their coats, or clutch them to them, often to the discomfort of those alongside or in the row in front or behind. There ought to be some elegance at concerts. Sitting on a coat or draping it over the back of your seat is not elegant.

I remember going to the opera, many years ago, in East Berlin. The work performed, Paisiello's *Barber of Seville,* almost never done because of the preference for Rossini's *Barber,* was less memorable than the fact that hat and coat checking was compulsory. The compulsion came as a shock, even in communist East Berlin, but the result added to the pleasure.

Now for the reasons buried deep in the human etc. Consider first the individuals who come in with more than one coat, and the couples who come in with more than two. Do they compete with the authorized coat checkers, offering lower rates and perhaps financing themselves with loans from the Small Business Administration, or are they wool and fur and polyester freaks who offer to hold the coats without charge, for the thrill of it?

Or if it isn't the profit motive at work, do they perhaps believe that clothes have souls that enjoy music, and do they dash into their closets for deserving coats before leaving for the concert? Perhaps the answer lies here.

Coat-toting may very well spread to the musicians, if only to establish that much desired kinship with the audience. They would have to wear their coats, of course, because they work on small chairs, unless they wanted to put them on the floor, where they would make exceptional sound absorbers. Wearing them would not, however, be feasible for the string players, who need freedom of movement. The brass and the woodwinds might just manage, but the most logical candidates for coat-toting would be the lesser percussionists, some of whom do no more in an entire evening than take a few swipes at a snare drum or tap out a few notes on the triangle. They might come on stage, coats and hats and scarves in place, just before their services are needed, do their stuff, and stroll off, straight to the parking lot. They would have to remove their gloves.

Near the end of Puccini's *La Bohème,* one of the characters sings a sad farewell to his beloved coat. Then he goes out to pawn it so that he can buy medicine for the dying Mimi. Maybe he should peddle it right there, and auction it off to the audience.

Benny Goodman
III
[14 June 1986]

Benny Goodman died last Friday; the obituaries have already appeared; these comments come a little late.

There was, however, one thing Goodman did—or, more accurately, said—that was not touched on in any of the stories about him. He was present one night at a rock and roll concert and after listening for a while to the performers and the frenzy they aroused, he turned to the young people near him. "Do you," he asked unbelievingly, "do you really dig this stuff?"

What this question amounted to was a confession not only of puzzlement but of sadness on Goodman's part that sizable numbers of people should have found rock and roll appealing. Given that point of view, we may surmise what he made of the stuff being pumped out today. He must have found it dreadful and inexplicable.

"Ah, well," someone will object, "it's a matter of generational differences. Old guys are always being left behind and out of step. Anyway, when Goodman was playing his swing music, didn't the older generation object to it and call it noise?"

They did, of course, and for that matter, nobody is saying that Goodman was impeccable. Listen to his recordings and you will find some that were noisy, raucous, with tempos too fast to be intelligible, and a good deal of self-indulgence masquerading under the name of improvisation.

Yet there is a difference. The glaring monotony now in fashion would not have been accepted then, nor would the limited techniques of so many of today's instrumentalists or the deliberately ugly sounds produced by so many of today's vocalists. Hoarseness, except for Louis

Armstrong's highly individual and joyful gravel-throated tones, was not considered an asset. What is more, when Armstrong sang, you could understand the words; you knew what he was singing about.

Another point: There was amplification then; microphones certainly existed and were used. The mikes were, however, employed in large halls so that audiences could hear what the bands were playing. They were not used to stun the audience or to produce volume for its own sake. By contrast, today's music is more technology than music. It has all the charm and variety of a wind machine.

The argument that generational differences are always with us is irrelevant. It goes without saying that they are; how could it be otherwise? But what is going on now must be distinguished from what went on before. Today's so-called music is single-dimensional and depressingly unmusical. The fact that young people profess to like it and welcome having their hearing impaired by it is no reason to hide the truth about it.

Benny Goodman, as noted before, had his lapses. Yet they were lapses, not the norm. The King of Swing, which he was, was always musical. He could hardly have recorded a Mozart clarinet concerto with the Boston Symphony and Charles Munch had he not been, or taken lessons from the great English clarinetist Reginald Kell when he wanted to change his technique. Or worked with that marvelously subtle jazz pianist Teddy Wilson had he been otherwise.

I know that I have turned Benny Goodman's death into the occasion for a diatribe against contemporary popular music. Perhaps that is not a graceful thing to do. Perhaps I should simply have have thanked Benny Goodman for the many hours of pleasure he gave me, in college and after, and gave to millions of others. On the other hand, maybe he would have approved of the diatribe. Faced with what music was turning into, he did say in disbelief, "Do you really dig this stuff?"

Afterthoughts on Music

A Soviet scientist, in the city of Ufa in the Ural Mountains, claims to have found evidence, among factory workers devoted to hard rock music, that it is educationally and industrially disastrous. He says it damages their memory, attention span, and reading speed, lowers their productivity, and makes them more stubborn and aggressive.

We have heard about soil erosion. These findings suggest a kind of soul erosion. Some of those addicted could not do without their hard rock for more than two days—they became irritable, their hands shook, and their pulse rates became irregular. The louder the music, the worse the effects.

The findings ought not to be accepted uncritically. They will require corroboration. Still, on the face of things, they seem not unreasonable. Rock musicians do not play their instruments so much as assault them. The audience is assaulted, too, and the more raucous the assault, the happier it appears to be. There must be deleterious effects, and not only on the sense of hearing.

It has been said that one of the worst things about prison is the constant noise, the din from prisoners' radios. Medieval artists portraying Hell—Hieronymus Bosch would be the best example—show the damned being tortured by fiends clanging cymbals next to their ears. In our day, people pay to have this done to them.

It is hard to believe that this does not somehow affect the general level of behavior in the United States, and the general intellectual level. If the Soviet Union is genuinely a menace to the United States, or even a rival, the best news to reach us lately is the growing popularity of rock in the USSR. For the sake of our industry and cutting the trade deficit, let's spread it around Japan, Taiwan, Hong Kong, and South Korea as quickly as possible.

As Only
We Can

■■■

Budget, Budget, Who's Got the Budget?
III
[11 February 1985]

In the mighty spectacle of American government, nothing is more remarkable and puzzling to outsiders, and insiders, than the federal budget. President Reagan has now submitted his proposed budget for fiscal 1986, that is, the year that begins October 1, 1985. He has just under $974,000,000,000 going out, and just under $794,000,000,000 coming in, with a resulting deficit of $180,000,000,000.

So Mr. Reagan and his team say—though if Congress did exactly what they ask, in every particular, the figures would not come out as forecast. To begin with, they can't; they are only estimates. Then too, much that is unforeseen invariably happens. Besides, presidential budget figures always err on the side of optimism. No bit of jargon is more popular in Washington than "worst-case scenario," but that is one scenario never employed in these exercises. So almost everybody not part of the administration believes the deficit will be larger.

That is only part of the problem. It is now the middle of February, more than seven months before the new budget is to take effect. That should be enough time to get it through. It probably won't be, for the procedure is almost inconceivably complicated. There are budget committees in the House and Senate that have jurisdiction, in theory, over the entire process. There are committees with jurisdiction over particular departments; these committees draw up the bills that authorize the appropriations under the budget (after subcommittees have done the spadework).

Hearings are held, stretching out over weeks and months. Charts are displayed, graphs deployed. Experts testify at paralyzing length, make arcane arguments, and disagree. There may be talk about "fine-tuning" the economy, although that brand of economists' arrogance is heard mercifully less often these days. Some committee members fall asleep; others yearn to.

After a while, appropriations committees with jurisdiction over particular departments, and also richly furnished with subcommittees, recommend the actual amounts to be provided. Eventually, all of this, which rests heavily on the labors of the Congressional staffs, is voted on in floor debate in the House and the Senate. Then conference committees reconcile the differences between House and Senate, and there are more votes on the floor. There are also budget resolutions that theoretically keep the whole thing in order. All the while, the White House is chipping in with statements about what is acceptable and what is not. Finally, if the budget isn't ready in time, other legislative devices are used to keep the government going.

The budget is a big undertaking, a very big undertaking, and nobody expects it to be easy. After all, it comes to something like a trillion dollars. But it is prodigiously and dauntingly difficult to follow, even to track a single appropriation. This breeds the well-known public reaction, apathy. Another reaction, cynicism, arises from other causes. President after president has promised to get the budget under control, bring down the deficit, even balance income and outgo. President Reagan, in 1981, spoke of a budget in balance in 1984. Instead, 1984 showed the largest deficit of all time, and the deficit for 1985 will be even larger.

The fault is not Mr. Reagan's alone, or that of presidents alone. Congress plays its part. So does the system, which spreads the responsibility over so many groups and individuals that almost nobody can be held to account. What we have is less a procedure than a maze. No other civilized nation has anything like it.

Spies
III
[12 June 1985]

Let's not convict the Walkers and Whitworth before a jury does, but perhaps it would not be out of line to say that there is something deeply disquieting about a spy case, any spy case. It throws us off balance. How can people do these things? What is wrong with our country? Why cannot it inspire more loyalty than this?

The country, and its ability to inspire loyalty, probably have nothing to do with it. There are always some people ready to turn against their country for any number of reasons—money; ideology; being a wise guy; some affront they have suffered, real or imagined; contempt for "ordinary people" who would never dream of doing such a thing. Look at last week's exchange of twenty-nine spies between the United States and East Germany and Poland.

So we should not be shocked. But we are, still more when the spying appears to have been done for money. One reason we are shocked is that soon after the Second World War, a style was set for spies. It was something upper-class people did. Thus the Burgess-McLean case, which shamed and outraged the British and caused resounding indignation in the United States, which actually considered ending the sharing of atomic secrets with London.

The names may not mean much now. Guy Burgess had been bounced from a position in the British embassy in Washington because of drunkenness and flamboyant homosexuality. Donald McLean had also served in the Washington embassy, where his duties included liaison on atomic matters. Later, he reached the position of head of the Foreign Office's American department. He was married to an American. When drunk, which apparently was often, he was bellicose.

British counterespionage eventually became convinced that leaks of information dealing with nuclear weapons had gone through McLean to the Soviet Union, but just before he was to be questioned, he was tipped off by his old friend from Washington and Cambridge University days, Guy Burgess. They caught a cross-Channel steamer and made their way to Moscow. The date of their departure was May 25, 1951. I remember going the next day to the McLean house an hour or so south of London. Only the gardener was there. What did he make of it? He had a heavy Somerset accent. "Oi were thoonderstroock," he said.

Burgess tipped off McLean, but who tipped off Burgess? Who was "the third man"? Years later, he turned out to be Harold "Kim" Philby, another friend from Cambridge. He had worked in Britain's Secret Intelligence Service and, in 1949, had been sent to Washington to be the liaison officer between the SIS and the CIA. He is said to have advised the CIA on counterespionage against the Soviet Union, which must have amused him and his Soviet friends no end.

In 1955, after a Labor member of the House of Commons publicly identified him as the third man, Philby was dropped by the British government. He held a news conference, at which the British journalists present declined to ask him whether he was the third man on the ground that to do so would be "McCarthyism." It fell to me to ask him. He not unexpectedly said no. He then became a British newspaper correspondent in the Middle East, and five years later he went off to live in Moscow.

This, as I say, is where the notion of high-toned spies pretty well set in, for they were, all three of them, Cambridge men, arrogant, and—there is reason to believe—scornful not only of "ordinary people," but of the United States. In 1979, it emerged that there had been a "fourth man." He was Sir Anthony Blunt, also from Cambridge, who became curator of the Queen's art collection. High-toned indeed.

When people of lesser social standing are charged with spying, it comes as a letdown. Rightly or wrongly, we expect better from them.

AFTERTHOUGHT

In November 1987, Philby turned up on Soviet television. The BBC, reporting this, remarked that he looked more like a retired university don than a spy in exile, which raised the question of just what a spy in exile looks like. *NBC Nightly News,* after kindly notifying me that it intended to do so, ran again the sound bite in which I asked Philby whether he was the third man. Some people who saw it smiled sympathetically as they told me that I had looked "very young."

Philby died in Moscow in May 1988 at the age of seventy-six. He was given a hero's funeral, in keeping with his honorary rank of general in the Soviet secret police, the KGB. The sound bite was used again, and more extensively, showing a longer exchange and the two of us chatting and shaking hands when the questioning was over.

It seems worth adding that when Philby went to Beirut as a correspondent, his employers took him on at the request of the British government, which was still, somewhat confusedly, on his trail. He went to Moscow when the British authorities were closing in.

The Ever-Rising Ceiling
III
[7 October 1985]

Maybe it's different at your house, but where I live, the ceiling is fixed. If it were to move up or down, or even quiver uneasily, I would call the superintendent. I might even look for shelter elsewhere.

Not so Washington's best-known ceiling, the ceiling on the national debt. It moves, indeed it leaps, and always in the same direction, up. When it last settled into place, the ceiling was $1,823,800,000,000. That seems worth repeating: $1,823,800,000,000. A year, however, is as long as the ceiling can hold still. The Treasury Department, seeing it twitching in anticipation, asked Congress to shove it up to $2,078,400,000,000, i.e., something more than two trillion dollars. The assumption was that the new ceiling would last through fiscal 1986, which began about a week ago, on October 1. After that, no doubt, the ceiling will become restless and have to be jacked up again. Two trillion will not be enough.

Congress usually does not want to raise the ceiling as much as the administration would like. It likes to strike a blow for frugality and fix a ceiling of, say, $2,075,400,000,000, or even less, maybe $2,069,400,000,000. This is done not so much to save money as to save face. In 1977, for example, the Carter administration wanted it raised by eighty-three billion. Congress refused to be pushed around. It taught President Carter a lesson and raised the ceiling by only fifty-two billion.

The debt ceiling is one of the silliest manifestations of government. It serves no purpose. When President Reagan took office, it was one trillion dollars. It will have been doubled in less than five years of his administration. Travel back through time: The ceiling stood at seven hundred billion in 1976. Before that, it was six twenty-nine. Before that, five ninety-five. In 1971, it was four hundred billion. And so on and so on.

Four hundred billion, by the way, is the so-called permanent ceiling. It is necessary to have a permanent ceiling so that there can be temporary increases above it.

Once upon a time—which is the way to begin a fairy tale and not inappropriate in the context—once upon a time there was no ceiling. There was almost no national debt. In 1910, the debt was hardly more than a billion dollars. The First World War brought vast government borrowing through Liberty Bonds, and that was when the first ceiling was imposed. It would not be easy to think of a more futile exercise, because over the years, whenever it has looked as though the debt would go through the ceiling, the ceiling has been raised to accommodate it. If it hadn't been, the government could not have paid its employees and its suppliers, and the Treasury could not have borrowed money with which to pay the debts coming due. It could not thereby have created more debts to be paid later with more borrowing. Hence the ever-rising ceiling.

There is a point in this charade: The request for the temporary increase, and the debate and the legislating, with figures like $2,078,400,000,000 being tossed around, give Congress and the President the illusion that they are maintaining some control over borrowing, and the further illusion that budget deficits are an aberration. The dictionary definition of illusion is "erroneous perception of reality," "erroneous concept or belief." That says it.

AFTERTHOUGHT

The ceiling did become restless again, so it was appeased by being moved up to $2,300,000,000,000, and then, in the fall of 1987, to $2,800,000,000,000. Further familiar twitching was anticipated, followed by the usual treatment for the symptoms, no later than May 1, 1988.

Unavoidable Tension
III
[21 November 1985]

There is a good deal of tension these days between the Central Intelligence Agency and Congress. The Director of Central Intelligence, William Casey, complains that Congressional oversight of intelligence "has gone seriously awry." Some Congressional criticism of his agency, he says, is "inaccurate" and "unfounded," and Congressional leaks "compromise sensitive intelligence sources and methods." If Congressional oversight is to work, Casey says, "It cannot do so on the front page of American newspapers."

On the Congressional side, there is Senator Patrick Leahy of Vermont, ranking Democrat on the Senate Intelligence Committee, saying that the CIA is "rejecting oversight" and calling Casey's remarks "unfortunate." The committee's chairman, Dave Durenberger of Minnesota, has said that intelligence agencies sometimes use secrecy as a way to hide mistakes. Other members of Congress have weighed in.

All of this came to a head over the affair of Vitaly Yurchenko, the KGB man who apparently defected and then apparently of his own free will went back. That, however, merely brought the tension to the surface. There was plenty of it before, but it only rarely became this public.

The tension is probably unavoidable. It is built into the CIA-Congress relationship, for there is an inherent contradiction in the idea that a legislature can regulate clandestine activities.

The difficulty is that there is no better way of handling the matter. Prime responsibility for what the CIA does rests with the president, but presidents do not always ride herd on the CIA as closely as many members of Congress would like. Also, Congress must authorize the money for the CIA's budget. The House and Senate Intelligence committees were therefore set up in 1976 to give Congress some degree of control. Committee members found themselves considering the propriety and effectiveness of covert activities against other governments, of sabotage, of a CIA primer that told the anti-Sandinistas in Nicaragua how to "neutralize" their enemies by "the selective use of violence." In effect, Congress delegated executive power to the committee members to okay or object to what the intelligence agencies do. Under the

Constitution, however, executive power is something Congress does not have.

So it has come about that the CIA is required to inform the Congressional committees of "significant anticipated activity." Suppose some of the committee members don't like the activity anticipated. Suppose they've told the CIA that and it is determined to go ahead, anyway. What do they do? Speak to the President, perhaps. Suppose he is determined to go ahead. What then? Tell other members of Congress about it? Try to get money for the CIA withheld? Leak word to the press? Go public?

If the CIA anticipates Congressional disapproval, does it hold back word? Evidently at times it does. It did not tell the committees that it intended to mine Nicaraguan harbors a couple of years ago.

What is the answer? There isn't any of a structural, systematic nature. Members of the Intelligence committees have to play it by ear. Unless they are prepared to go public from time to time, they are not so much monitors and watchdogs as they are captives. The CIA, for its part, will want to go on doing what it thinks it should be doing. From which it follows that the tension, the backbiting, and the cross-purposes will continue.

AFTERTHOUGHT

This column had a certain prophetic quality. What happened later, in the Iran-contra affair, went far beyond anything it foresaw.

Manhunt
III
[18 April 1986]

A book called *Manhunt* is about to hit the stands. It's by Peter Maas, and it tells the story of Edwin Wilson, the former CIA man who went to work for Libya and Colonel Qaddafi in the 1970s and who wound up with a net worth, according to Maas, of more than $15,000,000.

He also wound up with jail terms, for smuggling weapons to Libya and for conspiracy to commit murder, of fifty-two years.

In excerpts that appeared in the *New York Times,* Maas writes that for a long time, the CIA and the FBI had a good idea of what Wilson was up to in Libya and did "essentially nothing to stop him." He says that the inability or unwillingness of the various American intelligence agencies to police themselves threatens their integrity and endangers American lives and interests abroad. On that point, one of the things Wilson smuggled to Libya was the plastic explosive C4. Maas says it has a life of twenty years.

All of that is scary enough. But if Maas is to be believed—and he is an excellent reporter; many people will know his earlier book *Serpico*—the CIA was a danger to our system of government at home. For it seems to have functioned as a government within a government, an outfit off on its own, way beyond the popular control that is at the heart of our system. Here are some of the things Maas found the CIA had done or that took place under its authority:

It gave Wilson, at the outset of his career in 1956, a false identity as an international representative of something called Maritime Survey Associates, which had a mail-drop address at 80 Boylston Street in Boston.

In 1959, while Wilson was tapping the telephone of a journalist working for *Newsweek,* he recorded a call between the *Newsweek* writer and Vice President Nixon.

Wilson later became an undercover graduate student at the School of Industrial and Labor Relations at Cornell. As a result, he became the European representative of the Seafarers International Union of North America. While in that job, Wilson also still worked for the CIA, spotting cargoes destined for Cuba and spotting communists on the docks in Antwerp, near where he lived. He traveled to Marseilles to pay off Corsican mobsters who were keeping communist dock-workers in line.

After a year abroad, Wilson was found a job in Washington in the international department of the AFL-CIO. That took him to Latin America to oppose left-wing unions, and to Vietnam. In 1964, on the recommendation of the AFL-CIO and with the approval of the CIA, he became an advance man in Hubert Humphrey's vice presidential campaign.

The election over, Wilson set up a freight-forwarding agency that was a CIA front. According to Maas, he sent crowd-dispersion devices to Chile, Brazil, and Venezuela; arms to the Dominican Republic; communications gear to Morocco; weapons to Angola; electronic equipment to Iran; weapons for a coup in Indonesia; military supplies to Taiwan and the Philippines; material for the CIA's "secret war" in Laos; boats for raids on Cuba. All the shipments were intended to be impossible to trace to the CIA.

Very well, enough. All of this is history, and Wilson is in prison, largely thanks to an assistant U.S. Attorney, E. Lawrence Barcella, Jr., who refused to accept an FBI report that Wilson had done nothing for which he could be prosecuted. (The murder conspiracy charge on which Wilson was convicted was directed against Barcella.) Besides, what was done must have been intended to serve the interests of the United States.

Still, the question persists: Who controls the CIA? Does anyone, even its director? Sometimes, when the CIA is discussed, men of wisdom and experience will say that we must retain our "covert capability." Maybe so. If, however, you do keep your covert capability, should you be taking a high moral tone? Is it possible that covert action begets covert action? How much is done in the name of our government that we do not know about?

Maybe the CIA today is different from the CIA in Wilson's time. Maybe. How can we be sure?

AFTERTHOUGHT

Prophetic once more, but once more, mild compared to what was coming.

Stirring Speeches—To Order
[30 January 1987]

Maybe the time has come to put an end to State of the Union addresses. Not State of the Union messages. There is no reason presidents should not send messages to Congress listing their proposals for legislation and setting out what they believe the nation needs. Indeed, the Constitution calls for precisely that. It specifies that the president "shall from time to time give to the Congress information of the state of the Union, and recommend to their consideration such measures as he shall deem necessary and expedient."

The big, full-dress speeches, on the other hand, are almost always a letdown, and in the circumstances—the gathering of House and Senate, the justices of the Supreme Court, and diplomatic corps—it is all but inevitable that they will be. There is the compiling of suggestions and requests from the various departments. There are the stories, for days and weeks before, in the press and on radio and television. There are the "briefings" of reporters. There are the speech-writers, trying to bring forth something stirring, something winning, something significant, and yet reasonably in character for the person doing the speaking. There is the notion that what is said should bring those in the House chamber to their feet, roaring approval.

It is, however, not easy to be stirring and significant on schedule and to order, even for exceptionally talented speakers, which most of our presidents—and other politicians—are not. The burden that is placed on those who deliver State of the Union addresses is therefore extremely heavy, probably unreasonably so. The speech becomes a performance, to be reviewed as a star's performance on Broadway is. Did he measure up? Were there any flubs? Did the laugh lines work? Was the peroration suitably uplifting?

When President Reagan spoke last week, it was even more of a performance to be examined than it usually is. After his operation and his troubles over the Iran-contra affair, had he bounced back? Was it true that he was depressed? How did he measure up? These are legitimate questions. Beyond that, presidents have to be seen in public from time to time, so that the people can see for themselves that they are functioning. Still, it ought to be possible to do that without all the whoop-de-doo and manufactured drama.

State of the Union addresses should not be ruled out. If a president wants to give one, that should be up to him (or, when the time comes, her). The Constitution provides that the president may convene one or both houses of Congress "on extraordinary occasions." But note the "extraordinary occasions." It is the annual creation of such occasions that is wrong, for it results in what are generally fairly dreary recitals, of the "We can, we must, and we will" and the "We will, we can, and we must" school.

It may be objected that expecting presidents to come up once a year with something useful to say to the Congress and the nation is not unreasonable. It is also the case that a speech can at times be a considerable intellectual exercise, politically effective, and even inspiring. Some speeches have affected the course of history. Others still to come no doubt will.

With us, unfortunately, the process has become too studied. It is overblown, artificial, and out of control.

All Our Own Work

Watergate
III

What follows is an NBC radio broadcast, two minutes and thirty seconds long, dated June 21, 1972. The text may bring a smile of recognition from those who lived through Watergate. For those to whom Watergate is just a word, and a mysterious one at that, it may be instructive.

This is Edwin Newman, NBC News, New York, Emphasis Critic at Large.

The circumstances no longer matter, but I remember, years ago, a well-known California attorney's filing a suit for damages on behalf of one of his clients. "How much are you suing for?" he was asked. "Oh, the usual million," the lawyer replied.

The usual million is also the amount Lawrence O'Brien, the Democratic National Chairman, sued for yesterday. Given the erosion of the dollar, it is surprising that O'Brien did not try for more, but anyway he has filed the suit against The Committee to Reelect the President and against a company named McCord Associates. This arises from the most grotesque episode so far in the election campaign, the arrest last Saturday of five men allegedly trying to install listening devices in Democratic National Headquarters in Washington.

It is quite a story. The five men were said to have been wearing surgical rubber gloves, and carrying cameras, eavesdropping equipment, and tear-gas pens. All five appear to have had, at some time, a connection with the Central Intelligence Agency. One of them, James McCord, is a former CIA agent. Another, Bernard Barker, a Cuban now in real estate in Florida, took a hand in preparing the Bay of Pigs invasion in 1961. Furthermore, in address books of two of the five men the police are said to have found the name and home telephone number of one E. Howard Hunt. Hunt was from 1949 to 1970 a CIA agent, and he is said to have been the CIA man in charge of the Bay of Pigs invasion. That doesn't sound like much of a recommendation for further employment, but Hunt has been a White House consultant, part-time, last year and this. He is reported to have called on Barker in Miami about two weeks ago.

The Republican National Committee and the Committee to Re-elect the President deny having anything to do with the incident, and both have discharged McCord, who was a consultant on security to both.

Who might have ordered the bugging of Democratic head-quarters is a mystery. It is hard not to laugh at the whole affair, but if the affair is ever untangled, it may turn out to be more sinister than funny.

Edwin Newman, NBC News, New York.

Religion and Politics
III
[18 September 1984]

A good deal of nonsense is being talked about the church and state issue. We are told, to the point of boredom, about the wall of separation between church and state. To be sure, there are breaches in it; how else explain "In God We Trust" on our coins; the addition, at the insistence of President Eisenhower, of the words "under God" to the Pledge of Allegiance; the chaplains in the armed forces; the opening of sessions of the House and the Senate, and of state legislatures, with prayer?

Nonetheless, concede that the wall between church and state is substantially there. It does not follow that such a wall exists between religion and politics. Not at all.

Largely because of President Reagan and the candidacy of Ger-aldine Ferraro, attitudes to abortion have become an election issue. It is Ms. Ferraro's view, and that of Governor Mario Cuomo of New York, that they and other officeholders who are Catholic have no business trying to impose Catholic teachings on abortion on other

Americans. Cuomo, an unusually subtle thinker, put it this way in a speech at Notre Dame on September 13: "We know that the price of seeking to force our beliefs on others is that they might some day force theirs on us." He added: "There is neither an encyclical nor a catechism that spells out a political strategy for achieving legislative goals."

The argument is persuasive, but in a way it is more a matter of tactics than it is of principle. If people are genuinely religious, why should not their religious beliefs influence their political outlook? How can they fail to? Many churches played a part in the civil rights movement, as they did in the fight against slavery. They may have regarded both as moral questions, but the rights had to be established by political action, in the case of slavery by war. Last year, the Catholic bishops in the United States issued a pastoral letter on nuclear weapons. They may have regarded *that* as a moral issue, but again, their argument can prevail, or even be considered, only through political action. There are churches now, in various parts of the country, giving shelter to illegal immigrants. As for President Reagan, he has the vociferous support of many churchmen, including some usually described as evangelical or fundamentalist, who make voting for him a way of serving God. Thus Christians for Reagan, a project of the Christian Voice Moral Government Fund.

Is this deplorable? Not necessarily. It is simply another factor to take into account when deciding how to vote. Those who are offended or dismayed by the President's attitudes, or the support he gets, can vote against him.

Catholics must decide for themselves how far to push the abortion issue. But for those who believe that abortion is a crime, it is not un-American to try to have those beliefs enacted into law. Ill-advised, perhaps, as Cuomo insists. More trouble than it's worth. Dangerous to the goodwill among diverse groups that helps hold the country together. But that's another story.

Consider: There are millions of agnostics and atheists among the American people. Is it wrong for them to examine the religious views of candidates for office and the extent to which those views might affect their conduct in office? Is United States assistance to Israel a purely political question for all who support it? And is it out of order for elected school boards to decide what may be taught about the way the world came into being?

There is, it appears, a revival of religion in the United States, less in the mainline churches than in the evangelical, where feelings are more visceral and the desire to "save" others amounts almost to a compulsion. This has seeped—or flooded—into our politics. It could not have done otherwise.

Debates
###
[25 October 1984]

As the moderator of the final debate between President Reagan and Walter Mondale, I would have no business offering an opinion about who won. I am not precluded from offering an opinion about whether the debate was useful. I am sure it was.

The question about the debate is often put this way, usually as though it were a particularly clever formulation: "Is this any way to elect a president?" The answer is that indeed it is. Not the only way. Not necessarily the best way. But a perfectly valid part of the electoral process.

It may be thought that my point of view is colored by my having been the Kansas City moderator. Of course it was a flattering position to have. But if one were thinking of what is wrong with our method of choosing a president, the debate would come far down on the list. It has the virtue of possessing some element of reality. The candidates are there, face-to-face. True, they have prepared, studied, memorized, been briefed. It is almost as though they have been wound up and sent out to perform. But even the vast and specialized staffs that surround candidates these days cannot foresee everything. There are those unpredictable and revealing moments when comparative native intelligence, subtlety of mind, range of knowledge, and quickness of reaction are on display.

Should voters be considering how well the candidates conduct themselves in the debates, when there is no chance that a president will have to do anything like that during his term of office? Why not? Voters take all kinds of things into consideration, some of them less relevant.

Presidential campaign debates do have objectionable aspects. One of them is that it is almost impossible for those taking part to answer a question with "I don't know" or "I'll think about it." The impression—it's an illusion—is cultivated that the candidates have answers to all possible questions and positions on all conceivable issues. This is ridiculous on the face of it, but it is part of today's normal buildup. In fact, it is precisely this buildup that makes the debate valuable—again because of that occasional unpredictable moment when reality breaks in.

No doubt the debate has its unserious side. It is a gladiatorial contest, a form of entertainment not unlike the World Series, the Super Bowl, or a prize fight. We want to know who won. But compare it with campaign commercials, with what is churned out by the candidates' organizations, with closely controlled public appearances. The candidates are there, exposed and alone. It's hard on them, especially if they are not experienced debaters—and our politicians, compared with, say, the British, are not. But the rest of us may learn something about them. Isn't that the point?

Still, the objections continue. The debates are too theatrical, we're told. They trivialize the issues. What we are not told is how, in these respects, they differ from the rest of the campaign. Why single out the debates? Nobody would argue that the format is ideal, that it permits a deep and detailed discussion of the issues. Obviously, the format does not do that. The exercise might well be more illuminating if there were fewer intermediaries between the debaters, perhaps no questioners at all. But that is for the future.

Well, you will hear, the debates don't change any minds. That is almost certainly wrong. Common sense tells us that they change some minds, confirm some people in the choice they have made, cause others to think again, and for many make no difference at all. But forget all that. The test of the debates is whether they enlighten the voters about those running. That they undoubtedly do.

How to Be a Moderator
###
[22 October 1984]

There used to be an advertisement that began, "If I have only one life to live, let me live it as a blonde." I'd rather live mine as a moderator.

It's a wonderful assignment. It makes you at least a minor participant in a bit of American history.

Moreover, being chosen as a moderator of the second Reagan-Mondale debate makes you a celebrity, or, if you have already achieved that mysterious status, more of one. Heads turn as you go by, people smile in recognition and advise one another that you are about, and a few suggest that you should be running for president.

"Good luck," people say, or using the theater's equivalent, "Break a leg," or sometimes, "Keep 'em honest," and if they think you're a questioner, "Give 'em hell."

The following conversation also occasionally takes place and keeps things in perspective:

"Aren't you Mr. Newman?"

"Yes."

"Where are you going?"

"We're on our way to Kansas City" (a reference to my wife and to our daughter, Nancy Drucker).

"Something happening there?"

You are also interviewed by other people in the news business. They want to know what preparation the moderator does. In fact, it's fairly simple. You make yourself familiar with the rules governing the debate and the order of procedure. Familiarity with the issues to be discussed is desirable, if only to add to one's appreciation of the debate, but it isn't necessary. If anything, there's a danger in following the debate's content too closely. The moderator's job is to keep things on track, not to judge the wisdom of what is being said. He has, by the way, nothing to do with deciding which questions are to be asked; that is for the panelists.

What if the audience cheers and applauds and uses up debate time? Gentle admonitions at first, then firm admonitions. But what if the audience does not obey? There is no answer. It can't be expelled.

And if the candidates go beyond their alloted time in answering questions? Lights blink at them. If they continue, they are permitted to finish the sentence, but only the sentence, even if the thought isn't finished.

Six hours before airtime, moderator and panelists walk over to the Kansas City Municipal Auditorium, in company with The League of Women Voters members who are running the debate, the redoubtable Dorothy Ridings and Vicky Harian, and the League's producer, Wallace Westfeldt, a friend from the old days at NBC. This is done so that the pool network, in this case, CBS, can check the sound and the cameras and the lighting. You take along the jacket of the suit you are to wear to be sure it stands out against the background and isn't swallowed up.

After that you're free until two hours before airtime, when the moderator and the panelists gather in the League's headquarters suite in the headquarters hotel, the Radisson Muehlebach, Harry Truman's favorite of years ago. Makeup is applied and we walk two blocks to the Municipal Auditorium, cheered and waved at on the way. After arrival, we wait in the dressing room usually assigned to the chorus when the auditorium houses musical performances.

Twenty minutes before airtime, you go on stage. Your makeup is checked; you put on your telex, a wired device that fits in your ear and through which you get cues and other information from producer Wally Westfeldt, a model of calm and good sense, in the control room. You take note of where the floor manager is standing, for he may be flashing you signals too; look up at the audience; and smile at the questioners. There is also a telephone under the lectern connected to the control room; if the telex fails, it can be used, but you hope it won't have to be.

Finally, the candidates walk on stage, shake hands, get set, and the audience stands and applauds. The floor manager, who has been counting off the minutes, says, "Fifteen seconds." Fifteen seconds later, Dorothy Ridings comes out on stage. She speaks briefly, and hands over to you.

And then—but there's no need to go into that.

AFTERTHOUGHT

I said that if candidates go beyond their allotted time, lights blink at them and they are permitted only to finish the sentence.

It isn't always that simple. At the end of the second Reagan-Mondale debate, in Kansas City in 1984, Mr. Reagan, in his concluding remarks, ran over his time and showed no sign of stopping. I wondered what to do: He was, after all, President of the United States.

A calm voice came over the telex into my ear. It was the voice of Wally Westfeldt and it said three words familiar to everyone in radio and television: "Wrap him up."

I did the wrapping. Later, when I told Mr. Reagan that I was sorry but the rules had to be enforced, he grinned and said, "I had a great last line."

Walter, Walter
▪▪▪
[5 November 1984]

Now that the election is over, I feel free to confess that, as one whose mind is cluttered by musical references, I had a problem with Walter Mondale. The problem was Gracie Fields. Mondale probably has never heard of her, and she almost certainly never heard of him. But Gracie Fields was a British music hall performer and actress who was at her peak in the 1930s and '40s, and one of her more raucous and celebrated numbers, sung with a Lancashire accent and in tones of boozy despair, was "Walter, Walter, lead me to the altar, and make all my nightmares come true."

I found myself thinking of this tune, which sounds almost like a Republican marching song, as Mondale pressed his suit on the American voter. For an impartial observer, that was unfair, because no similar musical references were triggered by mention of President Reagan. There are, so far as I know, no songs about a Ronald, nothing like "Sorry, Ronnie, I'm marrying Donnie," or "Ron, Ron, if you can't turn me on, don't turn me off all the way."

It would have been possible, of course, to think of Mondale musically in another fashion, give or take a letter. The hero in Wagner's *Die Meistersinger* is Walther von Stolzing, a young knight (and, naturally, a tenor) who impetuously enters a song contest to be held on the morrow, which is when so many things happen in opera. The contest is organized by the goldsmith Pogner, and the prize is the hand of Pogner's daughter Eva. Why Pogner wants to unload Eva's hand in this way we needn't go into. In any case, Walther sings an aria that begins "Morning was blooming with roseate light," and even though "roseate" is a word pronounced aloud perhaps twice in a century, he wins the contest. Eva then crowns him with laurel and myrtle. No Ronald has done anything approaching this.

In the absence of songs about Ronald, it was clearly better to banish both Gracie Fields's Walter and Wagner's Walther from the mind. How to do it? There was a solution. Consider these lines from the report by Tass, the Soviet news agency, on the October meeting between Mondale and the Soviet foreign minister, Andrei Gromyko:

"It followed from what W. Mondale said that he, for his part, regarded a turn for the better in relations between the United States and the Soviet Union as important and, in principle, possible."

W. Mondale! There was the answer. No one had written a song about a W, which made it possible to ignore the fact that no one had written a song about an R. The impartiality of the impartial observer was restored.

Considering this now in postelection tranquillity, it does seem that the initial standing alone has other advantages. It's 1988. Picture one of those Sunday morning television programs:

"So, H. Baker," the interviewer asks, "you want to be president of the United States. Perhaps you will be good enough to tell us why?"

The candidate, giving as good as he gets, replies, "Well, S. Donaldson," or "Well, G. Will," or possibly "Gee whiz, G. Will," and, in an exercise required of presidential candidates, goes on to set out his vision of America.

Will this idea catch on? Perhaps not. Its having been borrowed from Tass won't help. And then there is the *New York Times*, which often sets the standard in such matters. All through the 1984 campaign, it insisted on writing about Walter F. Mondale, apparently so that he would not be confused with all the Walter Q. and Walter X. Mondales who abound in the land. It did the same with Geraldine A. Ferraro, to distinguish her from the numerous Geraldine Ferraros who had achieved prominence in fields other than politics.

All the same, H. Baker. J. Kemp. G. Hart. J. Jackson. M. Cuomo. We need something new in our election campaigns. This could be it.

AFTERTHOUGHT

The idea did not catch on. The 1988 campaign did not bring us G. Bush, B. Dole, B. Babbitt, R. Gephardt, M. Dukakis, and so on.

By the way—this is a tactical changing of the subject—the German for "roseate light" is "rosigem Schein."

The Rime of the Exit Poller

...

[9 November 1984]

It was an exit poller,
Who stoppèd one of three.
"By thy long gray beard and glittering eye,
Now wherefore stopp'st thou me?

The polling place is open wide
And I am here to vote.
The hour is late, the issues great,
Your hand, please, off my coat."

He held him with a skinny hand,
"There *was* a vote," quoth he.
"Hold off! Unhand me, gray-beard loon!"
Eftsoons his hand dropt he.

He held him with his glittering eye—
The citizen stood still,
And listened like a three years' child;
The poller had his will.

The citizen stood in the street,
A few yards from his goal.
His fate was sealed.
He was to be a digit in a poll.

"Now tell me, sir, your age and wealth,"
The exit poller said.
"Your economic status, please,
And whether you are wed."

The citizen now cleared his throat.
He faced the poller dour.
"I don't know what to say," he said.
"Just put me down, 'Not sure.' "

The poller looked a mite cast down.
His spirits seemed to droop.
He straightened up and tried again:
"What is your ethnic group?"

"I do not cast an ethnic vote,"
The citizen replied.
"My preference is not to be
So glibly classified."

"Well, what about the issues, then?"
The poller asked, a grim look in his eyes,
"Which issues mean the most to you?
In short, prioritize."

Once more the citizen drew back,
As if to pull away.
"I've got to go, I've much to do,
On this election day."

"I see your point," the poller said,
Then struck a kindly note:
"Just one last query, if I may;
For which one did you vote?"

" 'For which one did I vote?' you ask.
Dear Lord with me abide:
You've kept me from the voting booth.
I've not yet been inside."

The poller cried out in his pain;
He sobbed and moaned, "Not true!
With voters, voters, everywhere,
I have no interview."

His hair askew, his cheeks tearstained,
He fell and rent his hair.
Then, of a sudden, rose once more
And kissed his questionnaire.

The poller, though aghast at first,
Had found a newer role.
"A breakthrough here," exulted he,
"I've done an entry poll."

A Poet Laureate

Tolerance may now be called for. In 1983, I tried my hand at verse, in what was meant to be a guest column for a newspaper. The paper did not see it that way, but looked at now, the piece does not seem bad at all. The occasions referred to are self-explanatory, except, perhaps, the one involving Henry Kissinger. He had agreed to head a commission that would recommend policy in Central America for the United States.

This nation needs a poet laureate. Not, perhaps, on the British model, to bring forth compositions on great occasions; they come according to schedule and defeat spontaneity. We need a poet laureate for some of the smaller occasions that engage the nation's interest and call for celebration or lamentation.

There was, for example, the sad story of Ling Ling and her baby:

Was it Hsing Hsing's or was it artificially induced?
No matter. The panda babe came forth and Ling Ling loved
    it,
Nuzzled it, cradled it, mothered it,
And, after three hours, saw it die.
A buildup of fluids in the chest cavity, the doctors said,
    prenatal bronchopneumonia.
Through the land, in chest cavities beyond counting,
Broken hearts beat.
Joy was confined.

Another story worthy of a poet laureate's attention was that of the airline passengers who prevented a hijacking to Havana:

They messed up his plans and treated him rough,
Those Yanks on the plane who had just had enough.
With a "One" and a "Two" and a "Three" and a "Go!"
They pounced from behind on their unwitting foe.
The pilot, who'd had to announce the hijacking,
Now turned for Miami and got his craft cracking.
And they all landed safely, without much delay,
Thanks to Yanks on the plane who had simply said, "Nay."

Then there was the disputed home run hit by George Brett of the Kansas City Royals against the Yankees. Immediately after the incident, this would have been appropriate:

I must up to the plate again,
To the lonely plate and the sky,
And all I ask is a fat pitch,
And the light to see it by.
And a tie score, and a man on, and the pine tar d'minished,
On my stout bat, and a home run, and the ball game
        finished.

After the ruling by the president of the American League:

Freed of the umpires' raw decree,
Freed of my goatlike horns and tail,
I thank whatever gods may be
For AL Prexy Lee MacPhail.

To deal with someone of the stature of Henry Kissinger, it may be permissible to stand, as the saying goes, on the shoulders of Milton and Poe:

Kissinger, our chief of men, who through a cloud
Not of war only, but detractions rude,
Guided by faith and matchless fortitude,
To peace and truth thy glorious way has ploughed,
Turn now to Nic. and Salvador,

America's frontyard, southward spread,
Their villainies by Castro fed,
Though spake the Reagan, "Nevermore."
Go forth then, Doctor, and prescribe
A formula to save our tribe.
Pluck from your marv'lous expertise
A brilliant caper, if you please.

The British weekly *Private Eye* has its own poet laureate, identified as Eric Thribb, a schoolboy. Thribb, whose style is heroic, might have apostrophized Dr. Kissinger thus:

Hail, statesman extraordinaire!
The shade of Metternich hovers over you,
Whispering approvingly.
Or is it Talleyrand?
I forget.

If we can't get a Dryden, Wordsworth, or Tennyson, perhaps we can get a Thribb. It would be a start.

≡≡≡

No More Lovable Dogs, Please
▮▮▮
[5 February 1985]

Organized baseball has a commissioner. Organized football has a commissioner. Organized basketball has a commissioner. Almost all the sports that provide public entertainment have commissioners. One sport that does not is organized politics. It should, and the appointment should be made forthwith, while there is still time to head off the horrors that otherwise lie ahead.

We are in a lull now, but it won't be very long before—if we don't have a commissioner—we will be seeing politicians asked on television whether they will run for president in 1988. They will reply that they are mulling it over and that they will make their plans known at the proper time. There will then be a coy interchange about what the proper time might be.

Freedom to mull is the birthright of any American, but politicians ought to mull in private. A politics commissioner would set up the rules of discourse between politicians and reporters. Questions about politicians' intentions would be prohibited more than thirty days before the deadline for filing. No questions, no coaxing, no setting of traps, no what if this happens or what if that happens. No public mulling. When they're ready to announce, they announce. In short, no publicity help from us.

There are many salutary rules a politics commissioner could institute, so that all kinds of extraneous matter could be eliminated from American politics. No pets. If a politician's pet appears in public, said politician is docked a thousand votes in the next primary. No family. Any politician whose family lines up behind him—or her—at a political event is automatically docked five thousand votes in the next primary. And if a member of the politician's family shows up on the campaign trail or at the nominating convention, automatic disqualification from the contest.

Automatic disqualification also for saying—in any context, speech, press conference, interview—"We can, we will, and we must." Or for referring to one's own candidacy as historic. No more "speaking to the issues," or "speaking to the people's aspirations." Issues and aspirations are spoken "about," not "to." No use of the word "address" as a verb, and no use of the word "concerns." Anyone who addresses the people's concerns is silenced for forty-eight hours.

No eating so-called ethnic foods to get so-called ethnic votes. Any politician eating lasagna in an Italian district or knishes in a Jewish district is finished. And no putting on the garb of a religion of which the politician is not a member—or maybe even if he is. No name-dropping along the lines of "As I was saying to President Mitterand only last week . . ."

The theory behind such rules is that we could trim politics down to politics. Ability to smile while ingesting Irish stew or chitlins or grits would have nothing to do with being elected. Lovable dogs would be beside the point. Likewise lovable relatives, or unlovable relatives, who seem to be just as numerous. Our politics would be simpler. They would be less costly. They would be less obtrusive and less boring.

Maybe we could even shorten the process, and concentrate on the essentials.

Oops, sorry, one other thing that should have gone in above: No jokes from gag writers, unless attributed.

Italian Americans
[15 March 1985]

A fairly obscure item from Washington appeared last week in the *New York Times*. The National Italian-American Foundation was holding a reception for Senate and House aides of Italian descent. The Foundation, the *Times* said, telephoned the offices of the 435 representatives and 100 senators in search of staff members with "appropriate ethnic credentials." The calls produced between 600 and 700 names, and more than 400 accepted the invitation to the reception.

A question: What do being on the staff of a senator or representative and being of Italian descent have to do with each other? What difference does it make? Do the staff members do something they would not otherwise do because their forebears came from Italy?

But I am jumping the gun. According to the *Times*—and I did call the Foundation myself and check on this—the Foundation is dedicated to combating discrimination and stereotyping. Is gathering Congressional staffers and lumping them as Italian Americans a way to combat stereotyping? Pasta and zabaglione were served at the reception, and the wines were Bardolino and Asti Spumante. Is that a way to combat stereotyping?

No doubt I will be told that I am foolishly exercised at best, that it is at worst all in fun and harmless, and that Americans come from many backgrounds and should be proud of their heritage, whatever it may happen to be. But why be proud of your heritage? Don't apologize for it, certainly. But you didn't have anything to do with it. It is the merest accident that, whatever it is, it is yours.

Of course there are damaging stereotypes at large in the United States. There always have been, and sometimes more than damaging—vicious. People victimized by those stereotypes will naturally organize to fight them. There are Americans worried about relatives abroad, and Americans worried about the survival of cultures with which they identify. And there are Americans intent on retaliating for what they see as wrongs done to their ancestors. And I know that the United States has drawn strength and drive from its mixture of peoples and even from the competition among immigrant groups to establish themselves, often against heavy odds.

The National Italian-American Foundation, which answered my questions with the best will in the world, is an umbrella group of Italian-American organizations. It engages in "networking," that is, helping Italian Americans to get to know one another, on the theory that this will help Italian Americans with problems to get them solved. Finding Italian Americans among Congressional staffers was part of this exercise.

I write this more in sorrow than in anger: How long does "heritage" remain relevant? How long should we carry it around with us? Is it a sensible basis on which to organize? If we do insist on organizing according to "ethnic heritage," how do we stop short of letting it influence foreign policy? It often has. Are we now to decide our attitude to the Iran-Iraq war according to whether there are more people of Iranian descent than of Iraqi descent in the country? Should our Middle East policy rest on whether there are more Jewish Americans or Muslim Americans? Our Cyprus policy on the relative number of "Greek Americans" and "Turkish Americans"? Policy on Northern Ireland on whether there are more "Irish Americans" than "British Americans," the latter a group that does not organize anyway?

There are immigrant groups, newly arrived from Southeast Asia, from the Caribbean, from Mexico, in the country now. How clannish do we want to encourage them to be?

Politics and Television
III
[22 March 1985]

You remember Walter Mondale. He's the fellow who said it was necessary to master television to be a successful politician. He cited his own discomfort before the cameras and his defeat by President Reagan last November as evidence.

That is evidence, but it has to be seen in perspective. By any measure, Walter Mondale is a successful politician. He was a senator from Minnesota and vice president of the United States. Not bad. He won the Democratic presidential nomination in 1984 and made many appearances on television while doing so. It is true that once he got the nomination, his campaign was a forlorn affair. It is also true that compared to President Reagan, he was not effective on television. In understanding why, however, it is useful to bear in mind an old English music hall comedy line, "It isn't so much what he says, it's the nasty way he says it." Turn it around. It wasn't only Mondale's style. It was what he was saying. Too many voters had no patience with it.

Granted that a politician these days must cope with television, in the sense that everybody in public life must cope with television. Television is in everything. Politics could hardly be an exception. But what does coping with it mean? It surely does not mean that the politician must change personality and pretend to be something that he or she is not. If anything, it means being yourself in front of the cameras. It is too much trouble to do anything else, and those who try run the risk of being seen through. Being oneself will not guarantee success. There is also the matter of being persuasive. But then, that was the case before television, too.

Jimmy Carter was no master of television, and he became president. Gerald Ford wasn't, and he became president. Richard Nixon wasn't; the perspiration on his upper lip was a national joke. He became president. It may be objected that accident and chance helped all of them, especially Ford, who was, in effect, appointed president. Accident and chance are involved when anyone becomes president. How could it be otherwise?

Anyone who has worked on television knows that it does not treat all who appear on it uniformly. It is uniform in putting weight on everybody—say ten or fifteen pounds—but it is kind to some, neutral to some, unkind to some. The usual explanation is that this has something to do with facial bone structure. It may also have a good deal to do with the care that goes into makeup and lighting. I know that I looked better on certain programs than on others, or if you prefer to put it that way, worse on certain programs than on others. Lighting had much to do with it. For example, lighted from below, you look younger. Jowls are less likely to show.

For the candidates, experts are there to look after such things. Indeed, they are there to look after almost everything: the mailings, the appeals to pressure groups, the choosing of areas to cultivate and areas to skip, the polling, the advertisements, the television commercials, the writing of speeches, the coining of witticisms, the use or nonuse of relatives, the creation of "events" and "news." The pursuit of political office, especially the pursuit of the presidency, is a gigantic operation, truly a campaign as the term is understood in military usage, an exercise in organization, research, and marketing. Television, like the computer, is an indispensable part of all of this, but only a part.

I will return to this subject in my next column.

Television and Politics
###
[29 March 1985]

In my last column, I discussed Walter Mondale's rueful contention that to be successful, a politician these days must master television. I said that Mondale was a successful politician, as his career showed, and so were other politicians who were not outstanding television performers, Jimmy Carter, Gerald Ford, and Richard Nixon among them. What was really required, I said, was coping with television, which meant being oneself before the cameras. This did not guarantee success, but neither did being oneself in pretelevision days. Let's pick up there.

Television is said to place a premium on the ability to communicate. No doubt it does. What is wrong with that? Politicians have always been expected to have some ability in presenting a point of view. Television may make some personal qualities more valuable and some less so, reward a particular manner and penalize another. That is a matter of luck: there was a time when the candidate with the louder voice had an advantage. That was a matter of luck, too.

Nor does television necessarily increase the likelihood that phonies will be elected to office. There were phonies in the days before television, and misfits, and manufactured candidates. No names need be cited; anyone can draw up a list.

Perhaps it would comfort Mondale to know that there are people who are paid to be on television who have not "mastered" it. They are tense and nervous; they may insist on the services of one makeup artist and one alone; they may insist on the services of a hairdresser, and seek advice on what to wear. Some cannot ad lib and would be terrified to try. Some cannot memorize and would be terrified to try. Some do the same kind of report over and over again and trust themselves to do nothing else. There are those who cannot deal with a Teleprompter that goes awry, and those who abuse employees of lesser rank when something goes wrong in the control room or studio. I have been told of a few who sink into meditation to calm down before going on the air. My experience has been principally in news. The picture in other areas probably is not vastly different.

The point is that there are television naturals—Mondale had the misfortune to run into one of them—but they are not thick on the ground. Those who make their livings in television know that very well. The chances are that the American people do, too. They don't expect to be dazzled every time a politician makes a television appearance. They may expect a reasonable level of competence, confidence, and ease. Why not? Television does, after all, offer clues to ability to carry on under pressure. By the way, even the most celebrated television performers are not popular with everybody.

Television has had an effect on politics. It has had an effect on everything. Was Mondale a victim of television? He was not in President Reagan's class on the screen, but it's hard to believe that it would have made a large difference if he had been.

I do not deny that, as a general rule, television invites calculation and slickness. We speak, with good reason, of television "production." But our politics have been headed in that direction for a long time. Television may have accelerated the process. It did not begin it.

Kiss Me. I'm Irish
[17 April 1985]

It is well after St. Patrick's Day, but if someone should come along sporting the lapel button that says, "Kiss me. I'm Irish," you might do worse than direct the button wearer to Washington. There, if he or she can attract the attention of Donald Regan, the President's chief of staff, the desired kiss may well be supplied, and by said chief of staff himself.

Early in February, Regan appointed Patrick Buchanan, a broadcaster and columnist, White House director of communications. A couple of months later, he told the *New York Times,* "I like the guy. He's feisty, he's Irish, he's articulate, and has strong opinions. He's played it very sensibly."

Fair enough. Regan likes Buchanan. He finds that Buchanan has opinions, strongly held and vigorously expressed. To anyone familiar with Buchanan's work, that comes as no surprise. But note the "He's feisty, he's Irish." If Buchanan's descent were different, would Regan have pointed that out?

"He's feisty, he's Spanish."

"He's feisty, he's Portuguese."

"He's feisty, he's Chinese."

"He's feisty, he's Indonesian."

Regan himself, one supposes, considers himself "Irish" and so is pleased that Buchanan is "Irish," too. The President himself is no doubt regarded as "Irish." So Regan presumably feels more at home with another "Irishman." Especially a feisty one. In the grim days of prejudice against immigrants from Ireland, there used to be signs posted at some places where employment was available: No Irish need apply.

This seems to have been amended at the White House: Nonfeisty Irish need not apply.

Happily for all of us, there is no sign that says that feisty non-Irish need not apply, but what has the sort of attitude implicit in Regan's remarks to do with running the White House? To repeat a question asked in a previous column, how long do "ethnicity" and national descent remain relevant? Regan no doubt used the "He's Irish" line unthinkingly. And there are other and more important criteria by which to judge his worth as White House chief of staff. But are we to cling to these "ethnic" myths forever? President Reagan once said ungrammatically about himself and House Speaker Tip O'Neill, "Us Irish are given to oratory." Again the "ethnic" explanation.

From Geraldine Ferraro, as well. Last week, speaking in New York to the National Organization of Italian-American Women, of which she was a founder, Ms. Ferraro referred to reports that floated around during her vice-presidential campaign that her family had connections with organized crime. Most Italian-American organizations "remained mute," Ms. Ferraro said. She had been "shocked" by "the lack of solidarity in the Italian-American community."

Those thus reproached can speak for themselves. But if Ms. Ferraro was unfairly treated, "Italian Americans" had no greater duty to say so than anyone else. As for the solidarity Ms. Ferraro called for, it leads, by inherent logic, to bloc voting and ultimately to each of us searching for candidates whose forebears came from the same country ours did. What a prospect!

Ms. Ferraro, by the way, is considering a race against Republican Senator Alfonse D'Amato of New York in 1986. By that time, D'Amato will have accumulated twelve years of seniority in the Senate. What kind of Italian-American solidarity is that?

AFTERTHOUGHT

Ms. Ferraro did not run against D'Amato in 1988. Since 1984, she has not run for anything. That election, and her husband's legal troubles, may have finished her politically. As for the feisty Buchanan, he left the White House after a while and went back to television and writing a column. Regan also proved to be fairly feisty, leaving the White House with the help of a shove from Mrs. Reagan and writing a book about his experiences there. His account suggested that President Reagan, though "Irish," was so passive about most things as to be nonfeisty.

Ethnic Election Year
III
[9 January 1986]

1986.

Election year.

Polls, of course. Lots of them.

And ethnicity. Lots of it. The time may even have come to change the information that appears in those familiar parentheses after the names of most holders of elective office. Here is so-and-so, normally identified as (D, Wyoming). Under the new procedure, he would be Rep. or Sen. or Gov. So-and-So (Irish American, Wyoming). Or such-and-such, whose parentheses used to contain R, Ohio. Inside the parentheses would now be found Italian American, Ohio.

Given the cultivation of ethnicity in American politics, we may expect news stories to be appearing soon along these lines:

"In a sometimes fiery but inconclusive debate, the Senate last night worked into the small hours on the tax reform bill. As the weary members, Jews, Catholics, Protestants, and a few atheists among them, left the floor, there was no clear indication of how the vote on the bill would eventually go or when it would take place.

"Republican leader Claude Gerbigny of Rhode Island, one of the few legislators of French descent, acknowledged his disappointment and said he had indications from the White House that Basque American President Uzcudun would feel the same way. 'The country,' Gerbigny said, 'in its great ethnic variety needs this bill. Every American, whatever his ethnic derivation, needs this bill.'

"Minority leader Gunnar Jensen (Swedish American, Minnesota) charged Gerbigny with dilatory tactics. 'On this side of the aisle,' Jensen said, 'we have all been ready to vote, blacks and whites alike, first, second, and third generation Americans alike. Senators of Greek and Turkish descent have subordinated their differences for the greater good. I saw a Hispanic-American senator and a Hungarian-American senator talking about the bill and ignoring the gap in national origin between them, and this at a time when Hispanic Americans have reached twenty million in number, with a gross national income estimated at seventy-five to a hundred billion dollars. Yet our efforts have come to naught.'

"The night's least-heeded speech came from Senator Lewis Fulton, (Melting Pot, New York). Only three other senators were on the floor as Fulton spoke, and it appeared that his refusal to use an ethnic designation after his name and to champion countries from which his forebears came had cost him the standing with his colleagues he used to have.

"Senator Flora MacDonald (Scottish American, Pennsylvania) introduced an amendment that would give people more time to prepare for the tax changes proposed in the bill. ''Scottish Americans,'' she said, ''German Americans, Polish Americans, Welsh Americans, Haitian Americans, and all the rest, it makes no difference. We are all in this together, and as Scottish Americans, German Americans, Polish Americans, Welsh Americans, Haitian Americans, and all the rest, we need more time. Our forefathers, Scottish American, German American, Polish American—I need not go through the entire list—came to this country to find freedom. Let us not hastily fasten an ill-conceived tax bill on the people. Taxation without ethnic representation,' she concluded among cheers and applause, 'is tyranny.'

"As the clock struck two, majority leader Gerbigny and minority leader Jensen put forward a bipartisan, multiethnic motion to adjourn sine die, with the explanation that the use of a Latin phrase should not be taken as discrimination against, or offensive to, members whose language heritage was other than Latin. The motion carried by voice vote.''

See Samoa?
III
[10 February 1986]

Nobody else should be expected to remember this, but back in the thirties—that's the nineteen thirties, folks, ha ha; joke—there flourished a satirical magazine called *Ballyhoo*. The word was widely used in those days to mean sensational advertising and excessive claims, what we would now call hype.

Ballyhoo as a word has now almost disappeared, but the magazine remains in my memory for a drawing intended to suggest a travel advertisement. It showed a lissome young woman on a beach, against a background of sea and palm trees. She was naked from the waist up; from the waist down she was covered, as far south as necessary, by a sign that bore the question: "Would you like to see Samoa?"

Having held this astonishingly witty drawing in memory for five or so decades, I have now seen Samoa, at any rate part of it, the port town of Pago Pago on the island of Tutuila, in American Samoa. (There is also Western Samoa, an independent kingdom.) None of the young women, some of them lissome enough, followed the *Ballyhoo* prescription for dress.

The disappointment was, however, somewhat mitigated by the appearance of some hundreds of Republicans. I'll repeat that: Republicans. A dinner meeting to launch a fully organized Republican party of Samoa was being held in a hotel in the center of town. Representative Philip Crane of Illinois, the main speaker, had flown over with his wife.

It struck me that, Samoan reporters apart, I had stumbled upon an exclusive story about a development that might, ever so subtly, change the face of American politics. Then reality took over: A great Republican upsurge in Samoa was not going to have much effect in 1986 or 1988. Samoa's population is only about 35,000, and it is an unincorporated territory of the United States, so its people do not vote in United States elections, though they do send delegates to the nominating conventions.

Still, Representative Crane and his wife went at their task with vigor and goodwill, and there the G.O.P. was, among the palms and frangipani; the sharp green peaks; the tuna factories; the men—some of them gigantic, in wraparound skirts; the women likewise; the cricket played on a pitch bordering the ocean; and a land so fertile that local people tell you that if you stick a pencil in the ground, something will grow.

There was even a welcoming committee on the tarmac, complete with television camera crews, before the Cranes were taken through the landing formalities—*Fa'amaoniga o Pasese* is Samoan for Passenger Check-in—and to a reception in a notably modest V.I.P. lounge. The reception, I was told, was also being held "for the Chief Justice," but this proved to be as much of a letdown as the failure on the part of Samoan women to pick up the *Ballyhoo* dress cue. He turned out to be the Chief Justice of American Samoa, entirely amiable but not Warren Burger. Another exclusive shot.

Still, there were consolations. The enterprising Republicans were not the only sign of mainland life in Pago Pago. The hotel restaurant's dinner menu listed, among other things, Entree's. Even without the Republicans, that authentically misplaced apostrophe would have made any wandering American feel right at home.

And so we say good-bye to Pago Pago and the South Pacific. With kind regard's.

Porous Parties
III
[26 September 1986]

Question: Can you name an institutionally porous public utility?

Answer: The Republicans.

Second question: Can you name another institutionally porous public utility?

Second answer: The Democrats.

Surely there is some mistake here? The Republicans and Democrats public utilities? No, no mistake. See them in this way, as Professor L. D. Epstein of the University of Wisconsin does, and you understand why the two parties have been around for so long and why they have so little control over what goes on in their names.

In his book *Political Parties in the American Mold,* this eminent political scientist writes that each party "is regularly entered by individuals and groups who want its electoral label,'' who do not have to pay dues or do party work of any kind, who are not bound by the party platform, and who do not have to tie themselves to the national leadership. Our parties are, therefore, less ideological and less adversarial than those in European countries. So we have—to take a current example—a Republican administration but not a Republican party government.

In a way, this helps the Republicans and the Democrats. Third parties find it hard to get anywhere in the United States because, Epstein says, ''Each major party is so loosely defined that one or the other absorbs electoral protest that might otherwise find outlets in new parties.'' For the Republicans and Democrats, this means survival—without much power in the parties' central machinery, to be sure, but survival.

As for the parties' being public utilities, what has largely made them so is the direct primary. They are not self-governing associations that make their own rules and impose requirements for membership. They are really confederations of state parties, and these are regulated, principally through laws on the primaries, by the states.

What, then, is the outlook for the national parties? One view is that they will simply fade away, as they are increasingly bypassed by candidates who have organizations of their own and access to money from their own supporters and the federal government. Another view is that they will be strengthened because the health of our political system demands it.

Epstein looks for neither. He concedes that the national parties have been reinforced to a degree by the bolstering of the party apparatus in Congress, for example through the House and Senate campaign committees, and by the growing professionalism of the national committees. On the other hand, he finds state and Congressional candidates more and more able to win on their own.

So, says Epstein, the parties will not become significantly more centralized and will not give us something like party government on the European model. That is simply not part of the American way. Even in the nineteenth century, Epstein says, when the major parties were much more in control than they are now, it was partly because there were no real differences between them; they were Tweedledum and Tweedledee. What is more likely, he believes, is that our old friends, the elephant and the donkey, will ''survive and even moderately prosper.''

That outlook is not very dramatic, but the professor is a shrewd judge of these things. He is, by the way, a former president of the American Political Science Association, and he has taught in, among other places, Finland and Australia. He is also one of my oldest friends, but that should not be held against him.

Vote! Or Maybe Not!
III
[28 October 1986]

Would it be very far out of line to suggest that there is really nothing terribly wrong with not voting in an election, and specifically not voting next Tuesday? The air is full of appeals to people to vote, on radio, on television, in newspapers. As the election comes closer, the appeals become more numerous and pressing. The word "vote" appears before us, in capital letters and with an exclamation point after it. Those who do not vote, it is implied, are unworthy, and careless with their freedom.

It has long been a fact that Americans do not readily go to the polls. In presidential election after election, for example, the number of Americans who voted for the winning candidate was exceeded by the number of those who did not vote at all. It's an old story: Lyndon Johnson's landslide in 1964 was brought about by 38% of those of voting age; Harry Truman made it in 1948 with just over 25%; Calvin Coolidge won in 1924 with just under 24%.

In elections generally, we have not had turnouts as high as those in other practicing democracies, partly because our parties have never been as highly organized as theirs, or as well-defined ideologically. So party loyalty has been less pronounced. These days, of course, the parties count for even less.

There are other reasons: the length of the campaigns; the inflated claims made by candidates, which repel some people and lead others to consider politics a joke; a disillusionment that makes it seem not worth the trouble to vote; the sense that things are out of hand—the budget deficit is a contemporary instance—so that it doesn't matter who is elected; the fact that some groups were systematically prevented

from voting, with effects that linger even after these groups are en-
franchised. Still another reason: the growing use of television commercials by candidates, which risks having these political advertisements
thrown in with other commercials that many people suspect, reject, or
ignore. And two more reasons: the public opinion polls and the network
projections, both of which discourage some possible voters.

So there is a nonvoting tradition in this country. It is easy to
deplore it, but if voting is our birthright, so is the right not to vote,
just as is the right not to worship, and the right not to speak out, not
to assemble, not to petition for redress of grievances. Some argue that
the health of our system requires much larger election turnouts. That
is not quite the case. The system would not be healthy just because
people were taking part reluctantly, as a matter of form, and without
conviction or knowledge.

Those who do not vote are saying something about the system as
surely as those who do. Sometimes it is merely that they don't care
one way or the other, or that the outcome won't affect them anyway.
Sometimes they are saying that they don't see enough difference between the candidates to warrant taking the trouble to vote. This last
attitude is significant; it implies that, to use the current jargon, we
may need electoral contests that are more issue-oriented and less candidate-
centered.

All of that said, low voter turnouts do bespeak a separation between the people and the political process. That cannot be a good
thing, but equally, it cannot be cured by exhortation alone.

Bewildering Times
III
[18 November 1986]

Any American who isn't bewildered these days clearly does not know
what is going on. There was Reykjavik. What happened there? We
still don't know. There is SDI. Is it a dream, a fantasy? How can the
great mass of us hope to know? There is Iran, and what the administration has been doing in, with, through, and about it. There is also

the election, which has tended to be forgotten in the events of the last two weeks but which ought to be examined. It tells us much about the condition of the country.

In those elections, the Democrats took control of the Senate and held, and even slightly increased, their already large majority in the House. In the states where President Reagan campaigned, the Democrats did notably well. Still, the Democrats by and large did well by moving toward the center. At the same time, the Republicans substantially increased their governorships. In short, no clear picture emerged, but rather incoherence.

It isn't hard to see why. The electorate is somewhat disillusioned with President Reagan. Doubts have crept in. His luck seems to be running out. He no longer soars, unscathed, above the battle. Yet the disillusionment, the sense of letdown, has not reached the point that it did with, say, Jimmy Carter. The returns reflected that.

Those are immediate factors. Others go deeper. The parties are not ideologically pure, and in any case, party loyalty is not very strong. Then, too, the United States is home to a vast range of interests, many of them conflicting. The trade deficit with Japan, for example, came about because of the devastation of some of our most important industries. Japanese imports displace American products and destroy American jobs. At the same time, those imports bring prosperity to the Pacific Coast ports through which they come, and to those who bring them in and distribute them, and to those who sell them. How do you reconcile those interests? You don't.

The United States is, moreover, always going through change, often convulsive change, and the changes now come faster than ever. Some regions flourish, others decline. Population rises here and goes down there. Cities age and their centers deteriorate; as they do, their politics may be transformed. Agriculture becomes, for many, almost a disaster area. That has political consequences. Immigrants flow in from the Pacific area and from Latin America. That alters the political scene. Women go out to jobs and acquire a new independence. Political consequences again.

Technological advance transforms the economy. Some of today's unemployed will never work again. Genetic engineering lies just over the horizon, and so do biological weapons as frightening as the nuclear. To many people, AIDS and crack appear to be more pressing than any other issues. What have elections to do with them? Add to this the fact that the great majority of Americans do not bother to vote at all, which makes it statistically more likely that some contests will be decided by tiny margins. In one or another of those contests, an advertising genius pops up and makes the difference. Next time, the genius could work for the opposite side.

All of these things, and more, almost guarantee puzzling results. Granted that they do not apply in anything like the same degree when, as in presidential years, the elections are dominated by a couple of personalities. Even then, though, they count for something, and in off years, they can mean a great deal. In 1986, they did.

We are a big, complicated, uneven, and uneasy country. The result at times is something like incoherence. That is what the election showed. It was an accurate picture.

An End to Immunity
[24 November 1986]

A seemingly malign fate hangs over our presidents. We have not had a presidency that ended more or less satisfactorily since Dwight Eisenhower's. Our presidents are struck down or they are discredited and their administrations disintegrate.

There was John Kennedy—murdered. Lyndon Johnson was ruined by a barely believable stubbornness about Indochina and what the United States could do there. Richard Nixon gave the nation Watergate and gave himself a unique place in history—the only president to have resigned. Gerald Ford picked up the pieces after Watergate but was not thought to deserve a term of his own. Jimmy Carter never became a commanding figure. He puzzled people and was finally ruined by the Iranian hostage affair.

Now comes Ronald Reagan. For almost six years, he seemed to be immune to the disabilities the others had suffered. Various explanations were offered: his evident patriotism, his affability, his pride in his country, his gallantry when shot and in the face of illness, his marvelous "communicating." All those explanations were valid, but there was another, more important and more relevant now. This was that so many presidencies had been wrecked. It was painful to think about; even more, it was dangerous to the country to have so many presidents, for whatever reason, fail. A desire to see a president succeed took shape, because that would be good for the country. Mr. Reagan was the beneficiary of that feeling. People were lenient toward his mistakes and settled for his good intentions.

That period is now over. Things have gone too far—the budget deficit, the trade deficit, the murky goings-on over Nicaragua, the mixup over Reykjavik and what went on there, and then Iran and in particular, that sad, fumbling press conference. The sun that seemed eternally to shine on Mr. Reagan has gone down. The elections to the House and the Senate showed it setting even before Iran.

It would be wrong for people to complain that they were taken in by Mr. Reagan. If they were taken in, they did it to themselves. So did members of the press. With them, the reluctance to see another president fail must have been unconscious, but they also took it easy on Mr. Reagan. There was almost a competition in pronouncing him a "great communicator," indeed *the* great communicator. Reporters wanting to demonstrate how shrewd and savvy they were outdid one another in celebrating his persuasiveness. Now comes the turnaround, as it did with Nixon and as it did with Johnson. Now comes the competition in pronouncing him inarticulate, unconvincing, at a loss.

At the moment, the fashionable word is credibility—use the word and you show that you are a Washington insider—and the fashionable speculation is about how Mr. Reagan can restore his. The implication seems to be that the damage can be undone, if only the proper formula can be found, for example that the purpose of the Iran operation, which was to befriend and encourage "moderates" there, was sound, but that the execution was messy because the President was given bad advice. What happened was, therefore, not his fault.

There is one thing wrong with this plan: The advice may well have been bad, but it was the President who took it. There is another difficulty: Mr. Reagan's competence is in question as never before. Often, through the years, because of his lack of knowledge, he teetered on the brink of becoming a figure of fun. This time, he toppled over.

The prospect now may seem fairly grim. Congress is controlled by the opposition and the President no longer enjoys general respect. The fact is, the outlook is not so bad. Each side must know the limits of its power. Each will know that it faces a skeptical electorate. Both will have to rein in a bit, for the good of the country. Moreover, Mr.

Reagan will almost certainly get better advice from the Congressional leaders of both parties than he did from his staff. It's hard to see how he can get worse.

Doubtful Political Reform
III
[8 December 1986]

In the Broadway musical *Sweet Charity,* there is a song called ''Big Spender.'' The heroine sings it: ''Hey, big spender, spend a little time with me.''

She doesn't do badly, but she might find richer pickings if she turned away from the dance hall where she works and did her singing to politicians. They are truly big spenders. They put out staggering sums in the November elections, hundreds of millions of dollars in the Congressional races alone. On the House side, a million was not an unheard of sum. On the Senate side, a million made a candidate a pauper. Three, four, five, eight, even nine or ten million was not uncommon.

This has, naturally, brought forth calls for reform, among them limits on television advertising and contributions from political action committees, and federal financing and spending ceilings. One or two of these may be enacted in some form or other, though that would mean that members of the House and the Senate were cutting into one of the advantages incumbents have, the ability to attract more money than those who challenge them.

If they are enacted, the reforms almost certainly will not work. Agile legal minds will find ways around them. For politics cannot be separated from the rest of American life and elections turned into old-fashioned amateur contests, in which those who have most at stake make no effort to influence the outcome, or are prevented from doing so. Insulating politics against the power of money sounds like a good idea, but it would separate politics from the rest of American life and make it artificial. Nothing else in the country is so insulated; why should politics be?

The kind of politics we have is also determined by developments outside politics. The use of advertising and public relations techniques is such a development. So is the use of market research. So are advances in computer and other technology, advances that make the run for political office more and more calculated and less and less spontaneous. Another determinant of political style and content is education—or its absence.

All of this means that it is not logical to expect to have a level of political life generally—this includes the presidency—that is much higher than the broad level of popular culture in the country. A higher level once in a while cannot be ruled out; accidents do happen. It cannot, however, be counted on, and it cannot be artificially induced.

No doubt the country would be better off if some proportion were returned to our election campaigns; if the president, whoever holds the office, attracted less attention; if our political leaders rose more nearly organically from the system. If any of this did come about, however, it would result from profound changes in our society. It could not cause changes in that society. In other words, it could not come first. Politics reflects the society; it does not shape it.

The line of reasoning set out here may seem a counsel of despair. That is not the case. There is something that can be done, which is to convince the American people that politics is a serious business, to be treated seriously. They must learn to spot the phonies, to discount the television ads, and to judge for themselves. As solutions go, this one is not electrifying, but what other course is there?

Try Washington, George
[12 December 1986]

There was an extraordinary television news program on the air the other night. From beginning to end, it contained no footage of Secretary of State Shultz in foreign climes, on his way there, or coming back therefrom. There was also no such footage of Secretary of Defense

Weinberger. The conclusion appeared to be warranted that both men were working at their desks in Washington.

This was not quite unprecedented, but an inquiry at the Pentagon yielded the information that in the last year, Weinberger had been away from his office for seventy-seven days—that is more than twenty percent of the time—with six trips out of the country and twenty-one in the United States. At the State Department, the word was that Shultz had been abroad sixty-three days in this calendar year. (The number has gone up slightly since the query was put in.) On travel in the United States, the figure was twenty-four days. Total: eighty-seven.

Shultz's time (and probably Weinberger's) could be better employed. It is at least conceivable that Shultz would know more about what happened in the Iran-contra deal if he spent less time in the air and more time in Washington. He told the House Foreign Affairs Committee last week that he had been "shocked" to learn that the United States ambassador to Lebanon, John Kelly, had had secret communications through the CIA with Vice Admiral John Poindexter, then the national security adviser, without informing him. "Back channel" communications, these are called, and in this case they had to do with negotiations for the release of American hostages.

A secretary of state may be pardoned for assuming that he will be told about such matters. If, however, he is not told, he has a better chance of catching on in Washington, where these things are ultimately focused, than he does batting around getting jet lag. Nonetheless, as soon as his House committee testimony was over, he was off to London for a meeting with allies and with United States ambassadors stationed in the Middle East. Evidently he was keeping in practice.

Maybe, too, if Shultz spent more time at his desk, with time to think, he would not be reading to the House committee "special reports" from someone in the American embassy in Nicaragua. He did read one, written in a superior tone, describing the celebration of the anniversary of the Sandinista revolution. Part of the celebration was a performance by the Bolshoi Ballet. The report contained this passage: "Fragments of *Swan Lake* passed before the eyes of third world revolutionaries and rustic Sandinistas, whose sensibilities to the expression and synchronization of the dance are, to put it kindly, imperfectly developed."

There is a sneer in those words, an insulting haughtiness. Pity the poor "rustic Sandinistas" and "third world revolutionaries" forced to watch a ballet. What does the embassy in Managua think they should be shown—dirty movies? If third world representatives came here, what would we put on for them?

Writing this stuff is bad enough. That Shultz chose to read it in public, with evident relish, is worse. This lack of judgment and tact is the opposite of what we have the right to expect from someone alleged to be engaged in the practice of diplomacy. Maybe more thought and less travel would help.

Let's Pretend
⋮⋮⋮
[2 March 1987]

Few will remember it now, but the crippled Reagan presidency was foreshadowed six and a half years ago. It happened at the Republican nominating convention in Detroit in the summer of 1980, where it appeared for a while that Gerald Ford would agree to run for vice president on the Reagan ticket on the theory that he knew how Washington and the White House worked and that Mr. Reagan, if elected, would need such help. Also that Henry Kissinger would return as secretary of state, and that this would ensure that foreign policy was in competent hands.

Some hours after the negotiations became public, the Reagan camp realized that accepting Ford would amount to an admission that its man was capable of being president in name only. The idea was dropped. It has now, in somewhat different form, returned. It has returned because the job of president, in too many respects, has been demonstrated to be beyond Mr. Reagan. There were those who believed it was even before he entered the White House, before the Hinckley shooting, the operations, the passing of years, and the strain of office took their toll. For the good of the country, they may have hoped that they would never be proved to be right. They have been proved to be right, and now the impression of chaos at the White House, of silliness, ineptitude, and impropriety, is too strong to be wiped out, by speeches, news conferences, or anything else. Indeed, it would say something unpleasant about the American people—that we are self-deluding, sentimental patsies—if it could be.

If this is so, what chance is there that the country can have an effective government until the changeover in January 1989? A slim chance, resting on acceptance of what might be called a grand compromise. In other words, Mr. Reagan must be prepared to avoid confrontations and to cooperate to an extraordinary degree with the leaders of Congress.

In exchange, the Democrats will have to refrain from excessively exploiting the advantage that is now theirs. It happens that they probably would be wise to do so anyway, rather than appear to be picking on a defenseless old man. For the time must come when people tire of the Iran story and tire of having the nation look bad.

Mr. Reagan has taken a large step in the direction of a grand compromise with the appointment of Howard Baker as his chief of staff. Baker is a man of the Congress. His instinct will be to get along with the leaders on Capitol Hill. They will also want to work with him.

There is a crasser way of putting all of this, which is that for the next two years, we will have to pretend that we have a functioning presidency when in reality we do not. It won't be comfortable or inspiring, but patriotism requires that the charade be played out, if only because it is so much more desirable than any other course now in view. There could not, for example, be such cooperation if George Bush, with his own presidential ambitions, were in the White House.

Our allies will have to join in the pretense, but they appear to be ready to do that. They have been remarkably tactful in their public comments on the Iran affair. Even the opposition parties in Western Europe have largely held off. The Soviet Union will also have to be cautious, and do nothing that would obviously capitalize on the botch in Washington.

For Mr. Reagan, the charade will involve further humiliation, but he can hardly complain about that. Under his stewardship, the nation has been humiliated. Throughout the Iran-contra affair, he offered a simulacrum of the presidency, nothing more. He has to acknowledge that and, unless another illness or overwhelming discouragement forces him aside, get on with being president largely in name, exactly what was so bizarrely contemplated in Detroit six and a half years ago.

AFTERTHOUGHT

According to Larry Speakes, the former White House spokesman, it was not the Reagan people who eventually decided against a Reagan-

Ford ticket. In his book, *Speaking Out,* Speakes writes that it was Ford who went to Reagan and told him that he had "soulsearched" the idea and had concluded that it would be wrong for both of them.

Blaming the Press

[11 May 1987]

When Gary Hart made his withdrawal statement last week, it had a slightly familiar ring. It was reminiscent of the day in November 1962 when Richard Nixon, after losing the election for governor in California, told members of the press that they wouldn't "have Nixon to kick around anymore."

As it turned out, they did—and vice versa: Nixon did some kicking around, too. That, however, is beside the point. Nixon thought newspeople had been unfair to him. Hart thought so, too. They were making him the issue, Hart said. He would have to spend all his time talking about himself. There would be more rumors and gossip. It was "an intolerable situation." So he was pulling out.

Hart's complaints cannot simply be kissed off, especially his argument that "some of the best people in the country choose not to run for high office" because of what they and their families would be subjected to if they did. It is also true that the *Miami Herald*'s reporting on Hart left something to be desired in thoroughness and care, and that many people in the news business disliked it on principle.

Still, Hart overlooks some things. Ideally, a candidate's personal life should be private, should be his or her own business. Granted. And leave Hart out of it. Suppose, however, that that personal life contains elements that might come into play if the candidate was elected. Could those elements open him to blackmail? Do they tell us anything about the way he would conduct himself in office, the sort of people he would surround himself with, the care with which he would proceed? Would his pre-presidential habits and inclinations carry over?

It could be argued that these are risks worth taking for the sake of preserving some privacy in the lives of our public people and some dignity in our politics. They cannot, however, be preserved just by castigating the press and asking it to be calmer and more "responsible." Many parts of it are restrained and responsible, but the press—which of course includes radio and television—does not operate in a vacuum. It reflects the society it serves, or more accurately, by which it is bought. That society, taken as a whole, wants entertainment and excitement. The press has helped it to want them, but distribute the blame as you will, the deed is done.

This is also true of politics. Indeed, politics is more and more influenced by developments outside its immediate province, influenced, for example, by public relations and advertising and marketing methods, by the use of demographics, by the harnessing of technological advances, such as the computer. Politics has been tremendously affected by television, by the rise of the airplane and the decline of the railroad. Gary Hart, the story goes, met Donna Rice at a party given by a rock musician. Hart was interested in getting the rock musicians to help his campaign. That also is the stuff of politics.

It is easy enough to say what ought to happen. Clearly, our leaders should rise more nearly organically from the system, as they do in parliamentary countries. In those countries, there is time to get to know political leaders, see them in action, in triumph and adversity, over a period of years. Parliamentary politics does throw up some lemons, and it more and more borrows American electioneering techniques, but it is less convulsive than our arrangements. Still, we do not have a parliamentary system and we are not going to. It probably would not work in a country this large and complex, anyway.

Let's agree that we need more calm and continuity and seriousness in our politics. To get them, we will have to change more than the press, reform more than the financing of our campaigns. We will have to change some of the most basic attitudes in American life.

Tip's Commercials
|||
[31 August 1987]

Tip O'Neill, the former Speaker, is about to embark on a publicity tour to plug his book, *Man of the House*. Nothing objectionable there; the book tour is standard practice in the publishing business for authors on whom the publishers are willing to risk the costs involved. In O'Neill's case, the risk is unavoidable. The publisher guaranteed him $1,000,000 for his memoirs, so it would be foolish not to send him out, hitting the book-signing sessions and the news conferences and the talk shows.

To repeat, nothing objectionable there. Some of O'Neill's other recent behavior is more questionable, specifically his television commercials for American Express, Miller Lite Beer, and Hush Puppies. Maybe there were compelling economic reasons. O'Neill told the *New York Times* last week that when he left the House, after half a century in public life, he had only $2,900 in the bank. He also had his Congressional pension, of course, but let's not pry. Let's say he felt he needed the money the commercials brought in.

It was still a questionable thing to do. There is already enough cynicism in this country about politics and politicians. Seeing them doing commercials with the other pitchmen and pitchwomen can only increase that cynicism and strengthen the impression they are in it for what they can get. In O'Neill's case, it is made worse by the fact that he held the highest post the House can offer, indeed the highest legislative post in the country. Why should that be turned to the benefit of particular brands of beer, shoes, and credit cards?

O'Neill was not the first to do this sort of thing. After the 1964 election, William Miller, who ran for vice president on Barry Goldwater's ticket, did an American Express commercial. After the 1984 election, Geraldine Ferraro, Walter Mondale's running mate, turned up on television explaining the benefits to family life of Pepsi Cola. Perhaps there have been others, as well. That, however, makes what O'Neill did no more welcome. It also lends a certain unintended irony to his comment about President Reagan, that "Most of the time, he was an actor reading lines." So, now, is O'Neill.

American election turnouts, compared with those of other countries with representative forms of government, are strikingly and depressingly low. There are many reasons for this, among them widespread illiteracy and semiliteracy; the presence in the country of so many immigrant groups, newly arrived; and the lingering effects of the barriers erected against voting by blacks. These reasons are rooted in our history; Tip O'Neill's commercials will not make a great difference. One can, nonetheless, hear the comment, "Just another politician, cashing in."

Speaking of cashing in, maybe what lies ahead is members of the House and the Senate rushing off the floor during debates and into the television studios to give testimonials for the political managers who ran their campaigns. Maybe they will say a few words for the hair dye that made them look younger, or for the laxative that keeps them regular.

Imagine it: "I'm Senator So-and-so. When I'm not feeling just right—you know what I mean, sort of stodgy—I take _____. That's why I can say to the voters back home: You can count on me to be there when I'm needed. I've never missed a roll-call vote, and I owe it all to _____."

And, Senator So-and-so might add, to Tip O'Neill.

Biden My Time
[6 October 1987]

The principal purpose of this column is to work in the expression "Biden my time," which apparently went unused during the late flap over Senator Joe's withdrawal from the contest for the Democratic presidential nomination. A sad reflection on the state of American journalism, and a serious omission, now remedied.

With that taken care of, there they are: Gary Hart of Colorado, Joseph Biden of Delaware, and Patricia Schroeder of Colorado, all out of it. (Colorado seems to choose politicians who are accident-prone.) The Biden affair could also eventually knock off Michael Dukakis of

Massachusetts. Then there's Senator Albert Gore of Tennessee, who gave a "careless"—and magnified—account of his early career as a newspaperman. The way the Democrats are going, the Republicans may win in 1988 by default.

All the withdrawals had their piquant moments, that of Ms. Schroeder most of all. She had to stop a couple of times to collect herself so that she could go on. We know that public men also have become tearful under stress, but not to anything like this extent. Suppose some particularly stern message came over the hotline from Moscow: Would we want our president to cry? Or are there some allegedly female qualities, such as being a bit emotional now and then, that are acceptable? There is no answer, but the pollsters will no doubt be doing their stuff on the Schroeder weeping, wanting to know whether it hurt or helped her, and female candidates generally, in the eyes, teary or unteary, of the electorate.

These have been bad weeks for the Democrats. They give the impression that the party is full of unstable people, people such as Hart and Biden who are reckless and have no judgment at all; and Dukakis, the great manager who chooses a campaign director he has to dismiss; and Schroeder, who breaks down and cries under pressure; and the "careless" Gore. Only George Bush gave the Democrats any help, with his suggestion that Soviet mechanics were needed to raise standards of workmanship in Detroit. A joke, to be sure, but even joking is dangerous to presidential hopefuls. Everything seems to be.

That apart, the Democratic withdrawals do have consequences, and one possible interpretation is that they hurt Jesse Jackson. This is because Jackson, the only black among the candidates, is thought to be guaranteed a percentage of the primary votes below which he cannot fall. The more whites there are in the race, the more they split up the rest of the votes and make whatever Jackson gets seem larger. The fewer the whites competing with him, the smaller his advantage next March on Super Tuesday.

This may seem a racist interpretation. It isn't racist so much as realistic. Race plays its part in American politics, as it does in American life, and as it has, sometimes in perfectly horrible ways, for centuries. When Jackson's supporters chant "Run, Jesse, run," they are saying something about the place blacks have had in the United States, and they are expressing what has been called black pride. It tends to make Jackson a black candidate rather than a candidate who is black. That has consequences, too.

Back to Biden my time. The Seven Dwarfs, as such, are no more. Snow White has returned to her (I think it was) spinning wheel. What's left? Pirandello's *Six Characters in Search of an Author?* Kipling's "six honest servingmen"? Marryat's "six of one and half a dozen of the other"?

The Republicans ought to be able to get something out of those. Especially the last.

The Democrats, however, are not entirely defenseless. They have a comeback:

Bush league.

Americans
Look Abroad

Looking Outward

Going It Alone on Arms Control
###
[7 January 1985]

Last November, at the Hubert Humphrey Institute of Public Affairs in Minneapolis, I took part (as a moderator, not an expert) in a discussion of arms control. One of the ideas put forward there has stayed in my mind ever since. It is, essentially, that if the United States wants to reduce its nuclear arsenal, it can do so, even if the Soviet Union does not reciprocate, and can do so in safety. By implication, the Soviet Union could safely reduce its nuclear arsenal if it wanted to, even if the United States did not.

The idea was put forward in a paper by Jane M.O. Sharp, who holds research positions at both Harvard and Radcliffe. Ms. Sharp reasons that nuclear weapons can never be used: they are too powerful and destructive, and their use would be catastrophic to the world. This being so, she says, nuclear superiority is a delusion, for it can never be employed for any rational purpose. But could not a nation with nuclear superiority threaten its inferior and gain its ends that way? The answer is no, so long as the "inferior" nation has enough nuclear weapons to inflict unacceptable damage on the other. This does not require balance; it does not require having as many weapons as the other, or the same kinds. It does require having enough nuclear weapons invulnerably based.

How many would be enough? Ms. Sharp does not say. She did at one time think that one thousand nuclear warheads could do the job for the United States. Some others in the field thought the figure too high; others thought it too low. Whatever the figure is, it does not, in any case, affect the argument.

Ms. Sharp also tries to meet the objection that nuclear weapons can make up for inferiority in conventional forces. She believes that nuclear explosives cannot be substituted for conventional forces for the reasons already stated—that they cannot rationally be used, that the only point in having them is to keep one's adversary from using them. It follows, she continues, that if you reduce your nuclear arsenal, you will not necessarily have to increase your conventional strength. The one has nothing to do with the other. She even argues that if nuclear weapons now stationed with NATO ground forces were taken away, those forces would be improved, because men charged with custody of the nuclear weapons would be freed for other duties.

There is much more to Ms. Sharp's thesis than I have so far suggested. The title of her paper indicates that: "Arms Control, Alliance Cohesion, and Extended Deterrence." That last, by the way, means the ability to deter a Soviet attack on our allies in Western Europe, and Ms. Sharp believes that the key there is less a military matter than a political one, including a plain, continuing American commitment.

But I am not trying to reproduce her paper here. This is the kernel of her argument, in her own words: ". . . NATO doctrine should recognize that nuclear weapons can only serve a deterrent function, for which balanced nuclear forces are not required. NATO should decide on the absolute level of its deterrent force and withdraw redundant systems in as orderly a manner as possible, preferably in cooperation with the Soviet Union, but recognizing that unilateral reductions need not undermine either United States or West European security."

I have heard objections to this line of reasoning. One of them is that the Soviet Union might misinterpret what was happening and be tempted into doing something foolish. But that is not very convincing. If there is a case against a unilateral reduction in nuclear weapons, what is it?

AFTERTHOUGHT

Nothing that has happened since, including the arms treaty signed by President Reagan and Mikhail Gorbachev, undercuts Ms. Sharp's argument. It is clear, however, that the course she recommends will not be adopted by any administration. Cuts in nuclear weapons will have to come in tandem.

Radio Free Europe
•••
[21 January 1985]

In the middle of this month, the United States government "disso-ciated" itself from a broadcast to Poland by Radio Free Europe. The broadcast had implied similarities between present-day Poland and Nazi Germany, and between Adolf Hitler and Polish Prime Minister Wojciech Jaruzelski. Poland complained; the United States said it regretted the implications.

The broadcast could hardly have come at a less opportune time. The United States has been easing up on economic sanctions against Poland and even considering exchanging ambassadors with Warsaw after a gap of three years. In Poland itself, a public trial is taking place of secret police officers accused of murdering a dissident priest, Father Popieluszko. The fact of the trial itself is remarkable, and it suggests the existence of strains and rivalries inside the Polish government, and perhaps even an attempt by someone, possibly Jaruzelski, to rein in the secret police. This was the moment RFE chose to weigh in with the broadcast the United States has been obliged to "regret."

What is it we want the Poles to do? Be dissatisfied with their government? Millions of them are. Yearn for greater freedom and human rights? Millions of them do. Revolt? Suppose they did. Would we help them? The record, in East Germany, Czechoslovakia, and Hungary, does not suggest that we would.

Radio Free Europe is not formally an agency of the United States government. But it is financed by the Congress, and the board members are nominated by the president and approved by Congress. People in the five Eastern European countries that hear its broadcasts beamed from Munich are not likely to consider it an expression of American free enterprise. Of course it represents the United States, and it ought to be brought under control.

I would not argue that the task facing RFE and the United States in Poland (and elsewhere) is easy. We would like to see the Poles freer and more comfortable, and we want them to know this. We would like to see Poland out from under the Soviet Union. We would like this for the benefit of the Poles themselves as much as for ourselves. And RFE programs are said to be extremely popular in Poland. But how far do we go in encouraging them to detest their own government?

How far do we go in encouraging them to defy their own government and the Soviet Union? Whose responsibility is it? What consequences do we foresee?

There was, in addition, something distressingly sophomoric—which may be an egregious insult to sophomores everywhere—in the RFE broadcast. Is General Jaruzelski really to be compared with Adolf Hitler? Does it make sense to parody speeches by current Polish leaders and make them sound like speeches by Nazis? Is this, as RFE has said, satire? Satire should have an edge. This is childish name-calling.

The current Polish government is far from angelic. And when it comes to anti-Semitism, Poland in the 1930s needed lessons from no one. But Poland was invaded and carved up by Hitler and Stalin. It was occupied for six years by the Nazis. Something like six million Poles died in the Second World War. Reminders from us are not required.

If we want to broadcast to the Soviet bloc, it can probably be justified. Maybe the Poles are helped by hearing from us, the British, and others. But let's do what we do with some dignity, restraint, and intelligence. We owe ourselves that.

South Africa: No Hope?
[29 July 1985]

A word about South Africa:

It may be hopeless. It probably is.

The administration is sticking to its policy of "constructive engagement." The President and those around him argue that the opposite course—pulling away, ending American investment there—would deprive Washington of all influence and make conditions even worse for blacks, for whom still fewer decent jobs would be available. "Constructive engagement," the administration says, has the best chance of preventing mass bloodshed.

The President's critics reply that participating in South Africa's economy in any way is immoral, that the government in Pretoria has shown for decades that it is deaf to reason and moral suasion, that the blacks must be supported in their struggle for equal rights. To do otherwise, these critics say, is to put us not only on the wrong side but, in the long run, on the losing side.

Both arguments, as it happens, make sense. Contradictory as they are, both make sense. Yet both may be irrelevant, because nothing anyone on the outside can do seems likely to make any difference. Repression in South Africa has gone on for so long, and has been so inhumane, that accommodation may be out of the question. There is a center, moderates, brave people who have tried for years to bring the government to reason and so bring hope to the blacks. Unfortunately, the center is small and the hour late. South Africa shows every sign of being headed for tragedy on a grand scale. All that keeps what is left of the peace is the government's overwhelming force.

The ruling whites might have been able to buy time with concessions, but they see concessions as leading inexorably to their own fall from power, and to government by the black majority, which would have little reason to be generous to them. They are unquestionably right about that. So the explosion, and the bloodletting among blacks, whites, "coloreds," and Asians, though nobody can say just when they will come, draw nearer.

With the best will in the world, which is surely not present, there may be no way to dismantle a system such as South Africa's in an orderly, controlled way, even if those in power felt forced to do it. Passing out equal rights a little at a time, humanizing an oppressive regime, is tremendously difficult. Things get out of hand, the pace of reform speeds up, demands grow, the entire structure is threatened. The Russians saw that coming in Hungary in 1956 and in Czechoslovakia in 1968 and moved in in force.

From the point of view of the United States, it is possible to say that if black majority rule in South Africa is inevitable, then the sensible thing to do is to choose that side now and win whatever gratitude and goodwill we can. The Reagan administration clearly finds that course unacceptable, and even if it didn't, winning gratitude from South Africa's blacks would not necessarily follow. Too much has happened, and not happened, for that.

Where does this leave the United States? Governments do have to decide, they must make policy. Even doing nothing is a policy. The administration, which did recall its ambassador from Pretoria, may have to yield to the pressure in Congress for some measure that will show our disapproval in a concrete way, though without going very far. Broadly, however, it clings to the hope that somehow reason will prevail in South Africa, that compromise is still possible. It continues to use "quiet diplomacy." That course probably has as much chance to succeed as any other. Or as little. The sad fact is that what we think and what we do hardly seem to matter.

AFTERTHOUGHT

A visit to South Africa (page 223) did little to arouse the hope that anything we could do would make a useful difference.

Instant Analysis
▪▪▪
[7 October 1985]

American diplomacy has not been at its sparkling best lately. Two embarrassing incidents stand out—the reaction to the Israeli air strike against the Palestine Liberation Organization headquarters in Tunisia, and the invitation to some of our allies to a conference with President Reagan before his meeting with Mikhail Gorbachev.

Take them one at a time:

If Mr. Reagan has a model for "swift and effective retribution" against terrorists, it is Israel. The Israelis do hit back; that can be counted on. Which no doubt explains the quick statement by the White House that the Israeli raid appeared to be "a legitimate response" to "terrorist attacks." Asked whether the Israelis had retaliated against the right people, the President replied that he had great faith in Israeli intelligence.

Now twenty-four hours pass. Other governments do not have the same faith in Israeli intelligence, and there has been unhappiness at the State Department, where Secretary Shultz had incautiously offered an opinion obviously not cleared with the White House. Said he: "We need to be clear in our opposition to the acts of violence from whatever quarter they come, and without respect to the presumed rationale for them.'' Presumed rationale. There is a pregnant phrase. For the presumed rationale was set forth by the White House—that the raid appeared to be a legitimate response to terrorist attacks.

All of this leads to yet another statement, a gem of its kind, in which the air strike is described as deplorable but also understandable, and yet, although understandable, distressing and not to be condoned. This statement reads like broad comedy. It also provides the basis for the United States position during the unanimous vote in the United Nations Security Council condemning Israel. The United States abstains.

There is still more. PLO headquarters are in Tunis at least in part because of the United States. We asked Tunisia to take in the PLO after Israel forced it out of Lebanon in 1979. Tunisians as well as Palestinians were killed in the Israeli raid. Moreover, we have long had friendly and useful relations with Tunisia. The fact is, the French regarded us as excessively friendly to the Tunisians when they were seeking their independence from France in the late 1950s. There were even suggestions that the Tunisians were being helped by the CIA. As a reporter who worked in both Paris and Tunis, I have some personal knowledge of this.

Nor is that the end. Forty-eight hours after Mr. Reagan's first statement, there were reports that William Buckley, one of the six remaining American hostages in Lebanon, had been killed as a reply to the raid. The reports are unsubstantiated, and Buckley might have been killed, anyway. Still, at a time when the President has said we are doing everything possible to free the hostages, endorsing the raid could hardly have helped.

That is not the end, either. The day before the Israeli raid, four members of the Soviet embassy in Beirut were abducted by a Muslim group that wanted Moscow to press Syria to stop the fighting in the Lebanese city of Tripoli. One of those abducted was killed. Suppose Moscow declares itself free to retaliate and becomes, however briefly, militarily involved in Lebanon. That is not a complication Washington would welcome.

While all of this was going on, the administration was being impulsive about another matter of importance. That was the meeting President Reagan wants to have with Britain, France, West Germany, Italy, Canada, and Japan later this month, before his meeting with Mikhail Gorbachev. President Mitterand of France declined, evidently because he was not consulted in advance. Belgium and Holland were displeased because they had been left out, which gives Gorbachev help he does not need and strengthens the hand of those in Belgium and Holland who don't want NATO nuclear missiles stationed there.

Considerations such as these are elementary. They make it amusing that commentators on television are criticized for engaging in "instant analysis" after a presidential speech or some other event. It appears that the truly dangerous instant analysis is that being done at the highest levels in Washington.

At the Summit
[21 October 1985]

In Geneva, on November 19—not very far off now—President Reagan and Mikhail Gorbachev are to have their summit meeting.

Does anyone remember where that term, "summit meeting," came from? Winston Churchill used it first, in 1950, when it seemed to him that the world was in a dangerous state. He thought it would be well for the leaders of the West—Churchill himself was not prime minister at the time—to have a meeting with Josef Stalin, to "parley at the summit." The idea was not taken up.

In 1953, by now back in Downing Street, Churchill tried once more. The occasion was this announcement by Moscow Radio: "The heart of the inspired continuer of Lenin's will, the wise leader and teacher of the Communist Party and Soviet people, Josef Vissarionovich Stalin, has stopped beating." Stalin had died just in time to prevent him from carrying out another of his murderous purges, this one of physicians, most of them Jewish, he believed were plotting against him and the Soviet state. His despotic presence was gone, and his successor, Georgi Malenkov, was in place.

As things worked out, Malenkov did not last long. He was put out to pasture, running an electric power station, in September 1953, and became one of the world's most thoroughly forgotten figures. But in those bright, barely believable days after Stalin's death, Churchill saw a chance to come to an understanding with the Soviets and to make the world a safer place. He proposed a meeting of Malenkov, President Eisenhower, and himself. "A meeting at the summit," he called it.

Eisenhower had been in office barely six weeks and hung back. His secretary of state, John Foster Dulles, devoutly anti-communist, believed that the Soviets should earn their way to international respectability. He believed also that meeting them might give an impression of weakness and of being "soft on communism." Churchill considered meeting Malenkov by himself, but fate intervened. He had a stroke.

It wasn't called that at the time. All that was said publicly was that Churchill's doctors had warned him that if he did not take a complete rest, away from work and out of the public eye, he risked a "collapse." (In that same month, June 1953, Britain's foreign secretary, Anthony Eden, underwent a bile duct operation in Boston. That was kept secret, too.) Rumors that Churchill had had a stroke did circulate, but all that could be established was that he was incapacitated. Two years later, in April 1955, Churchill stepped down as prime minister. He said that he had considered going to the summit alone, but that—and here he gestured dramatically—a stroke that had paralyzed him down the left side had made it impossible.

It was with this announcement that the phrase took off, and the idea, too. Of summit meetings since, there has been no shortage. Now it is Mr. Reagan's turn.

Summits are contests in appearing to be firm yet reasonable, peace-loving but no pushover. They are performances, elaborately and painstakingly planned. There is, nonetheless, always a possibility that something unexpected will happen, something unforeseen. Much depends on how the principals size each other up, whether one or the other lets slip something that had not been intended. The consequences may not become evident until later. They are not without risk.

The change in Moscow now is not so dramatic as it was after Stalin's death. Stalin, after all, was one of the most malign tyrants ever known. Still, there are new and different conditions in the Kremlin now that might be turned to advantage. Gorbachev, a more complicated sort than we are used to from Moscow, may be able to bring off changes in policy and attitude that his predecessors could not. Churchill would surely have thought this "parley at the summit" well worth trying.

Meet Me in Geneva, Eva
▬▬▬
[4 November 1985]

Have you ever been tempted to rewrite old songs? Take "My Defenses Are Down," from Irving Berlin's *Annie Get Your Gun*. An up-to-date version, to judge by the number of times one hears it, might be "My Computer Is Down," or on a happier note, "My Cholesterol's Down." The first line, by the way, is easier to get than those that follow, as in the case of the Bing Crosby hit "Sweet Leilani," turned into "Sheikh Yamani."

In deference to the upcoming meeting between President Reagan and Mikhail Gorbachev, we might rewrite that good old song, "Meet Me in St. Louis, Louis." It could go like this:

> Meet me in Geneva, Eva
> Meet me at the lake.
> Meet me in Geneva, Eva,
> Everything is jake.

A note to younger readers: "Everything is jake," now fallen into disuse, means everything is all right, everything is fine. A further note to all readers: Eva has nothing to do with the Reagan-Gorbachev meeting; I know that; it's just that rhymes for Geneva are hard to find. It could work for an opera singer: "Meet me in Geneva, diva," and still in an operatic mood, for a drinking song: "Meet me in Geneva"—and here glasses are raised—"Viva!" If the summiteers' wives were brought into it, we could have a variation: "Meet me when you fancy, Nancy." Raisa (that's three syllables) Gorbachev does, however, create problems. Nothing in English rhymes with Raisa. "No one need be any waisa, Raisa" is straining too hard.

Some of course think the summit a mistake. They might hark back to "Meet Me in Dreamland" and suggest that the title calls for no rewriting at all. Likewise with "Dancing in the Dark."

There is no end to the old popular songs that could apply to the summit. The following list is alphabetical, and the circumstances in which each song would be appropriate suggest themselves:

Anything You Can Do I Can Do Better
Alone Together
Better Luck Next Time
Big Noise From Winnetka (Sorry. Mr. Reagan's from Eureka,
     Illinois, not Winnetka.)
Can't We Be Friends?
Do Nothing Till You Hear From Me
Don't Be That Way
Embraceable You
Hallelujah!
I Can't Get Started With You
I Guess I'll Have to Change My Plans
I'll Be Seeing You
Johnny One-Note
Let's Begin
Let's Call the Whole Thing Off
Let's Do It
Make Believe
The Man That Got Away
My Buddy
Russian Lullaby
Say It Isn't So
S'posin'
Strike Up the Band
Stumbling
There'll Be Some Changes Made
Things Are Looking Up
Why Can't You Behave?
You're Driving Me Crazy

Hold on a minute. Getting back to Raisa Gorbachev, there was
a song in the musical *The Bandwagon* called "I Love Louisa." That
might be adapted to Mrs. G. We shall see.

Truman and the Greeks
###
[7 May 1986]

Among the other heartwarming events of this spring was one that largely escaped notice. It was a decision by the City Council of Athens not to put back on its pedestal a statue of Harry Truman. The statue, a gift from a group of Greek Americans, was blown up by a leftist group in March by way of greeting an official visit by Secretary of State Shultz. It was to be put back. Now it won't be.

Not all members of the City Council voted against restoring the statue. The Socialist majority and its Communist allies, however, carried the day, with the somewhat puzzling explanation that the vote "should in no way be considered to be directed against the principle of friendship" between Greeks and Americans. Rather, the statue "conflicted with the sentiments of the Athenian people because of the policy that was expressed and carried out by Truman."

The roots of the council's vote go back a long way. They were explained to me fourteen years ago by Andreas Papandreou, now the Greek prime minister and head of the Socialist party that dominates the Athens City Council. Papandreou, an economist, was then teaching at York University in Toronto. He had earlier taught in Sweden and at three American universities, Minnesota, Northwestern, and Berkeley. Five years earlier, in 1967, when the Greek military seized power, he had, as a cabinet minister in a government headed by his father, been put in prison and then sent into exile.

Simply stated, Papandreou blamed the United States for what had happened to him and to his country. His reasoning went like this: President Truman in 1947 enunciated the Truman Doctrine, under which the United States announced that it would not allow Greece or Turkey to fall to communism. By 1949, the threat had been dispelled, in part because Yugoslavia stopped helping the Greek communist guerrillas. Then, according to Papandreou, came "a decade of direct . . . supervision of the political and economic life of Greece by the United States . . . Greece was run, basically, by the American mission."

Greek intelligence and the Greek military, Papandreou went on, were adjuncts of the United States. In 1967, when it appeared that the Papandreous would win a national election, and this was deemed inimical to the interests of the United States, Washington gave the signal for a military coup. The dictatorship that followed was described by Papandreou as "a covert occupation" of Greece by the United States. It lasted until 1974, when the Greek military supported a coup on Cyprus. That brought a Turkish invasion of Cyprus, and it brought the Greek colonels down.

Papandreou's view explains not only why the Truman statue won't be put up again. It explains Greece's general attitude to NATO and to the United States. Papandreou came into office in 1981 speaking of ending United States military bases in Greece. Though he has never done that, the future of the bases is in doubt. He has not cooperated in actions against terrorism to a degree that Washington would like. Relations are difficult at best.

All of this may seem hard on the United States, which Papandreou himself says spent something like a million dollars a day for ten years to hold off communism in Greece, and that at a time when a million dollars was a lot more than it is now. It is also hard on Harry Truman, who made a fundamental decision that Greece and Turkey were to be held and was prepared to do whatever was necessary to hold them. Still, there is no understanding Greek policy now without taking account of Papandreou's interpretation of history. The Truman statue is a casualty of that interpretation.

AFTERTHOUGHT

The statue was, after all, put back up, in the spring of 1987, with the pedestal surrounded by iron railings more than six feet high, and with two policemen on guard day and night.

Mexico and the Free Market
iii
[19 May 1986]

The Reagan administration is distinctly unhappy these days with Mexico. It is unhappy about an apparent increase in illegal immigration, about drug traffic, and about corruption. The corruption, it is strongly implied, is so pervasive that it frustrates attempts to do anything about the drugs and the immigration. So unhappy is the administration that these things were said publicly last week during a Senate hearing. In a closed hearing, it was even noised about that relatives of President Miguel de la Madrid were engaged in the drug traffic.

There is no small irony in this. The administration is devoted to the free market as the key to national well-being. It urges the free market on others, including the nations of the Third World. What it complains of in Mexico, however, is the free market at work. In that kind of market, people go where the jobs are, wherefore the illegal immigration. Supply goes where the demand is, wherefore the drugs. The free market does not pay much attention to borders, especially borders 1,600 miles long. It operates, and lets things go at that.

If this is so, then the question is not so much Mexico's curtailing or not curtailing the supply of marijuana and heroin. It is more a matter of cutting the demand. It is the pronounced goofiness of so many Americans that is the root of the trouble. People here, in large numbers, use drugs. Doing so is thought to be clever and sophisticated, though probably no longer daring. For millions of Americans, drugs are all but routine.

One could wish that the Mexicans were more efficient at stamping out their marijuana and opium, and that they were less corrupt, for their own sake as well as ours. If, however, there is money to be made from drugs, there are those who will produce them and those who will traffic in them. If we want to stop that, we will have to stop it on our side of the border. Less of our time and effort might go into lecturing others, and more into reforming ourselves.

The immigration problem arises because, roughly speaking, we are rich and Mexico is poor. There are jobs on our side of the border and no jobs on theirs. Again, there is money to be made not only by the immigrants themselves but by those who get them across the border, and by those who employ them here. If Americans did not employ illegals, the illegals would go away, or certainly diminish. For that to happen, working conditions might have to be improved, and some of the unemployed would have to accept the kind of work that is available. Granted that that last is easy to ask—especially by those of us who have never done such work or anything like it—and not so easy to do.

Some self-examination is in order. Why are so many Americans using drugs? Why is there such a mismatch between those who don't have jobs and the jobs that are open? How much corruption is there on our side that ties up with theirs? Incidentally, what would happen in Mexico if there were no safety valve for the illegals?

Finally, there is the diplomatic aspect. United States customs and drug control and immigration officials who deal with these matters are understandably exercised, but denunciations of Mexico by the United States are not likely to help. They will not cause Mexicans generally to become indignant about their government and to force changes on it welcome to us. What the denunciations already have done is to cause Mexico to accuse us of spreading misinformation and of violating Mexican sovereignty.

For reasons embedded in history and inherent in the imbalance between their wealth and power and ours, the United States is not exactly beloved in our neighbor to the south. It's tiresome to keep that in mind, but kept in mind it has to be.

Mikhail, Meet Vegas
[11 June 1986]

Americans like to say that if Soviet leaders could just see how the average American working man lives, they would change their minds about capitalism and the United States.

Very well. Mikhail Gorbachev may still be coming to this country sometime this year, probably after the election. To see the average American working man, where should he go? There can be only one answer: Vegas, also known as fabulous Las Vegas. There Gorbachev would see working Americans at play, amid many wonders. One wonder is Al Capone's car, the bulletproof limousine that carried around the country's most celebrated gangster until Scarface Al ran into trouble over income taxes in 1931 and was put away. Security makes strange bedfellows: the car does not look very different from the limos leading politicians are obliged to ride around in today.

If Gorbachev likes flowers, there is Bugsy Siegel's rose garden. Bugsy was a gangster who, because of the antigambling laws in

California, had much to do with making Vegas a gambling center. It is said that nobody dared call him Bugsy to his face, except possibly after he had been rendered extremely dead by shooting. His garden is preserved in the grounds of a Vegas hotel, and a whimsical sign explains that the roses bloom so bountifully possibly because of a nutrient Bugsy used years ago, said nutrient having been the remains of three of his associates, Big Howie Dennis, Mad Dog Nevills, and Filthy Frankie Giannatasio, all of whom vanished without trace.

The sign says also that if you stand in the garden at midnight, under a full moon, you may hear three muffled voices asking, "Bugsy, how do you like the roses, Bugsy?" Gorbachev and his wife, Raisa, might want to try it. It would make dinner conversation in the Kremlin, from which disappearances without trace are not unknown.

Enough of crime, unless arrangements can be made for the Gorbachevs to watch a skimming operation.

For culture, there is classical statuary on the main street, placed there by hotels reminding visitors of the grandeur that was Rome; and there is Liberace's piano museum; and for employment opportunities for exceptionally tall Soviet athletes, in case Gorbachev wants to send some this way, the University of Nevada at Las Vegas basketball team.

Other Vegas attractions might be considered: the Flying Dutchman restaurant, which—in Vegas, this seems perfectly logical—specializes in Basque food; and the preschool center called The Lit'l Scholar, which evidently specializes in prespelling and may have offered technical advice to the condo that says forthrightly on an outdoor sign, "If you don't like, don't by." Precisely. Gorbachev would be impressed by the democratic spelling.

The Lit'l Scholar may also have assisted with the spelling on a hotel restaurant's menu that offers a Mamouth Malt. Unless, that is, the malt was devised by a chef named, perhaps, Pierre or Jean Claude Mamouth. Anyway, it is mamouth and thick, and Gorbachev might like to try one. He might also be tempted by one of those fixed-price Vegas buffets, a form of private enterprise benevolence, where the customers help themselves and are gently admonished, "Take all you please, but please eat all you take." And by the breakfast available at midnight. Starting the day that early—breakfast costs less then—leaves more time for recreation, i.e., gambling.

The creators of Vegas have made the desert bloom. Not as the

Mormons who founded it in 1855 might have hoped. What mainly grows is neon. Still, bloom Vegas does. Give Gorbachev a break. Let him see it.

AFTERTHOUGHT

Gorbachev came and went. No Vegas.
Maybe next time.

Go Back to Normal Channels
ııı
[20 October 1986]

Not the least striking aftermath of the Reagan-Gorbachev meeting has been the unprecedented confusion it generated. Ever since the meeting ended, administration members from the President down, and with Secretary of State Shultz getting more airtime than Phil Donahue, have been all over the papers and all over the screen, trying to explain what happened at Reykjavik and where it may lead. (When Shultz has not been at it, or Assistant Secretary of Defense Richard Perle, as often as not Donald Regan has. Regan should not have been. White House chief of staff is, as the title suggests, a staff job. The person who holds it cannot be anonymous, but he or she can be silent.)

It may be that the approach of the election has something to do with the administration's zeal in retrospectively finding good cheer in Reykjavik. All the same, it almost seems that the spokesmanless Shultz and the others have been talking on every available program to help themselves understand what happened.

From this flood of talk, little has emerged to promote so-called summit meetings as a useful diplomatic procedure. The confusion that has followed Reykjavik is an argument against "summits." The fact that there was an all-night session on the last night at Reykjavik is an even stronger argument against them. Great issues—momentous issues—ought not to be dealt with in that way. Nor is there any reason to deal with them in that way, especially in the absence of Secretary of Defense Caspar Weinberger, when the issues fell overwhelmingly in his domain. What was the hurry? The Geneva arms control talks have been going on for years. Unless they have been a complete waste of time, in which case they ought to be terminated, can't discussions continue through normal channels?

The answer, of course, is that those who go to "summits" want to go away from them with tangible achievements. Otherwise the meetings may be described as failures, the principals may be so described, too, and a mood of gloom, justified or not, may be induced. So, once a "summit" is held, the pressure for success crowds out almost all other considerations. This is another count against them.

"Summits" have yet another drawback. They worry allies, who may feel that their interests are being ignored. And another: They become personal duels. Again, this is not a sensible way to conduct the business of diplomacy, which ought to be, as far as possible, impersonal and unaccompanied by foolish talk about who blinked and who stood tall.

At Reykjavik, one measure of success was whether it would lead to another "summit," this one in the United States. Demon interviewers on television, when not busy winning Nobel Peace Prizes by suggesting compromises on SDI testing, have been asking whether Gorbachev might be coming over in April. May, then? What about June?

If Gorbachev wants to come to the United States, by all means let him. Let him talk with the President and go about and see some of the country. He might learn something, and we might learn something about him. It would not be necessary to conduct negotiations. We have people who are paid to do that. If Gorbachev and Mr. Reagan want to sign something, they can give instructions to their representatives at Geneva that might lead to an agreement. Nothing earthshaking is required; measurable progress on arms control that might lead on to further progress would do. Then they can go to Geneva, or anywhere else they please, and sign away to their hearts' content. The agreement could contain a provision stating that the signing definitely constituted a "summit," and everybody, especially the newspeople who find that term irresistible, can go home happy. For those still not satisfied, maybe Mr. Reagan and Gorbachev can arm-wrestle.

The Cost of Overconfidence
III
[13 November 1987]

In late January 1985, this space was occupied by a dirge for the British pound. It was worth about $1.10 and appeared to be heading further downward. Its decline from $5.00 in 1939, and from about $4.00 after the Second World War, was taken as a sad reflection of Britain's decline.

Not quite three years later, the pound is worth about $1.80. The dollar has faded, and fast. Is that a reflection of the decline of the United States?

Let's begin by acknowledging that the dollar may have gone too high for our own good. Almost all economists, whatever their other beliefs, agree on that. More fundamentally, let's acknowledge also that the dominant position we held when the Second World War ended and for years thereafter could not be maintained. Other countries had to be restored to health. Indeed, we helped in that restoration, through the Marshall Plan in Western Europe and the benevolent occupation of Japan. As these countries recovered, joined by others we helped, such as South Korea and Taiwan, some adjustment became inevitable.

Not everything was inevitable, however. There was a tremendous overconfidence at large in the United States. For one thing, we did not see the coming industrial challenge. It seemed not to be understood that our competitors were equipping themselves with the newest machines and techniques. Their older industrial plant had been destroyed. Ours had not. We were still using it. Obsolescence set in.

We also overspent militarily. True, we did have to bear the main burden of discouraging Soviet aggression and expansion. A happy idea was at large, however, that if the Soviet Union tried to keep up with us, we could spend it into economic collapse. This attitude was never formally stated as policy, but it lay behind much of what we did.

There was also Vietnam. Consider it only as it relates to the American dollar. Vietnam built a hefty deficit into the federal budget. We have never come out from under that shadow.

Other factors can be identified. American industry seemed not to think in the long term. Its taste was for takeovers and mergers and golden handshakes for executives who lost out. And waste was not confined to government. Not all American industry was lean and mean.

There was a national mania for going into debt. It was thought to be un-American, for the country, states, counties, cities, businesses, individuals, not to be in debt. Hold off expenditures until you had enough money to pay for them and you were considered simpleminded.

Nor was that all. We permitted the development of a tremendous underclass, poor, unemployed, and often illiterate, which contributes nothing to the nation's production and, because of the social problems it throws up, acts as a drag on the economy.

In Washington, we have a budget process that is without flexibility. The tax system is, too. They handicap us.

Somewhere behind all this lurked a basic overconfidence. It may have been understandable in the late forties and the fifties, even into the early sixties. After that, it was sheer recklessness.

That overconfidence cannot conceivably continue, in view of what has happened. It is time for Americans to do what we once did best. Let's get down to business.

AFTERTHOUGHT

In the summer of 1987, my wife accompanied me to a meeting in Copenhagen on economic issues arising between the European Community and the United States. There was much discussion of countervailing duties, escape clause provisions, key process issues, and the like, but what really got her was the calculations stated in that wonderful concept of the economists, constant dollars. She wrote a brief ode:

You were constant once, none more—
Constant as the Northern Star.
And then? Weakness, fading into a distant spark.

The dollar that is only a distant spark may well promote exports and reduce imports, but how many people can make poetry of it?

≡ Vietnam and Nicaragua

≡ Private Military Action
III
[7 September 1984]

At the request of the State Department, the Customs Service is investigating the organization known as Civilian Military Assistance. That is the group, based in Huntsville, Alabama, and made up largely of Vietnam veterans from Alabama, Mississippi, and Tennessee, two of whose members were killed in late August when their helicopter was shot down by forces of Nicaragua's Sandinista government. The Customs investigation, into whether flying weapons to Central America violated the Arms Export Control Act, may mean that there will not be one by the Justice Department. If so, that is disappointing. Because the Justice Department probably would have had to check into possible violations of the Neutrality Acts of the 1930s, and the word "neutrality," in the circumstances, carries with it a certain irony.

For, it might have been asked, How can the Neutrality Acts be invoked when the United States is not neutral? Should the Justice Department investigate the CIA? Should it investigate the administration as a whole? And if the administration insists that the government of Nicaragua is dangerous to the United States, how can the men of Civilian Military Assistance be blamed for wanting to do their part in protecting their country?

The administration, it is true, has not called for private military action in Central America. Still, the example it sets is unmistakable. It is hardly a secret that the United States supports the "contras" in Nicaragua. The CIA's "covert action" there must be among the least covert covert actions of all time. Indeed, there are overt Congressional debates about authorizing and financing it.

The men in Huntsville, one supposes, agreeing with the admin-

155

istration and troubled by Congress's hesitations, felt they were doing no more than their duty. "If we don't fight them there, we'll have to fight them here," one member of CMA explained. That isn't very different from the administration's description of Central America as this country's front yard. "Everytime we heard about the communists doing something somewhere," said another, "we got ticked off real bad." Not very different, either, except perhaps grammatically, from what the administration has said. Moreover, members of the United States Military Advisory Group in El Salvador, attached to the embassy there, helped CMA to meet Salvadoran officers, including the army chief of staff. They helped in other ways in getting materiel donated by CMA to the Salvadorans. Why would the CMA representatives have felt they were doing anything wrong?

So the men from Huntsville conducted their filibuster. "Filibusters"—not the Senatorial kind—were private military activities in Latin America, conducted by citizens of the United States. They reached their peak around the middle of the last century, during the Latin American wars of independence. By those standards, the Huntsville expedition was a small one. But its size has nothing to do with whether it was legal, and—leaving aside the wisdom or unwisdom of President Reagan's policy in Central America—nothing to do with whether it is desirable for United States citizens to be roaming around Central America more or less on their own, carrying out their own foreign policy and not under official control.

In effect, the Customs Service investigation amounts to the administration's saying, "No private enterprise, please. Leave it to us." But the voice in which it is saying that is very small.

Vietnam and Nicaragua
###
[7 February 1985]

President Reagan is not exactly sweeping all before him with his policy on Nicaragua. He is running into a reluctance to do anything that might get our men involved in shooting and being shot at.

On its own merits, Nicaragua may well be a place to stay out of, but some of the reluctance comes from memories of Vietnam. The Vietnam syndrome, it used to be fashionable to call this cautious attitude; the term carried a certain scorn, an implication that Vietnam was making us cowards and blind to our own interests.

The fact is, Vietnam did make Americans wary about intervention overseas, wary even about the use of American advisers where fighting is taking place. With good reason. It may be salutary to remember some of the pronouncements handed down by those in authority. They help to explain why official statements, and still more reassuring official looks into the future, are not readily believed.

General J. Lawton Collins, at the time chief of staff of the United States Army, said this: "There is no question that the communist menace in French Indochina has been stopped." That was in 1951, when the Vietnamese were fighting the French. In 1953, Secretary of State John Foster Dulles said, "We would all like to think the war might be successfully concluded next year."

Next year was 1954, when Admiral Arthur Radford, chairman of the Joint Chiefs of Staff, said: "The French are going to win. It is a fight that is going to be finished with our help." Vice President Richard Nixon also was heard from: "The Vietnamese lack the ability to conduct a war by themselves or govern themselves."

Jump to 1962. The Vietnamese were no longer fighting the French, but us. Attorney General Robert Kennedy, visiting Saigon, said, "We are going to win. We will remain here until we do win." A year later, in 1963, General Paul Harkins, United States commander in Vietnam, said, "I can safely say the end of the war is in sight."

This next quotation became widely known: "Secretary McNamara and General Taylor reported their judgment that the major part of the United States military task can be completed by 1965, although there may be a continuing requirement for a limited number of United States training personnel." That was a White House statement in October 1963, after the second visit to Vietnam by the secretary of defense. McNamara made many more visits, and by his fifth, in May 1964, he thought it might be necessary to increase the 15,000-man American military training group in Vietnam—though not substantially.

And so on and so on. There is no great satisfaction in running through this litany of error. Civilian officials make mistakes. So do the military. So do other people. But this country had a hemorrhage of confidence in government because of Vietnam. The danger that people in power will be cut off from reality and delude themselves has rarely been made so clear. The price that was paid was fearful.

No country, deciding what to do in the present, should be paralyzed by its past. Equally, however, no country can fail to be influenced by its past. The Vietnam experience cannot be set aside. Grenada, so far as we can tell, worked. But there was the failed attempt to rescue the hostages in Iran. Lebanon, though not on the Vietnam scale, was a disaster. Skepticism about American adventures overseas is healthy. And understandable.

Our Past in Nicaragua
[11 March 1985]

Nicaragua is an intensely difficult problem for the United States. Glib answers come readily enough, especially from the administration. Effective courses that are also decent and defensible are another matter.

There is, however, one ingredient that could be stirred into United States policy without act of Congress and without costing us a cent. It is called humility. Nothing would become us more. If humility is too much to ask for, then some understanding of the past. The press in particular has an obligation to set out that past, and the obligation has not been met.

Washington is altogether too indignant about Nicaragua. We are indignant about the absence of a true multiparty system, about violations of human rights, about the company Nicaragua keeps. What we seem never to ask ourselves is why things turned out this way and whether we had anything to do with it.

It isn't necessary to believe that the Sandinistas are angels. They may be very bad people. Given the circumstances in which they came to power, that is distinctly possible. The Somoza dictatorship, which they—and their allies, some of them now cast aside—displaced, was vile. It would hardly have bred a moderate opposition.

But the United States does not enter the situation carrying no baggage at all. We have a past. Our motives may not seem as pure to others as they do to us. We helped to impose perfectly horrible governments on Guatemala (Somoza helped us here) and Chile.

In Nicaragua, we intervened militarily as early as 1912. Sending in the Marines during the 1920s was almost standard operating procedure. In 1927, President Calvin Coolidge dispatched Henry L. Stimson to Nicaragua to try to end a civil war there, a humane enough act. In the event, we agreed to supervise an election, and American Marines stayed on for years. When we left, in Franklin Roosevelt's time, the Somoza family translated control of the Guardia Nacional, which we helped to create, into control of the country. It is not possible to believe that this could have been done without at least our acquiescence. Every United States administration supported them until they were overthrown in 1979. The last straw apparently was their diversion of earthquake relief supplies to their own profit at a time when, by some estimates, they controlled fifty percent of their country's wealth.

Now, who are the Sandinistas? They named themselves for a national hero, Augusto Cesar Sandino. Why was he a national hero? In 1927, he proclaimed his opposition to United States intervention in his country. A guerrilla fighter and, it appears, a socialist, he managed to stay out of the way of the Marines until they left. In 1934, the Americans gone, he emerged, and the Somoza government had him shot. Professor Lester Langley, of the University of Georgia, writes in a forthcoming book, *Central America: The Real Stakes:* "In kicking out Somoza, they (the Sandinistas) proclaimed the expulsion of, not a Nicaraguan tyrant, but an American lackey."

To repeat, Americans must know these things. How can we judge United States policy, and its chance of success, if we don't?

Should we, then, do nothing about Nicaragua? Doing nothing is one course that might be followed, one among many. It is not being recommended here. What is being recommended is a recognition that an attitude of outrage is out of place and futile. There may be much to be said for letting others carry the ball. That would not guarantee success; nothing can. But it might help.

Remembering the Tonkin Gulf
■■■
[17 April 1985]

Wayne Morse.

Ernest Gruening.

Two names worth remembering as we mark the tenth anniversary of the fall of Saigon to the Viet Cong and North Vietnamese. Morse, Democrat of Oregon, and Gruening, Democrat of Alaska, were the only members of Congress to vote against the Tonkin Gulf Resolution. They did that much more than ten years ago. The precise date was August 7, 1964. As we look back on our misadventure in Indochina, that is a date worth remembering. Morse and Gruening, both of them stubbornly independent, are worth remembering, too.

It was on July 30, 1964, that the South Vietnamese Navy raided islands in the Gulf of Tonkin, north of the 17th parallel, which was the dividing line between North and South. As the operation continued, two United States destroyers patrolling nearby came under unprovoked attack by North Vietnamese PT boats. One, the *Maddox,* was hit. Two PT boats were sunk, and United States aircraft bombed their bases, the first American attack on North Vietnamese territory.

That, at any rate, was the official version, according to which there was also a second torpedo attack on our ships on August 4, though neither was hit. It is necessary to say official because, as reporters have dug away over the years, another version has emerged. This was that the *Maddox* and the other destroyer, the *C. Turner Joy,* were sent into the Gulf and into what North Vietnam considered its territorial waters, to draw an attack. The Resolution, so this version has it, was ready and waiting before the incident occurred.

Whichever version you accept, there is no doubt that a joint resolution was submitted to Congress. It authorized the President "to take all necessary measures to repel any armed attack against the forces of the United States and to prevent further aggression." On August 7, the House, after forty minutes of debate, passed the resolution, 416 to 0. The Senate, after nine hours of debate, passed it, 88 to 2. A number of senators had misgivings about it, Republicans Jacob Javits of New York and George Aiken of Vermont and Democrats George McGovern of South Dakota and Gaylord Nelson of Wisconsin among them. So did some House members. The feeling that they had to support

160

the President and show no disunity overcame their doubts. So, at a guess, did the idea that the President and his advisers knew something they did not, that "intelligence" information existed that they did not have.

At this time, the United States had 15,000 advisers in Vietnam. In March 1964, Morse and Gruening had demanded total United States withdrawal. Faced with the Tonkin Gulf Resolution, Morse argued that evidence had been accumulating for months that the Pentagon and the State Department "were preparing to escalate the war into North Vietnam." For ten years, he said, the United States has been "a provocateur every bit as much as North Vietnam has been a provocateur." Moreover, he and Gruening said, the Resolution was "a predated declaration of war" and therefore unconstitutional. (It was later called "the functional equivalent" of a declaration of war by Attorney General Nicholas Katzenbach.)

Constitutionality aside, Morse and Gruening weren't far wrong. Congress appropriated $2,400,000,000 for the Vietnam war effort in 1965. Also in 1965, the United States began bombing military targets in North Vietnam, and the first American ground troops— Marines—were sent to DaNang to protect American bases. All of this, and everything that followed—including the 58,000 names on the Vietnam Memorial in Washington—without a formal declaration of war.

But there was the Tonkin Gulf Resolution, of which, it was said, President Johnson carried a copy in his back pocket to show that he had legal backing for what he was doing. On June 24, 1970, the Senate repealed it.

No More Vietnams
III
[24 April 1985]

President Reagan has joined Richard Nixon in pushing the line that we did not lose the war in Vietnam, we won it.

Here is how Mr. Nixon put it in his latest book, *No More Viet-*

nams: "We won the war in Vietnam but we lost the peace. All that we had achieved in twelve years of fighting was thrown away in a spasm of Congressional irresponsibility."

Here is how Mr. Reagan put it at a White House luncheon for editors and broadcasters: "Well, the truth of the matter is that we did have victory. We continue to talk about losing that war. We didn't lose that war. We won virtually every engagement."

Suppose it is granted, as Mr. Reagan and Mr. Nixon would like it to be, that we did not lose the war but rather withdrew from it, gave it up, and that this eventually left the way open for the North Vietnamese and Viet Cong to displace the government we left in Saigon. Grant also that, as Mr. Reagan and Mr. Nixon tell us, promises had been made to our South Vietnamese allies and that these promises were broken.

How did this come about? The people of this country—not all of them but as a whole—were sick of the whole business, sick of throwing away lives and treasure, sick of killing people half a world away who had done nothing to us. They had despaired of the regime in Saigon and were weary of being misled. Maybe that last was the most influential: being told, as they were over the years, that our participation would be limited; that every statistical index showed that we were winning; that it was possible to see our military effort coming to an end; that all we would have to do was leave a training mission behind; that—Hubert Humphrey said this—we were building the Great Society in Southeast Asia.

Eventually, the American people, again not all of them but as a whole, recognized reality, called their government to account, and imposed a policy on it. What could be more democratic? Mr. Nixon writes that he gave two guarantees to President Thieu of South Vietnam: "We would continue to send enough military aid to maintain the balance of power, and we would respond swiftly to North Vietnamese attempts to subvert the terms of the agreement. South Vietnam would handle minor violations of the cease-fire, and the United States would retaliate against major ones." He also writes: "We had to maintain a credible threat of American retaliation against an invasion from North Vietnam." Give these guarantees Mr. Nixon may well have. They were politically impossible to carry out. It was too late.

Mr. Nixon argues, and others argue, that we must never again enter a war we do not intend to win. Most people probably would agree, though it is not impossible to conceive of circumstances, in a nuclear age, in which something short of victory would be tolerable. What is more important is never again to enter a war as unnecessary and ill-chosen as the war in Vietnam. Our intervention in Indochina was based on, as much as anything, the view that all communists were the same, that when you fought the Vietnamese you were really fighting the Chinese, and that if we didn't fight the communists in Asia, we would soon be fighting them in California. Not much later, the Chinese and the Vietnamese were fighting each other. The only Indochinese who landed on our shores were refugees.

Of course there would have been damage to our side if we had let South Vietnam fall without a fight. Of course it is horrifying to watch people being subjected to communist rule. Still, some things happen in this world that we cannot prevent. Our resources, human and material, are not infinite. They should be used wisely, not squandered. In Vietnam, they were squandered. The fact is, the American people were tremendously patient with their government over Vietnam. The wonder is that they did not force the pullout sooner.

A Particular Piece
Of Real Estate
ııı
[7 June 1985]

During hearings on the war in Vietnam, the chairman of the Senate Foreign Relations Committee, J. William Fulbright of Arkansas, put a question to Secretary of State Dean Rusk. What was it, Fulbright wanted to know, what was it that made Vietnam—he would sometimes exasperatedly use the phrase "this particular piece of real estate"— special? Why were we so willing to pay the price we were paying? Why the gigantic United States undertaking there?

Somewhat the same question might now be asked about Nicaragua. What is it about Nicaragua that so offends President Reagan,

Secretary of State Shultz, and some others in the administration? Are the Sandinistas such a threat to the United States that we are truly considering using force against them? There are more and more leaks that we are.

White House spokesman Larry Speakes said last week that "to raise the specter of direct U.S. involvement is wrong, wrong, wrong." He said also, "The President has no plans to use U.S. military forces in Central America, period." All the same, Shultz said last month that if administration recommendations for aid to the contras in Nicaragua were not accepted by Congress, we could eventually face "an agonizing choice about the use of American combat troops" there. According to the *New York Times*, President Reagan, in a secret report to Congress, described the use of American military force as "an eventual option in the region, if other policy alternatives fail." Mr. Reagan said only last week, "Soviet bloc nations and their terrorist allies are pouring in weapons and ammunition to establish a beachhead on our own doorstep." "A beachhead on our doorstep" sounds serious. It sounds as though it might warrant military action.

A settlement in Central America is unlikely to come from the course the administration is following. The Sandinistas cannot give way publicly to American indignation and denunciations. They may be able to back away from Cuba and the Soviet Union in negotiations with us, more likely in negotiations with other Latin Americans. For the anti-Somoza revolution was also an anti-American revolution. The administration is unwilling to see this and accept it. But it was. Our demands for a "pluralistic democracy" in Nicaragua must seem the height of cynicism to the Sandinistas. Not that they want one. But we were not insisting on that during the more than forty years of the Somoza dictatorship. We did not insist on it when Somoza worked with us in 1954 to overthrow a leftist government in Guatemala.

None of this makes the Sandinistas angels. They seem not even to be smart: Why announce a visit to Moscow by President Daniel Ortega Saavedra the very day the House votes down aid to the contras? The Sandinistas are nasty and doctrinaire. Of course, one would like to see the Nicaraguan people, after so many years of dreadful government, first by the Somozas, now by the Sandinistas, with something better. The question is, how to get it for them, or more properly, how to help them get it for themselves?

Is this a recipe for inaction? No, it is an argument for letting others get out in front to see what they can do. It almost seems that wounded vanity in Washington stands in the way of this, just as there were times when wounded vanity seemed to be at work with President Johnson over Vietnam. But the United States is not the only country in the Western Hemisphere with a stake in Central America. Some of the others have credentials that we do not. One of those credentials is that they are Latin American. We are not. Let's understand that and use it.

Rambo
III
[12 June 1985]

Ever ready to quest anew in the cause of journalism, I took myself off to see Sylvester Stallone's latest movie, *Rambo*.

It was, said *Variety* in varietese, Socko in Detroit, Rugged in Pitt, Muscular in D.C., Flashy in Balto, Husky in Mpls, Explosive in L.A., Bold on B'way, Fancy in Cleve, Big in Miami, Smash in Philly, Dynamic in Chi, Brawny in Bay Area, and in K.C., Pow. Over the Memorial Day holiday, *Rambo* posted the third-best weekend box office of all time.

With Mr. Stallone, I had been advised, the key thing to note was how much time went by before he took off his shirt. By stopwatch, it was eight minutes and forty seconds. Even with his shirt on, however, Mr. Stallone does most of his acting with his chest and arms. This is just as well, for as an actor—if that is not a misuse of the term—he is a man of few words, and most of them come out as grunts. He also has two facial expressions. In one, he glowers. In the other, he looks resentful.

The key thing to understand in *Rambo,* and no doubt in all his other movies, is that whoever shoots at Mr. Stallone misses. Mr. Stallone, by contrast, never misses. This may seem one-sided, but then, Mr. Stallone is the good guy. Bad guys cannot possibly hit him.

What is astonishing about *Rambo* is its dullness. Guns go off, bombs go off, explosions and fires are set off by bow and arrow, houses blow up, huts blow up, boats blow up, helicopters blow up, men are knifed, strangled, clubbed, riddled with bullets, almost all of this brought about single-handed by Mr. Stallone. Mr. Stallone himself (still in Vietnam) is tortured by sadistic Russians; so is another American. It is all paralyzingly dull. I was embarrassed for those who made it, until I thought of the socko, pow, and brawny box-office figures cited above. In less than three weeks, *Rambo* pulled in $70,000,000. Its budget was $30,000,000.

"Brawny" is of course the word for Mr. Stallone. He is powerfully built. His pectorals, biceps, and triceps are remarkable, but not of abiding interest. Which leads us to the plot. The full title of the movie is *Rambo: First Blood Part II,* so evidently there was a Part I with first first blood, which landed former special forces soldier John Rambo in prison. He is let out to go on a mission to Vietnam, to see whether any Americans are still held in prisoner of war camps, and if so, to take photographs of them to prove it. The Defense Department's computers have come up with him as one of the three men in the country best qualified to do the job.

As it happens, a villainous bureaucrat from Washington, apparently under villainous orders from Washington, has chosen a camp he knows is empty, so that concern about missing Americans will be put at rest. The mission, in short, is a fake. But the camp isn't empty, and Rambo brings out some prisoners to prove it. In the course of doing so, he kills enough Vietnamese to solve any overpopulation problems that country may have, wipes out considerable numbers of Russians, and raises the question of why we had as many as half a million men in Vietnam when all we had to do was send in this one.

He also meets a beautiful Vietnamese girl, another agent for the United States, who saves his life. He promises to take her back to the United States with him, but immediately thereafter she is shot to death by the same people who never seem able to hit him. All of this to the accompaniment of deafening combat music.

The implication in all of this, we are entitled to suppose, is that just as Rambo was betrayed by a bureaucrat from Washington, so were our fighting men let down and kept from winning the war itself. If this is the message Mr. Stallone wants to convey, he is certainly free to do so. He is not alone. President Reagan and Richard Nixon have lately argued that militarily, we won in Vietnam; the losing was done back home. Whatever one thinks of the argument, the movie is childishly silly. The producers acknowledge at the end that the persons and events portrayed in *Rambo* are fictitious. It's gracious of them to say so.

Violence and Terrorism

The Beirut Bombing
III
[21 September 1984]

There is no pleasure in writing this, but the latest bombing attack on the United States embassy in Beirut has provoked some remarkably foolish comments from those who govern us and those who would. Walter Mondale called it "irrational." Geraldine Ferraro spoke of "the senseless loss of life." To President Reagan, the attack was "cowardly." George Bush said something about those who want to "snuff out any light that is the symbol of freedom," which can be ignored. None of these comments is in the slightest degree helpful. Quite the opposite.

Begin with President Reagan. He called it a "cowardly" attack. How so? Is it cowardly to drive a truck loaded with explosives into a heavily guarded compound, through a maze of concrete barriers and antitank defenses, being shot at and knowing you are going to certain death? In what way is that cowardly? We cannot know the personal motivations that drew those who drove the truck into their suicide mission. But how many of us would do it?

As for Mondale and Ferraro, at the time he was denouncing the attack as "irrational" and she was denouncing it as "senseless," they did not even know who the attackers were. Calling this kind of thing senseless and irrational has become an almost automatic response that contributes nothing to our understanding. Indeed, if you truly believe such attacks to be senseless, you deny yourself any hope of understanding them.

Moreover, whatever one may think of those who made the attack, and however profoundly we may wish that it had not taken place, from the bombers' point of view, what they did was not senseless. It is reasonable to suppose that they knew what they wanted to accomplish, which was to get the United States out of Lebanon. President Reagan says we will not be pushed out by terrorism. Very well. At least that suggests that he understands the reason for the bombing. And no doubt he means what he says. But we were pushed out of Lebanon by precisely such an attack as this, the one that killed 241 Marines while they slept. Not long after that, our Marines were withdrawn. The administration tried to present that as somehow a strengthening of American resolve, but withdrawn they were, and they have not gone back. Against that background, was this latest attack "senseless" to those who brought it off?

Consider a further fact. The embassy annex that was attacked had only recently been taken over by the United States. It was chosen because it was thought to be less vulnerable than the site previously used, and it may well have been. It is possible that with the new location, the casualties and damage were less than they would otherwise have been. Nonetheless, the bombers were telling the United States that there is no safety for its people in Beirut. They were trying to make the price for staying higher than we want to pay. That is a calculated act, not a senseless one.

Politicians are forever being asked to comment on such events as the bombing. Especially during an election campaign, they cannot avoid being asked. They may even want to comment, out of outrage or because they think their campaign requires it. But what is there to say on this subject? That you're sad, and angry, and that you offer such sympathy and comfort as you can to the families of the dead and injured. But don't call the attack cowardly. And don't say it's senseless. Saying that is.

The Lebanese Charnel House
[28 May 1985]

Over the years, as a newsman, I have reported from many countries, some of them grim and sad, a few dangerous. I have never reported from Lebanon. The newsmen and newswomen who work there now deserve our thanks. They are risking their lives trying to explain the increasingly unexplainable.

For Lebanon is a charnel house, a building, room, or vault in which the bones and bodies of the dead are placed. More than that, the bones and bodies are also made suitable for being placed there. Lebanon is a slaughterhouse.

In a strange way, the world is becoming used to it. Not hardened to it. Not unconcerned about it. But used to it. Read about Lebanon often enough, see it often enough on television, and you come to think it hopeless. At first, you watch in disbelief, and wonder why these people are so set on murdering one another. You look for clues that might lead to understanding and eventually to a solution. You are horrified and full of pity, especially for the women driven half-mad, some of them wailing, some struck dumb. After a while, horrified and pitying though you still may be, you come to terms with it, conclude that nothing can be done. Forces are loose in Lebanon that are beyond control.

It is possible to learn about Lebanon, learn something of its history, trace the events of the last years. Once upon a time, and not long ago, it was a center of trade and tourism. For those who were connoisseurs of such things, Beirut airport was a particularly advantageous place for shopping. (I can remember congratulating myself on being there long enough between planes to buy a wristwatch.) Beirut was wide open and one of the world's great fleshpots. From the time Lebanon threw off the French mandate, late in the Second World War, it was delicately balanced internally—the recitation is familiar—its population divided almost equally between Muslims and Christians, with the Muslims themselves broken into three sects, Sunni, Shiite, and Druse. And so on and so on. In 1958, President Eisenhower sent in the Marines to put down a revolt against the largely Christian government we helped win the election in 1957. And so on again.

Yet read what you will, the bombings, shootings, killing of the wounded, have their own being. A matter-of-fact insanity seems to be at large, and some of those in the fighting appear to be enjoying it. Evidently there are those for whom it is fun to step out into a street of wrecked buildings and let loose a stream of automatic-rifle fire, those who get a kick out of tossing a hand grenade into a crowded house, those who are thrilled when they lob artillery shells into a sector of the city that is not theirs. For those who drive the suicide cars and trucks, if it isn't fun, it is salvation.

Still, you try. Read about the Syrians, the Palestinians. The Shiites want the Palestinians out because their presence in force might bring back the Israelis. There was also the Israeli invasion and occupation, which, whether out of self-defense or not, made Lebanon's internal politics even more venomous. And the "peacekeeping" by outside powers, among them the United States. Still more venom.

So you read, and decide, finally, that the past is less and less relevant to what is going on now. What is going on now feeds on itself and is nourished by its own evil.

Will it ever end? Yes, this kind of thing always does, if only through exhaustion. But when, and how?

Terrorism: Here to Stay
[27 January 1986]

The St. Louis *Post-Dispatch* now has a department headed "Violent Deaths." Does this have anything to do with terrorism?

Does this? Prison sentences of life with no possibility of parole were imposed on four Las Vegas youths, two of them sixteen, the others fifteen. One had pleaded guilty; the others had gone to trial and been convicted of kidnapping a newspaper deliveryman, then shooting and beating him to death, the while robbing him of nine dollars. On the same day, they shot and wounded four other persons. When sentence was pronounced, they showed no emotion. The prosecutor said they lived in a fantasy world, committed crimes for thrills, and had no fear of being caught or punished.

Is there any connection here with terrorism? A sixteen-year-old boy, according to Compton, California, police, was shot and killed by a fourteen-year-old during a fight outside a junior high school. The fourteen-year-old was arrested. So was a thirteen-year-old identified as the gun's owner.

Or here? The Los Angeles Police Department has 145 officers assigned to CRASH—Community Resources Against Street Hoodlums. They work to suppress an estimated 160 street gangs with 12,500 members. The Los Angeles Sheriff's Department has 52 officers assigned to OSS—Operation Safe Streets. They work to suppress 239 gangs with 25,000 members. In 1984, the two units reported not quite 8,000 major gang-related crimes, i.e., homicides, attempted homicides, felony assaults, battery on a police officer, rape, kidnap, robbery, arson, and shooting at inhabited dwellings.

What is the connection with terrorism? Just this: All of these items tell us that terrorism is not an isolated phenomenon. It may exist for, so to speak, its own sake. That is another way of saying that people may choose a violent way of life for many reasons. Nobody doubts that economic and social conditions, as well as political ones, may play a part. But violence and a life outside the law themselves have an appeal for many people. They may commit crimes because they like to, because they enjoy it.

How else shall we explain the martial arts expert in Washington, Pa., who was convicted of robbery, of theft, and of killing three widows, one eighty-four, one eighty-seven, one eighty-eight, with karate chops? Or the young man ordered out of a Brooklyn, N.Y., doughnut shop because he was making trouble. As he left, he pulled a gun and fired into the shop. A sixteen-year-old girl was killed.

In the case of the four young Las Vegans, the prosecutor said they committed crimes for thrills. Imagine the thrill that must come from raiding an airport and randomly shooting people down, or from hijacking an airliner and taking hostages, or even, as we have seen, hijacking a cruise liner.

Obviously we must do what we can to defeat terrorists, just as police forces do what they can to defeat more typical criminals. We should also understand, however, that even if we do catch up with some of them, terrorism is likely to go on. It may be part of the temper of the times, in the same way that street gangs are. Moreover, technological advances make spectacular coups, of the kind we have seen in Rome, in Vienna, in TWA 847, in the *Achille Lauro,* ever more feasible. Terrorism may be with us for a long, long time.

Violent Times
III
[19 May 1986]

We are told that we live in violent times. It's true. We do. There are hijackings, bombings, assassinations, coups. President Reagan is shot; the Pope is shot; in Egypt, Anwar Sadat is shot and killed; in Sweden, Olof Palme. There are South Africa, Lebanon, Indochina. Iran and Iraq engage in mutual slaughter for six years and the world hardly notices except when the supply and price of oil are affected—not that there seems much to be done about it. In our own country, guns are everywhere and arson is commonplace.

So, yes, we do live in violent times, and it frightens, saddens, and oppresses us. But who did not?

Think back to the thirties: Hitler in Germany, Mussolini in Italy, Stalin in the Soviet Union, Japan attacking China, the Spanish Civil War, the merciless Gran Chaco war between Bolivia and Paraguay. The chancellor of Austria was murdered; the king of Yugoslavia was assassinated, and the French foreign minister with him. An unemployed bricklayer tried to shoot President-elect Franklin Roosevelt and killed the mayor of Chicago, Anton Cermak, who was standing next to him. Who remembers now that Puerto Rican nationalists tried to kill President Truman in an attack on Blair House, where he was living while the White House was under renovation? Other Puerto Ricans opened fire from the gallery of the House of Representatives and wounded some members.

Violence? It is almost impossible to conceive of this now, but when the explorer Henry Morton Stanley (the "Dr. Livingston, I presume?" Stanley) explored the Congo for King Leopold II of the Belgians, the Congo became, for all practical purposes, Leopold's private property for more than twenty years. International horror at Leopold's brutality there forced him to turn it over to the Belgian government in 1908.

Think, too, of how other colonial empires were established and maintained. Think of the American Civil War, in its time the bloodiest war ever. Many countries had human slavery. After it was abolished in the United States, we had frequent lynchings.

Perhaps you like the song by Kurt Weill "Mack the Knife." Mack was a highwayman. They are less often encountered now, though a contemporary version has turned up of late in Mexico. Some American tourists have been victims. And where did the term "riding shotgun" come from? That is how stagecoaches were protected in the American west.

Violence? How far back shall we go? To the days when women thought to be witches were burned at the stake? When capital punishment was part of almost every country's criminal justice system? (Interesting that it is coming back, in a comparatively small way, in this country.) Torture is still widely practiced; imagine what it was in less sensitive times.

All of this barely scratches the surface. What is different now is that the weapons used are deadlier, that the airplane and other technological developments have made violence easier and—because in some circumstances the killer need never actually face his victims— impersonal, and that modern news organizations make the violence more immediate and graphic. Also, more people know about it, so that it seems to be going on all the time and everywhere. Most people did not have that knowledge before.

Nothing else is new. The word "assassin" shows that. The first assassins were members of a secret Muslim order that killed Christian crusaders who were trying to take the Holy Land back from "the infidels." The word "assassin" comes from hashish, from which the assassins drew some of their courage. It dates back to A.D. 1090.

Clean Hands
■■■
[26 January 1987]

Hostage-taking is an outrage. The personal agony it imposes apart, it brings about a kind of national humiliation and presents governments with difficult, even agonizing, decisions.

On all of that, everyone will agree. Perhaps we can also agree that the events that have come to light in the last few months—the dealings with Iran and Israel and the contras and Saudi Arabia and Portugal and Brunei and who knows whom else, the unsavory go-betweens, the arms shipments and secret bank accounts and disappearing millions—shed a good deal of light on hostage-taking and other forms of terrorism. They do not justify it or mean that we should limply accept it. They do help us to understand it.

We denounce terrorism, especially when it claims innocent lives, and call for international action against it. Our last two secretaries of state, Alexander Haig and George Shultz, have been particularly forceful advocates of such action. There is, however, an old saying about coming into court with clean hands. We do not. We have overturned governments, as in Guatemala, or helped in their overthrow, as in Chile, or tried unsuccessfully to overthrow them, as in Cuba. We have allied ourselves with despots, as with the Somozas in Nicaragua. We restored the Shah to the throne of Iran in 1953, after he had been deposed (a fact not often mentioned, but one that helps to explain some things in Iran). We have intervened over the years in Greece, Guyana, Zaire, and many other places.

These actions are in the past, but we have clandestine activities under way now in various parts of the world, helping the rebels in Angola, for one, and helping the resistance forces in Afghanistan. That is what the CIA, in part, is for. We may say that we carry out these clandestine activities in the cause of peace and freedom and for our own security, and so the end justifies means that may at times be grim and even brutal. Very well. The basic fact, however, is that we, too, operate in this world of intrigue and double cross and bribery and violence. Enter this world—which for individuals it may take no small amount of courage to do—and you cannot fairly claim to be exempt from its habits and practices.

We do at times seem to suggest that the CIA should be free to act as it pleases, handing out manuals of instruction in assassination and sabotage in Nicaragua, for example, and mining harbors there. It is reported that we fed what is gently called disinformation to both sides in the Iran-Iraq war. If we did, and if death and devastation resulted, is no one in those countries to want revenge?

Use the weapons available to you, and you must expect other people to use the weapons available to them. The weapons are not lovely. They may include—especially for those whose resources are more modest than ours—acts of terrorism. When these occur, outrage and indignation from our government, which is the sponsor of our own "covert activities," will not help. We try to hit those we take to be our enemies where they are vulnerable. They do the same to us.

What course, then, do we follow when Americans are taken hostage? Do we let them languish? No, we do what we can to get them out, taking account of other necessities of policy and the fact that some of the hostages surely knew and accepted the risks of being where they were. That is not a pleasant process, but it is more acceptable when not accompanied by self-righteous blather. The White House, out of weariness and a long overdue realism about what we can and cannot do, seems at last to have understood that.

≡

Just the Facts, Please— The News Business

■■■

Polls, Polls, Polls
III
[7 September 1984]

Political campaign reporting seems pretty simple these days. It goes like this:

"The polls say . . ."

"The polls show . . ."

"According to the polls . . ."

"It's still early, but if the polls are anything to go by . . ."

"The polls show that if the election were held tomorrow . . ."

"That big a lead in the polls can cause overconfidence, so . . ."

"The candidate's own pollsters are telling him that . . ."

"Polls to be published tomorrow . . ."

"The polls show a gap between the candidates of . . ."

"He is saying that the only poll that counts is the one on election day, but that may be whistling in the dark, and his own polling organization . . ."

"The polls reveal . . ."

"That kind of lead in the polls at this stage of the campaign doesn't necessarily mean much, but . . ."

"The polls have been wrong before, but . . ."

"An NBC poll just completed gives . . ."

"A CBS poll just completed puts . . ."

"An ABC poll just completed has . . ."

"We commissioned a poll, and the results, while not conclusive, suggest . . ."

"Given a margin of error of three percent either way, the poll . . ."

"If you take these polls and project them nationally, you find . . ."

"Polling is not an exact science, and people can change their minds. All the same . . ."

"We put together the poll results of the last two months, and they show a definite trend toward . . ."

"The polls show some weakening in the position of . . ."

"It's not unknown for front-runners in the polls to be overhauled. Still . . ."

179

"Our polls indicate . . ."

"We have polled a number of key districts, and . . ."

"If the polls can be trusted . . ."

"You might expect him to be discouraged by the polls, but he claims to be confident about the eventual outcome."

"There is an interesting divergence here between Gallup and Harris."

"Polling by the candidate's own organization, so his people say, reveals a much more hopeful picture."

"That big a margin in the polls is almost without precedent."

"That big a margin in the polls repeats the pattern of . . ."

"The polls support that view."

"The polls show some erosion of the lead hitherto enjoyed by . . ."

"There have been some ups and downs, but there hasn't been any really significant change in the polling figures for the last . . ."

"The polls themselves may become a factor, as the contest goes down to the wire."

"The advantage in the polls continues to rest with . . ."

"They believe—at least they say they believe—that as time goes by, the polls will tell a different story."

"Polls can be wrong, but for what they're worth, they show . . ."

"A poll is a snapshot taken at a moment in time. Today's snapshot can be changed by tomorrow. Bearing that in mind, here are the results of our latest . . ."

"With the election just six weeks (five weeks) (four weeks) (three weeks) (two weeks) (a week) off, the polls . . ."

"Well, here we are at last, election eve, and as the nation prepares to vote, the polls show . . ."

Shelf Life
III
[22 October 1984]

There is still plenty of time in the election campaign. Surprises and excitement and—who can say—even entertainment may lie ahead. Yet it seems unlikely that these last weeks can produce anything that will eclipse that immortal moment when some genius in the public opinion polling business reached into the world of retailing and came up with the term "shelf life."

This came about, it will be recalled, roughly halfway through the Democratic primaries. The experts (who may be distinguished from pollsters by the fact that they do not themselves conduct polls; they are merely obsessed by the findings of those who do) had pronounced Walter Mondale virtually a sure thing; then, when he proved not to be a sure thing, they explained with undiminished authority why he wasn't. They also explained why Gary Hart had done so well, although they had not been able to spot these factors before. The experts are never disqualified or even, it seems, abashed. They simply go on being experts.

The pollsters, however, who also had their problems, like to believe that there is something "scientific" in what they do. They had to come up with an explanation. The explanation was "shelf life." That is, the claim was made that the polls were accurate; they did reflect the views of the electorate; but not for as long as had been supposed. The voters changed their minds so quickly that the shelf life of the polls was shorter than had been assumed; it was not weeks but days, perhaps not days but hours. The implication seemed to be that the voters were excessively volatile and that it was their fault that the polls did not foresee the results.

This raises a question: What good is a poll with so limited a shelf life? What purpose does it serve? Which leads to another question: Even if the polls had a longer period of applicability, and even if they were accurate, what good are they? What purpose do they serve? What do you do with the information, or misinformation, that they give you? You still have to wait for the election. In the meantime, there they are, creating impressions, establishing favorites, and risking affecting the outcome of the vote. They also help to determine the way in which the outcome will be judged, which during the primaries may affect the contests that follow.

Is this unfair to the candidates? Perhaps not. They enter the struggle with their eyes open. Besides, the politicians themselves, at any rate those who can afford to, employ their own pollsters full-time and often plan their strategy accordingly. They contribute to this madness.

Why, it may be asked, do news organizations place so much emphasis on polls? Their semiscientific aura, of course, and because they've become part of the competition. And they're easy; when you can't think of anything else to do, take a poll; it is, by now, an instinctive reaction.

Should they, then, be outlawed? They can't be. Polls are not, in any sense, illegal. Nor is there any reason to believe that, however boring and pointless they may be, they will disappear, or even be reduced. They won't. Things are moving in the opposite direction. Polling failures don't lead to less polling; they lead to more. The only remedy for all of this nonsense is for people to ignore it.

AFTERTHOUGHT

Much political reporting has been reduced to telling us what the pollsters say. On election night, you might get the impression that the elections are held almost entirely to see whether the polls were right.

Fiesta in Madrid
[25 January 1985]

One of the useful theatrical innovations of the last few years is the surtitle. Not subtitle, which goes below, or at the bottom, but surtitle, which is used in opera and is flashed above the proscenium arch. Thus, when Tosca, at the end of the second act, stabs the villainous police chief Scarpia, and he cries, *"Aiuto, aiuto!"* the surtitle flashes, "Help, help!" No help comes, and when he expires, Tosca's sardonic exit line is *"E avanti a lui tremara tutta Roma."* subtitle, "And before him, all Rome trembled."

I am wondering whether something of this sort might have helped *Fiesta in Madrid,* a show that has remained in my memory for more than a decade and a half. It dates from my days as a New York play reviewer, or as the job is more grandly known, drama critic. Most of these nights have gone beyond recall, which is just as well, but not *Fiesta in Madrid.* I must have wanted to remember it, because I kept my notes. I even did a wondering broadcast about it years later.

Fiesta in Madrid opened in May 1969, a Spanish show of the type called zarzuela, an operetta, really, and its libretto should be placed in a museum where it will be preserved forever. According to the libretto, when the curtain rises, all of those on stage, boys and girls, cry "Ha, ha." "Ha, ha" is a form of shorthand: it means that those on stage are to carry on in an animated way, showing how happy they are. This may well take several minutes.

While they are crying "Ha, ha," which could be flashed above the proscenium arch untranslated, a vendor of cream puffs appears. The girls ask, "How many cream puffs may we have?" The boys reply, "All you want. Forty pounds." At this point, the cream puffs inexplicably drop out of the action.

Surtitles or not, some of the flavor of any show is lost in translation. Consider the song sung by three girls dressed as sailors: "We are the sailors who love the wild sea, we are very brave and face the fiercest gale. Each time we ride the green waves, we love the sea. Ahoy, ahoy, we are the sailors who are so brave and have no fear of exciting storms."

Now the love interest enters, carried by Julian and Susana. Susana, however, is ignoring Julian, which unfortunately leads him to sing: "Even a working man like me has a heart and knows how to cry. My heart is like a blacksmith's anvil; the more blows it takes, the stronger it gets. I am so disturbed by this dark-haired witch that you can read it plainly on my face."

Julian's outburst annoys an older woman, who says, "If I can read it on your face, it is time to forget the dark-haired witch and snap out of it." She has hardly delivered this line when another vendor appears, this one selling strawberries, and we are back where we began, facing the same problem that we did with the cream puffs.

How did *Fiesta in Madrid* come to be put on in New York? That is an abiding mystery. How did it turn out? My notes do not say. Probably there was a lively finale, with everybody crying "Ha, ha," and the critics getting the last laugh. They earned it.

Heinrich Böll
III
[22 July 1985]

"Who was the most interesting person you ever interviewed?"

An impossible question to answer, but somewhere on the list of most interesting, and most gracious, would be the West German novelist Heinrich Böll, who died last week at the age of 67.

The interview took place soon after he won the 1972 Nobel Prize for Literature, which he said was bringing him publicity that he thought he would in time enjoy, although he would also "go sort of underground, disappear, and write."

Early in the interview, he used the expression "law and order," and smiled. He had, after all, once said that the perfect expression of law and order is in the cemetery. Did he accept a certain degree of law and order for himself?

"I even accept it for the society," Böll said, "and I'm ready to pay my taxes for it. I don't mean it ironically. It is just that my experience with so-called law-and-order people in my lifetime was so terrible that I'm very suspicious when I hear the words. Because the law-and-order people in my memory, they are absolutely lawless and disorderly people. An author and an artist has a very great affinity to order. You need a great sense of order to paint a picture, to compose a novel. . . . A lot of misunderstandings about artists and intellectuals comes from that point."

As a German soldier in the Second World War, Heinrich Böll was wounded four times. "If you say wounded, I was—but you join a very big attack. Sometimes it was attacks with fifty, sixty, a hundred thousand soldiers involved. . . . I was very happy when I was wounded. Most soldiers were because they came back into hospitals, they got a leave and so on. . . . And it was very quickly most times. I was sent to the Soviet Union somewhere, let's say for three weeks or four or two days, and I was wounded and went back, and I went again. I didn't really fight."

Here is Böll on military life generally: "I was surprised about military life. All these people say that it has an educational effect on a young man. I never found that. Making every boy clean and proper—I never found that. The contrary was the case."

On being a German writer: "It was a new German literature

184

after the war. It was very difficult to deal with the German language after the corruption it had for twelve years—corrupted by propaganda, by terribly aggressive"—he paused—"barbarity." German intellectuals, he said, were sensible enough to welcome the Bonn government after the Second World War. During the Weimar Republic, after the First World War, the intellectuals were too critical and unfair.

On whether the German people should be reminded periodically of Hitler: "It depends on the way you do it. It's very difficult. It is a problem even for me to explain to my sons, who were all born after the war. If they see a picture of Hitler or see a bit of him in a television documentary, it's absolutely impossible for me to explain to them how this man could become so important. There is a, let's call it, mysticism, irrationalism involved as soon as Hitler comes into discussion. And that is very dangerous. . . . You can explain to a certain degree, maybe to a very high one. But not completely. There is a residue that is not explainable. Even for me."

Would a Hitler have come to power in any other country?

"Impossible to think of a Hitler as a person—I wouldn't say a fascistic phenomenon—but Hitler as a person, the man he was, talking, shouting, writing, I think it would be impossible in Great Britain or America. I'm sure. That's what makes me suspicious about the unexplainable part."

On the censorship of his books in communist countries: "It's not political passages, it's erotic passages. Because they have a terrible fear of pornography—what they call pornography."

Böll denied the story that he never read what critics said about him. He read them after a year, because by then "You have said goodbye to the book. It's finished. It's printed. So I sometimes read them later, to come back to the subject."

A final point on the Nobel Prize: When Böll won it, he gave much of the money to an international fund for the families of writers in prison.

Interviewing Hirohito
###
[22 July 1985]

Would anyone object to a small amount of self-glorification?

Ten years ago, I became the first journalist ever to interview an emperor of Japan: on September 8, 1975, I interviewed Emperor Hirohito in the Imperial Palace in Tokyo. No credit belonged to me; the interview had been arranged by the NBC News bureau in Tokyo in advance of Hirohito's visit to the United States; I was sent over from New York to do it.

My opening moves were not auspicious. I arrived in Tokyo without a visa, and my explanation at immigration, that I was there to interview the Emperor, was not on the face of it likely to be convincing to many Japanese. Fortunately, someone from NBC's Tokyo bureau was waiting at the airport, and he managed to get me through, on the condition that I not leave my hotel until the visa matter was settled. It was settled in a day or two with the requirement that I write a short biography of myself and promise never to try to come in without a visa again.

The Imperial Palace was a new building, a replacement for one that had burned down some years before, and it was remarkably beautiful, using traditional Japanese materials and contemporary design. The rooms I saw had no pictures on the walls; the palace's landscaping, seen through the windows, was used instead. I went first into a waiting room that was perhaps four stories high. Then, outside a ceremonial hall, where the interview was to take place, I was met by the palace's Master of Ceremonies, whose son, it turned out, was studying journalism at the University of Houston.

There was a knock on the door from inside; the doors slid open (all the doors I saw were in pairs that slid apart and together, which enabled palace employees, peering through the slits between the doors, to see whether the Emperor was approaching), I bowed slightly, as instructed, and was handed over to the palace's Grand Master of Ceremonies. He escorted me across the room to the Emperor; I bowed again. The Emperor was small, slightly stooped, and wore a blue business suit, blue-striped shirt, and blue-figured tie. He said, in English, that he was happy to have me there. I replied that it was an honor to be there. Then I clipped a microphone to my lapel, and the interpreter, a Japanese diplomat with the rank of ambassador, did the same. There was no question of anyone's touching the Emperor to clip a microphone to him; for him, a microphone lay on the table between us.

The questions had been submitted in advance, with one follow-up allowed for each, and a time limit of thirty minutes. The Emperor seemed earnest, though expressionless. His answers were guarded, but he was plainly eager to be understood on one point: It was he who had ordered and insisted on the surrender in August 1945. There were three cameras, operated by Japanese crews; the sound crew, and everyone else from NBC, was hidden behind a screen. Three representatives of the Foreign Ministry sat ten feet or so to the Emperor's left; they never looked at him but stared straight ahead.

The interview over, we shook hands, as we had when I entered, and I turned and bowed again at the door. It had been an impersonal experience, but a large gesture of friendship to the American people before Hirohito's visit, and it made me something of a celebrity in Japan, with requests to write accounts of it for Japanese newspapers, and invitations to broadcast on American affairs to Japan for some years thereafter. A Japanese employee of NBC in Tokyo put it in perspective. "Is it true," he asked, "that you shook hands with the Emperor?" Yes, it was. "My God!" he said.

AFTERTHOUGHT

The "My God!" attitude persisted. Toward the end of 1987, when the Emperor was seriously ill, a Japanese television network interviewed three Americans for an obituary program. I was one of them.

Dreams of Glory
iii
[30 July 1985]

The Eastern shuttle from Boston had landed at LaGuardia and the exodus down the aisle had begun with, as usual, some people carrying pieces of luggage larger than themselves, including a few garment bags that apparently contained folded grand pianos. A fellow passenger paused long enough to speak to me. He pointed to the airline's in-flight magazine. "You're a clue in the puzzle," he said.

Signal honor though this may seem to be, I took it in stride. I had been in crossword puzzles before, and more than once. Usually the clue was "TV's Newman," in five letters, or "TV's Edwin," in six. Occasionally it was "*Strictly Speaking* author," which came in six letters or eleven.

I do not scoff at this. What one does not know is how many people who, rather than smiling with satisfaction and filling in the boxes, said "Who?" with some indignation, and cast the puzzle aside. All the same, it does not fall to everybody to be a clue. There is no reason to be unduly modest. The time may well be approaching when, like so many other public figures, I will have to make a full disclosure of my financial holdings.

Or the time may be coming when I will set up, as Van Cliburn has done for aspiring pianists, an annual competition for aspiring news-casters, with the implicit message: "You, too, can be an Edwin Newman." There would be the obvious points to be demonstrated—the ability to sound grave; to sound breezy; to say, "We'll be right back after this"; to avoid gulping and looking lost when the Teleprompter breaks down; to tease the sportscaster about an incorrect prediction and the weather man or woman about a forecast of sunny skies just before enough rain came down to cause urban flooding, electricity to fail, and the airports to close down; and the ability to smile at the end of the program and to sound especially sincere when wishing the viewers a good day, morning, afternoon, evening, night, weekend, week, month, year, and decade. Substituting "terrific," "wonderful," or "marvelous" for "good" would not count; indeed, it would result in a penalty; the test is of the way the "good" is delivered.

Nor would that be the end of it. The contestants would have to show that they can look interested while making conversation with other members of the team, perhaps with the weather forecaster leaning nonchalantly on the newscaster's desk and laughing uncontrollably, with the cameras still on and the credits rolling. This is essential, because it shows that the team is one big happy family.

Appearance of course counts, so there would be extra points for those who used their own teeth, uncapped, and their own hair, and additional points if they had no hair and brazened it out. The judges would be hooked to electrodes—or vice versa, electrodes would be hooked to the judges—to see which of the contestants made their palms perspire. Perspiring palms are thought by many television executives to be a sign that a broadcaster is "getting through." Finally, the prize: an anchor job, with agent attached, and beaming congratulations from the competition's founder.

Ah, well, dreams of glory. Full financial disclosure. An endowed competition for newscasters. Such are the dreams that come when you find yourself a clue in a crossword puzzle.

AFTERTHOUGHT

As things worked out, I did not endow a competition for aspiring newscasters. Movement was in the opposite direction: On Home Box Office's satirical show *Not Necessarily the News,* I did a "commercial" for the Edwin Newman Center in California, where anyone with an addiction to news could go to be cured.

Davis, Latch, Hangen, Clay ...
[16 September 1985]

From time to time, people are kind enough to come up to me and thank me for the work I've done over the years in television news.

The sensible reply, of course, is "Thank you very much." The thanks are sincerely intended, and it is better to leave unsaid the fact that those who become prominent in the news business are doing a job for which they are paid, that they are doing something they enjoy, and that there are other rewards, among them exactly that public recognition that led to the thanks being proffered in the first place. We are, in short, not selfless and not heroes.

Yet there are those among us who have earned the thanks of the public, for they have, in the course of doing their jobs, seeking out the information the American people should have, lost their lives. The deaths in Thailand early this month of correspondent-cameraman Neil Davis and soundman William Latch were only the latest in a startlingly long list of NBC men who have been killed on the job.

Davis and Latch, it will be recalled, were shot during a coup attempt in Bangkok. To judge by the television footage—Davis's own, for his camera went on working even after he fell—the crew of a rebel tank opened fire directly on them. Davis was killed instantly; Latch died in a hospital six hours later.

It was, in a way, not easy to understand. Davis—an Australian, as it happened—was as experienced in covering wars and in that part of the world as anyone could be. Yet, in a coup attempt in which a total of four people died, he and Latch, also a veteran in that part of the world, made up half the casualties.

It brought to mind George Clay, a name admiringly remembered. Again, Clay—a South African, handsome, even debonair—was a vastly experienced war correspondent and knew the area he covered intimately. If you were going into combat, he was a man you would want to be with. In November 1964, in the Congo, as he rode in a truck, a stray bullet passed through his head and killed him.

NBC—and it is used here only as an example—has had other such losses. Producer Ted Yates knew as much about covering wars as anyone. In Israel, in June 1967, as he lay on the ground, taking what cover he could from the firing, he was killed as Clay had been, by a bullet through the head.

A few years later came Cambodia, and the invasion by American and South Vietnamese forces. Cameraman Peter Bellendorf was killed there in April 1970. Within two months came a still heavier blow. Correspondent Welles Hangen had been sent to Cambodia to apply his extremely sharp intellect to finding out what was going on there, and to appraise the chance that the United States would succeed. Hangen was another man with a good deal of combat experience. He and his camera crew drove out, probably unknowingly, into what proved to be enemy territory. They were taken prisoner. His driver escaped, or was released. Hangen, cameraman George Colne, and soundman Yoshihiko Waku were never heard from again.

The Jonestown affair in Guyana in November 1978 took two NBC lives. Representative Leo Ryan of California had gone there to investigate the People's Temple cult, and when he left, some members of the Temple chose to leave with him. An NBC crew was at the airport, heading for the aircraft that was to take them out. Other cult members, angered by what had happened and perhaps foreseeing the end of Jonestown, opened fire. Correspondent Don Harris and soundman Robert Brown died with Ryan and three others.

Covering the news in many parts of the world is no joyride. It can be hazardous. Not that these men did not go into the business with their eyes open. They did. Still, they deserve to be remembered, especially by those of us who, by luck or design, have had less dangerous assignments.

What, No Eyeballs?
[21 November 1985]

The Reagan-Gorbachev meeting has come and gone, and there seems not to have been a single reference to Mr. Reagan and Mikhail Gorbachev's being eyeball-to-eyeball. Then, when the President returned to Washington, not a single news broadcaster reported that the chief executive was back in the nation's capital or that the head-to-head summitry had brought hope of a deepening U.S.-Soviet dialogue.

Something is wrong with the new generation of journalists. They may be snobs. They clearly have no respect for their elders. Aren't these honored clichés good enough for them? They served the older generation faithfully and well.

Surely there are still suave diplomats on the job, and their well-known colleagues, the striped-pants diplomats and the tea-drinking, cookie-pushing diplomats. Why do we no longer hear about them? The roving envoy does turn up now and then, when somebody is designated to do the roving. He may even be doing double duty as a troubleshooter. One way to tell a troubleshooter, by the way, is that he does not wear striped pants or push cookies. Troubleshooters are expected to mean business. One could almost wish for trouble somewhere, so that a roving envoy could be sent out to shoot it.

Some clichés are gone because there are no longer the circumstances that nourish them. We are without an energy czar, for example. You cannot have an energy czar and an oil glut at the same time. At the moment, we have an oil glut. Ergo, no czar. We also have no inflation fighter because, relatively speaking, we have no inflation. One species of trouble ripe for shooting was the bottleneck. We don't get many of those, either. Bottlenecks tend to be a wartime phenomenon.

All is not lost. We do still have a traveling pontiff. The current pontiff has outtraveled all the traveling pontiffs of the past, and he is far from finished. Picture the headline: Pontiff's travels not at an end. If the Pope traveled on the Concorde, we could have the traveling pontiff winging to wherever he is winging to aboard the sleek, needle-nosed airliner. Once there, maybe he could meet a roving envoy. This seems worth bringing about.

It would also be worthwhile for the President to designate a few key aides. They have tended to drop out of sight of late. ("This door is locked," the President said. "Call my key aides.")

Key aides and traveling pontiffs, however, cannot do the job alone. When did you last hear Saudi Arabia referred to as the desert kingdom? Japan as the island nation? Marxist president. There's another. The term used to be applied so often to Salvador Allende of Chile that you might have thought the office of Marxist president figured in the Chilean constitution. The term could now be applied to Daniel Ortega Saavedra of Nicaragua. It is mystifying that it has not been. Even Fidel Castro isn't being billed as the bearded revolutionary, or the cigar-chomping Cuban. What is wrong here? Luckily the British are still around to help, with a bewigged Speaker to control parliamentary wrangling.

Ailing prime minister and aging prime minister, often mentioned in the same breath as the bewigged Speaker, are also among the missing. Their principal task used to be to aver, as in "His doctors had assured him of a complete recovery, the ailing prime minister averred." There is no longer such averring.

The reason for these lost clichés may be that journalists of the new generation do not think of themselves as seasoned scribes. Here is a piece of advice for them: Think of yourself that way and everything else, beginning with the confrontational eyeballs, follows.

AFTERTHOUGHT

Even a seasoned scribe could not now bring back a cigar-chomping Fidel Castro. He's given them up.

The Old Refrain

III

[9 May 1986]

There is a song called "The Old Refrain," which for humanitarian reasons I do not sing but which is brought to mind by the latest groan about leaks to the press.

The latest rendition comes from William Casey, Director of Central Intelligence, who says that five publications violated a 1950 law that makes it a crime to reveal information about American codes and ciphers or about the way we monitor and break other countries' codes and ciphers. This they allegedly did in stories about what the United States knew about Libya's connection with recent acts of terrorism. The five are the *Washington Post, Washington Times, New York Times, Time,* and *Newsweek.* The *Washington Post* has, in addition, a story that it has not yet published, because Casey asked it not to, about a former employee of the National Security Agency—that is the code-breaking agency—who has been fired and is charged with passing information to the Soviet Union.

Whether the five are to be prosecuted is up the Justice Department, which is said to be reluctant to take the cases to court. The reluctance is understandable. There is the matter of freedom of the press. There is the potential embarrassment in setting out how the five got the information they did—who gave it to them, and why. There is the danger that if legal proceedings do begin, even more information will come out. It could be a thoroughly unseemly affair.

Besides, the leak is part of the system of government. The state of Wisconsin calls itself Land of Lakes. Washington, D.C., could put "Land of Leaks" on its license plates. The leak is used to put out information unofficially, to see what the reaction may be. It is used to let other governments know which way thinking in Washington is moving. It may be used to intimidate other governments, make them think twice. It is used to cultivate reporters and make them friendly. It is used by people in government who see ideas taking shape that they don't like and want to kill. It is sometimes the only way to keep government from being too secretive and to give the public information it ought to have.

All of this is ingrained in Washington. Any hope of stopping it is illusory. Also, much information about government intentions comes from members of Congress and their staffs. They are beyond the reach of the White House.

In January 1982, President Reagan called leaks "a problem of major proportions." He made it a rule that anyone connected with national security policy get permission from a senior official before speaking to a reporter, and then submit a memorandum about what was discussed. Yet here we are, with the old refrain being played once more.

Speaking of old refrains, in 1946 a former secretary of war, Patrick Hurley, went on a mission to China for President Truman. A determinedly colorful New Mexican, Hurley returned with a pet name (unprintable) for Mao Tse-tung and in a state of outrage. He bellowed over the telephone to a reporter (not me), "I will not be leaked on by civil servants." The phrase caused much delight in Washington and elsewhere, but Hurley had been leaked on. If he had hung around, he probably would have been again.

It is easy to understand why administrations are annoyed, and more than annoyed, by leaks they do not intend, for those leaks reduce a president's control over events and dilute his power. Nonetheless, a leakless Washington is out of the question. It won't happen.

AFTERTHOUGHT

Why so squeamish? Hurley's name for Mao Tse-tung was Moose Dung.

In the Chapel
▪▪▪
[22 June 1986]

Newspeople are sometimes privileged. This newsman recently was. The assignment called for spending two days surrounded by some of the greatest works of man—Michelangelo's frescoes in the Sistine Chapel.

The reason for the assignment was that the frescoes, of the Creation on the ceiling and the Last Judgment on the wall over the main altar, are being restored. The hope is that when the twelve years of restoration are over, in 1992, Michelangelo's work will look as it did when completed, and it was said, "It was as if the world were rushing from everywhere to see it, and it was enough to amaze people and leave them speechless."

There is, perhaps, something of more than symbolic significance in the fact that the rights to make a record of the restoration were bought by a Japanese television network. The results of their labors will of course be seen all over the world, in versions tailored to the various national markets. That is where this newsman came in.

The restoration has aroused some controversy. Wash away, with the utmost care and deliberateness, and with a special detergent, the layers of dirt and soot, and the deposits of candles and oil lamps, and the animal glue used in earlier rescue work, and Michelangelo is revealed as a painter who used color almost as the Impressionists did. Some of those who object to what is being done argue that what is being revealed was not originally there at all. The predominant opinion, however, is that the restoration, undertaken by the Vatican art authorities, is proving to be tremendously successful, thrillingly so, and does fairly reveal what Michelangelo painted more than four and a half centuries ago.

Michelangelo climbed ladders to get to the ceiling and to his specially constructed scaffold. The holes in the wall into which the scaffold was placed are still there and are being used for the metal scaffold on which the restorers perch. Now a temporary lift takes you to the ceiling and you stand within an inch or two of the frescoes, crouching at times to get under them and comparing the fifth of the ceiling already restored with the rest. The difference is startling. You can also see the dilapidated state of the section not yet done—the cracks, the corrosion caused by rain, the effects of earlier restorations, some of them ill-advised, even including metal clamps driven into the plaster.

The ceiling is wavy, because water's leaking in. Some of the earlier attempts at cleaning resulted only in fixing dirt in place and making it harder to remove. Spotted on the ceiling are chalk circles designating areas that had been retouched, but whether by Michelangelo himself after the plaster and paint had dried or by someone much later, perhaps in the eighteenth century, cannot be known until the paint inside the circles is analyzed. That knowledge in turn will dictate the kind of cleaning material to be used.

In a way, the high point of the assignment may have come when a box lunch was brought in by a local caterer. *Cucina mobile,* it was called, and it was not *cucina Italiana* at its best. Still, gulping it down under the eyes of the prophet Joel and the prophet Zacharias and Eleazar and Jacob and Joseph and Ezechiel, with David hacking away at the neck of Goliath just above you, isn't an everyday ambiance for a meal. You have to remind yourself that it is really happening. You look up from the food and there is the Last Judgment, illuminated by the television lights and showing shades of color, especially blues, you had never dreamed were there.

There are only a few of you—camera crew, lighting men, the rest of the production team, and of course a representative of the Vatican, and a few Swiss Guards looking in from time to time. You have it all to yourself.

Privilege.

AFTERTHOUGHT

Left out of this column was the date of the frescoes. They took four years, 1508–1512.

Give Me That Microphone!
[3 July 1986]

It's flattering, in a way. Journalists have been found to have the third-most stressful job of all. They tie with construction workers and civil aviation pilots, it is true, but all the same they are well up there, behind only miners and the police.

The research was done by the Institute of Science and Technology at Manchester University, in England, and was not purely statistical. The researchers—in the field of organizational psychology—used their judgment. Still, it is a proud moment. It's pleasant to have the public think of us as working under tremendous strain, hoarse with tension and fatigue, shouting, "Tear out the front page!" and in the broadcasting end, "Give me that microphone!" and "Get that camera on! I have a big story here!"

The fact is, this is hooey. The really valuable people in the news business are those who don't shout and carry on, those who do not show the strain and on the whole do not feel it.

Early in my career, if that is not applying too grand a word to it, when I was working for a wire service, a reporter one day tore a phone out of the wall in the Navy press room in Washington (it probably was not very securely fastened) because the man in the office taking down the story he was dictating could not get it straight. A little later, a man on the night desk, never seen without a hat on the job or off (because he was bald, not because it was what hard-boiled newspapermen were thought to do) became so exasperated with a subordinate that he took off his hat and flung it against the wall. He also very nearly wept when he realized what he had done.

Calm is, however, what is needed. Say that you are on the air with a breaking story. The producer has to tell you, through your earpiece and while you are talking, to switch to the White House because the president is about to make a statement. It does not help if he shouts. Quite the opposite; the calmer and quieter, the better.

This does not mean that you are not affected by the events you are describing. Of course you are. You are a citizen of the country; how can you not be? Some of those first on the air with the shooting of President Kennedy were in tears, or close to it. I heard a recording of myself later, announcing Mr. Kennedy's death. Of course I sounded troubled and somber.

I don't know what it is like now, but in the old wire service days, when somebody out on a beat picked up a phone, got through to the desk, and shouted "Flash!"—meaning he had the hottest kind of story—and the desk man sang out "Flash!" and prepared to take it down, everybody's pulse picked up a beat and everybody who could crowded round to see what it was. It was exciting, enjoyable.

That, however, depended on the kind of story it was. I was working in the Washington bureau of the United Press on December 7, 1941. On that day, there was no enjoyment, but rather anger and sadness. All the same, what newspeople have to concentrate on is how the story is shaping up, what angles should be pursued, what they are going to write and say. That is what the news business is about. In print or on the air, you cannot waste time thinking thoughts that cannot be used.

Maybe what the Manchester researchers say is true. Maybe journalism is a stressful calling. If you are in the business, however, it is a mistake to keep reminding yourself of that. Moreover, many of us manage to live quite long lives—as long as the dentists, advertising people, actors, politicians, tax collectors, stockbrokers, doctors, astronomers, clergymen, and bus drivers, who trail behind us, and maybe even museum workers and librarians. They have the least stressful jobs of all—though they probably don't think so.

CBS News
▪▪▪
[9 March 1987]

CBS News has fired 215 employees. It is trying, in a few weeks, to cut its $300,000,000 budget by ten percent. All of this while newswriters are on strike at CBS, and at ABC, possibly to be joined at the end of the month by those at NBC.

To understand these events, it helps to put aside the term "the media." Nothing is happening in "the media." Something is happening in a part of the news business. Understanding begins there, with the point that news is a business, a competitive business. It does, of course, have its peculiarities, one of which is that its freedom is constitutionally protected. News is, nonetheless, open to many of the pressures that other businesses are. It also displays some of the habits and practices that other businesses do. What are they? Good management, mismanagement, nepotism, cronyism, competent people, incompetent people, overstaffing, empire-building, featherbedding, ability rewarded, ability unrewarded, insane overestimation of some who work in it, underestimation of others.

In television, there is a star system that greatly inflates news department budgets (and may antagonize large numbers of potential viewers by making the news appear to be the personal property of a select few). There are executives of talent and imagination, and there are so-called "hands-on" bosses trying to show how tough they are. Some have gone from one failure to another, having been hired by people who do not have the faintest idea of what journalism is about and would never dream of asking.

Television news departments also have occasional staff buildups when a demand arises for particular kinds of programs—documentaries, for example, or campaign and election specials—and then, through no fault of their own, these people may sit around for months and years with nothing to do when the demand for these programs falls off.

These are grim days at CBS, which has had three mass firings in eighteen months; a lot of good people have been given the axe. They have been grim at NBC and ABC, too, for a year and more, although the layoffs there have not been as explosive as those at CBS. Something like this probably had to come, brought on by smaller audiences, more national and international reporting by local stations, and competition from Ted Turner's Cable News Network. It has also been brought on by a larger development—television networks becoming part of giant corporations, and the news departments becoming less sacrosanct and untouchable, meaning that money pressures and considerations of profit increasingly determine what is done, and by whom.

The fact that the staffs are leaner does not necessarily mean that the news will not be as well-presented; a focusing of responsibility and less production of material that never gets on the air may be a good thing. There is, however, likely to be less news on the air—we have already seen a tremendous shrinkage of documentaries—and there may be less willingness to put on programs that draw comparatively small audiences. This latter tendency has, in fact, been visible for some time, most recently in the elimination of religious program units.

The process the network news departments have been going through newspapers in the United States have been going through for decades. The result is that we have fewer voices, more uniformity, more emphasis on the package and less on what is in it. This is the saddest, and most damaging, part of what is happening in—there's that term again—not the media. The news business.

AFTERTHOUGHT

The grim days continued. Late in 1987, NBC lopped off people wholesale. The grimness continued in another way: No amount of trying could get people to stop talking about "the media." They added insult to injury by making media singular. "Why does the media do this?" they wanted to know. "Why doesn't the media do that?" One reason is that they is part of the news business.

Where'er I Roam

At the Feeding Center
■■■
[13 December 1984]

Mauritania is one of the famine-stricken countries of Africa. (There are said to be twenty-six.) Nouakchott is its capital. One of the first Americans I met there, after two Nebraskans working on a U.S. A.I.D. road-building project and a former foreign service officer now with the Red Cross, was Mel Blount. Blount is a large and personable man who was for years a defensive back for the Pittsburgh Steelers, and one of the NFL's best. He was in West Africa with an American Red Cross delegation that wanted to draw attention to the famine and help feed the starving.

Blount and I had much the same mission. I was in Nouakchott early this month working for World Vision Incorporated, a religious group that feeds the hungry. The members of the team I was working with were old hands. They had been, among them, in Mozambique, Chad, Senegal, Kenya, Mali, and Bourkina Faso, which used to be Upper Volta. But Ethiopia was their touchstone. What they saw in Mauritania—a baby with arms like matchsticks, for example—they measured by what they had seen there.

In the early afternoon, we left our hotel and drove past arid land and sand dunes, past slums where people lived in tents, and in huts made of wooden slats, corrugated iron, and burlap bags, and past better sections, too, and street markets, until we reached a feeding center. It was one of our shooting locations. Children who are admitted there, such as the one with matchstick arms, "qualify" by weighing less than seventy percent of what they should in relation to their height. The building at the center was full, so the mothers sat in the shade of some trees, though trees, especially with leaves, are not easy to come by in Nouakchott. The mothers sat on the ground all day. Their only purpose, and their only activity, was exactly that—to sit there so that their children could be kept alive by being fed six times a day. Catholic Relief Services, we were told, had supplied the food.

It was not something to take in stride: flies everywhere, more flies than you believe the world could support; the women holding babies in advanced stages of decline, many of them not moving at all, some strong enough only to let out an occasional whimper or wail. To do your "stand-upper," you sat or crouched among them, resisting the natural temptation to attract a baby's attention, obeying strict instructions not to touch any of the women, even accidentally. They were, by the way, nomads, but their land had gone dry, their animals were dead, the husbands of many were away, working wherever they could find jobs, and the city was the last hope of survival.

It was not clear whether they understood what we were doing; some may have been too tired or weak or discouraged to care. Or perhaps they had seen television teams before. Still, they cooperated, moving when asked to, turning the babies toward the camera, remaining silent, which they seemed disposed to do, anyway. So there are you, well fed, clothed, and shod, a hotel room—rudimentary but clean—to go to, and an airline ticket out after a few days, speaking now to a camera, touching the shoulder of a particularly wasted child as you used the words "millions of children like these."

The feeding center was less bad than I had expected. There were the flies, millions of them, it seemed—"Don't brush away the flies when we're shooting, Ed," the director said. "I'm not seeing them." The children were not only emaciated; their hair, or lack of it, or its washed-out color, said something. Many had shaven heads, because of infection. Many had sores. Some drooled and dribbled. Most only stared. But there was no smell of death or disease; some of the children were said to be improving; and devoted people, local and foreign, were running things.

Yet the picture lingers, of dozens of women, sitting on the ground for hours on end, cradling their babies, willing them to remain alive. At sunset, they left the center for whatever they called home, to return in the morning, if they still had a reason to.

The Beggars of Haiti
###
[13 May 1985]

One of the hardest things about being in Haiti—I have just returned from there after working on a television documentary—is saying no to beggars. Or, more precisely, ignoring them. They come in dismaying variety. There are old women, thin, bent, and toothless, saying one unintelligible syllable over and over again. There is a boy who puts out his left hand; his right arm ends above the wrist. Other boys and girls seem to be all eyes; some rub their stomachs to show that they are hungry. Other adults do not beg overtly but stand around, hoping. Some tell you they are ill—*"Monsieur, je suis malade."* Usually, they look it.

Out in the countryside, people come up near your vehicle, holding out a hand, saying "Dollar." One young boy shouts, *"Des sous, des sous!"* The *sou* was the smallest French coin; it went out of use long, long ago. In a market area, a small woman comes up alongside us and holds out her hands. There are no fingers, only palms. For blocks, as the bus moves fitfully, she has no trouble keeping up. Every time we stop, her palms are raised toward us. "Mister," she says. "Mister." You don't look at her but you can't help hearing her, and involuntarily you begin hoping that she will fall behind. After a while, you begin to dislike yourself for not helping her, and to dislike the place that is making you feel this way.

Suddenly a memory comes back, brought on by the boy with the stump, of a beggar in Cairo, perhaps thirty years ago, who stationed himself at a busy intersection. When the traffic stopped, he chose the nearest car that looked promising and pushed an arm through the open window. The hand was cut off, the arm a stump but bifurcated, a lump on the left, a lump on the right. Why this memory should persist, among various horrors seen, it is impossible to say.

Very well, then, why ignore the pathetic beggars of Haiti? Why not give away a few coins. One reason is self-protection. Many of them are diseased, often on the skin. Another reason is that once you begin to hand out money, there is no end. It's better not to start. Finally, those who know about these things—missionaries, for the most part—insist that giving out pittances doesn't do much good.

Organized help is what is needed, something that will enable the people to help themselves.

Those who know put their money into, say, well-digging equipment, take requests from villages, sometimes make arrangements with other aid groups to bear part of the cost or supply materials, go where they are wanted, and sink a well. A team sponsored by the Southern Baptist Convention said it had hit water 125 out of 150 times.

Maybe more important, they teach local people to do the work themselves. The Baptists' foreman was a shy young man named Samson Fenelous. He was a mechanic who had been taught well-drilling by an American engineer. It had taken two months. Now he ran the job himself.

The Baptists' teams also cap mountain springs and channel them into villages. One village, I was told, now had its own water supply for the first time in two hundred years. This is water for household use, not agriculture. Water for irrigation requires projects on a much larger scale. But the small-scale efforts also meet pressing needs, and there are no middlemen, just people helping directly.

This is then, among other things, a rationale for ignoring beggars. As a rough guide to conduct, in some circumstances, ignoring them is almost unavoidable. Thinking of the wells and springs may help. You still feel like a heel doing it.

Memories of Haiti
[13 May 1985]

Haiti has a strange effect on a visitor. The poverty is so hard to get away from that statistics that would elsewhere be forgotten are fixed in the mind. Per capita income, about $300 a year. Population with access to clean water, twenty-five percent, some say ten percent. Infant mortality, 110–150 per thousand. Unemployment, fifty percent. Illiteracy, sixty percent, maybe higher.

Then you ask yourself: In a country that is so vastly illiterate, what can these figures be worth? It may be better to rely on impressions. These were some of mine:

The bus carrying our television team crosses bridge after bridge. The streams beneath are usually dry. Women crouch or go down on all fours searching among the stones for puddles large enough to do laundry in.

In a village where a visiting American medical team sees and treats 1,800 people in three days, a boy carries a live chicken, its feet tied. It is clearly destined for the pot. After a village woman whispers to him, the boy spares our sensibilities by going behind a well to wring the chicken's neck.

The presence of the medical team is a reminder of the Haitian brain drain. There are more Haitian physicians in the United States than in Haiti. Most people, when they are treated at all, go to healers. Some Haitians advocate training these healers, called *houngans,* to expand their knowledge and make better use of it. The argument is that Western medicine will not be practiced on a large scale in Haiti for a long, long time; with the healers, there could be quick improvement. The idea has not been adopted.

Four years ago, an epidemic of African swine fever hit Haiti. The pig population was wiped out. Replacements are being shipped in, by the United States Agency for International Development and by nongovernment charities. Question: Will these pigs be hardy enough to survive in Haiti? And what will they eat? The old ones ate anything they could find, and furnished a rough equivalent of pest control and garbage disposal. Will the transplanted pigs be able to do that?

Also shipped in are seedlings, so that trees will grow on Haiti's ravaged hills and stop the erosion. The experts choose fast-growing varieties, to provide lumber and charcoal, and to protect food crops planted among them, and to enable the Haitians to see quick results.

Money is shipped in from the United States, as well, and not only public and private aid. Haitian émigrés remit $80,000,000 a year. Jobs come in, too, as American toy and textile and electronic manufacturers set up assembly plants. The Haitians are industrious and the prevailing wage is about three dollars a day. Japan, Korea, and Taiwan may feel the effects, too.

Lasting memories of Haiti? Two. First, the loads the women carry on their heads, carry everywhere, even weaving nonchalantly through the racket and hubbub of traffic. A female cranium not bearing a burden is evidently thought to be wasteful, so they carry laundry, pots and pans, cartons full of goods to be sold, wood, charcoal, sisal, baskets, food, drink. In one case, a woman strolled by casually toting on her head plastic trays holding four dozen eggs. The loads are balanced on coils of cloth, which makes it no less impressive. Little girls carry smaller loads, learning the technique, and using a steadying hand the veterans disdain.

The second lasting memory is of neatly uniformed school children, who in spite of everything are fairly numerous, gathered outside our bus. Bursting with smiles, they sing the Haitian national anthem.

AFTERTHOUGHT

The pigs survived, and they do eat the same scraps their predecessors did. In the interest of increasing their numbers quickly, supplementary feeding is provided, and attempts are under way to grow fodder for them, something that had not been done in Haiti before.

Soon after this column appeared, the government of Claude "Baby Doc" Duvalier, which presided over the misery described, was overthrown. The United States flew him out, and he and his family settled in France, the French having given him temporary refuge at our request. They then found that nobody else would take him. It would be pleasant to report that things are better in Haiti, economically or in matters of personal liberty. The evidence is that they aren't.

Memories of Guinea
[8 July 1985]

It did not make many front pages, but there was an attempted coup last week in the West African country of Guinea. A former prime minister tried to return to power, displacing a president who had displaced him just eight months before. The army was against him and he failed.

Guinea is not a country that attracts much attention in the United States, even from the point of view of hunger. Although it does have a food shortage, it is not one of the African countries suffering most. For me, however, it does have a particular interest, and it has its place in the colonial and anticolonial history of our time. When Charles de Gaulle took power in France after the uprising by the French settlers and military in Algeria in 1958, he turned the French colonies into independent nations, but free to keep a special connection with Paris in a "French Union" if they wanted to. All did want to, at least for a while, except Guinea, a supplier of bauxite and bananas that sits on the southern part of Africa's bulge into the Atlantic. That sounded like a good television story, since nobody could remember having seen footage of Guinea, so off we went, I from Paris, a cameraman and a soundman from London, to make a half-hour program about it.

On the way, there was a small shock. The plane made a stop at Dakar, in Senegal. A newspaper in the airport headlined *"Le pape est grave,"* the Pope is gravely ill. As a former Rome correspondent, I would have been sent there to help, but now it was to be Conakry, Guinea's capital, instead. Still, that's the news business. In Conakry, we soon ran into Tom Johnston of the *New York Times,* who covered that part of the world. He had beaten us there. That also is the news business.

Guinea proved to be memorable in a number of ways. Its national dance company, which had some reputation outside the country, had been forbidden to perform for a month after independence, as a measure of the seriousness of what was happening. The ban was lifted for us, meaning that we could dress up our program with what were, in those days, still called "native dances." A party was organized, and a roasted pig, of extraordinary size, was brought in on a pole carried by a team of men. After the initial cuts were made, the serving technique was to walk up and grab a handful.

Many of the Frenchmen we spoke to told us that the country would dissolve into chaos after they left. They were wrong: what followed was not chaos but dictatorship, run by Ahmed Sekou Toure, who took the title of president and remained in power until March 1984, when he died in the United States, where he had gone for a heart operation. Sekou Toure was a handsome, smiling man, and an avowed socialist. When I told him that it was common talk in Paris that he was a communist, he smiled more broadly than ever. The smile was not extended to political opponents, many of whom wound up in prison or dead.

Guinea's principal resource was and is bauxite, of which it may have more than any other country in the world. It also has, among other things, bananas, and banana plantations make good pictures. We went to one, where I asked the French manager whether he employed any Europeans. He said no. Why not? His answer, in the English he was struggling with for our camera, said much in a few words: "Yoo-rope-ee-ans is too expensive."

We also filmed a shopping expedition, which is to say we went into the Conakry branch of a French Woolworth's-style chain to buy a pad and a pencil. The salesgirls wore skirts. Period. It was somewhat disconcerting when you reached over to take a pencil and a salesgirl moved in to help. This did not speed up the shopping process. Nor, in those primmer times, did it get into the program. But the film editors were grateful.

Finally, there was a Guinean civil servant who had a suggestion for how the United States could help his country. He wasn't asking for much, he said, just that any cars we Americans were ready to toss on the junk heap be shipped to Guinea instead.

Guinea rarely figured in the news; Sekou Toure kept it under strict control and out of international controversies. It was an unhappy and oppressed country, in its corner of West Africa, the hope of freedom and prosperity once the colonial power had gone sadly disappointed. It would be pleasant to think that somehow, things will be better now.

AFTERTHOUGHT

They do seem to be better. One hears that life in Guinea is less oppressive.

Good News
III
[25 October 1985]

"Why don't you ever give us any good news?"

The plaint is familiar to anyone in the business.

All right, here is some good news, good news about diarrhea.

Fewer children will be dying of it, that is, of the dehydration it brings about. This is because of a medical development called oral rehydration therapy, ORT for short. ORT is effective and inexpensive. The trick is to get it where it is needed.

To begin at the beginning, something like 14,000,000 children in developing countries (a number of which, as we know, do not develop; they go the other way) die each year of malnutrition and disease. Almost four million of those deaths are caused by dehydration, which in turn is caused by diarrhea. Worldwide, that works out to one child dying every ten seconds.

ORT, which is most often a solution of sodium chloride, sodium bicarbonate, potassium chloride, glucose, and water, does not cure diarrhea; it does offset dehydration. It was first used successfully in 1949, in an experiment in the United States. Its first large-scale use came in 1971, among refugees from the war between Pakistan and India. After that, much of the work on ORT was done in Bangladesh. According to the United Nations Children's Fund (UNICEF), the Bangladesh government now distributes 17,000,000 ORT sachets a year. Where ORT is not available, mothers in rural areas are taught to use a combination of salt, molasses, and water instead. Even so, almost ten percent of Bangladeshi children die before the age of five from the dehydration and malnutrition brought on by diarrhea.

There are two principal problems in getting ORT where it is needed. One, as always, is money. When ORT is described as inexpensive, that is relative. In the Third World, nothing is inexpensive. Alongside the traditional treatment for dehydration, however, which is hospital-administered intravenous infusion of lost fluid and salts, the price is low. Nor does it require trained hospital personnel; it can be administered by local health workers and by mothers. Still, most of the countries that need it are too poor to produce it or buy it in sufficient quantities. This despite the fact that UNICEF has been able to buy ORT for as little as four American cents a packet. (UNICEF itself distributes 65,000,000 packets a year.)

The second problem is making those who need ORT know that it exists. Again, these are poor countries; they don't have ready means of getting the information around. Nevertheless, radio and television do spread the word; so do churches; governments and aid groups post signs and set up shops where ORT and instruction in using it are made available. When I was in Haiti early this year, there was a wealth of signs for Serum Oral, which is ORT's local brand name.

Solve these problems, and another will remain. That is producing enough ORT. It is now being made in forty-one countries, at a rate, in 1984, of 160,000,000 packets a year.

If ORT is so effective, what can be done to get it where it is needed? That is to be the subject of a conference being held in Washington from December 10 to December 13. Representatives of more than eighty countries are to be there, under the sponsorship of the United States Agency for International Development, the International Center for Diarrheal Disease Research in Bangladesh, the World Bank, and three UN agencies—UNICEF, the Development Programme, and the World Health Organization.

If the conference proves to be more than an occasion for junkets, and actually produces useful results, there will be more good news to report.

Unique Sydney

[14 February 1986]

Sydney, Australia, arouses great expectations. It should: one of the key characters in Dickens's novel of that name was Magwitch, the escaped (and framed) convict; Magwitch was known to those who helped him as "the gentleman from New South Wales"; and Sydney is New South Wales' capital. Beyond that, one is told that Sydney has one of the world's most magnificent harbors, crowned by the celebrated opera house, created in the 1970s with a roof intended to suggest sails bellying out with the wind.

Sydney, as I learned on a recent visit, lives up to the expectations. The harbor was superb; the opera house, which is really a complex of theaters, was all it was cracked up to be; and our ship nosed in past sailboats by the score, running before the wind and under a bright, blue sky.

Sydney may be unique in the world. It has more than 3,000,000 people, which is about a fifth of Australia's population, spread out over vast suburbs overlooking the harbor. It has industry. It has a downtown business center with the usual high rises (it became unacceptable some years ago to describe a building as tall) mixing with Victorian buildings whose ironwork rivals that of New Orleans' French Quarter. It has an underground railway system, first-class museums, and marvelous parks.

Yet, big and booming as it is, Sydney also has the air of a resort city. The mild climate has something to do with it, and the parks, and the beaches, most notably Bondi, without whose undressed girls publications in many parts of the world would go out of business. Sydney might be described as an idealized version of an English seaside town, for it is neat and decorous and clean, with golf courses, cricket fields, and lawns for bowling. It is full of healthy-looking people, and squalor and dilapidation are hard to find.

The people are, of course, not all splendidly built "bronzed Aussies." There is a high incidence of beer bellies, for Australians pride themselves on their capacity for beer and, when they have drunk too much of it, for "chundering"—which is to say, throwing up—"in the old Pacific sea."

There was some evidence of discontent, signs complaining about oppression of various kinds, mostly of the poor and the unions. There were also mysterious signs. "Xmas OK, Santa No Way" was one. Mysterious only at first glance was "You've got to be bonkers not to go via Honkers," an airline advertisement that meant you would have to be crazy, if going to Europe, not to take a "shopover" stop in Hong Kong.

Newspaper stories sometimes sounded familiar: OUR HOSPITAL SYSTEM IS SICK: SOARING COSTS, LACK OF NURSES. A suggestion that all was not paradisaical was contained in an advertisement aimed at Aussies who wanted to spend a year in Fiji "away from the rat race" building vacation bungalows they would own and rent to—who else?—Americans when not occupying them themselves.

At times, it was tempting to think of Sydney as a city disfigured by the Australian (pronounce it Strine) cockney accent. We passed a nyvel byse, and a syfe area, watched syleboats in the bye, and were driven through a part of town where some night clubs had femyle impersonyters. Still, unless you got too much of it, the accent could be chalked up to local color.

One thought did intrude: What is a section of the Western world doing in the South Pacific? How long can it remain Western? The Aussies must worry about that, too. Maybe that's why they're so glad to see you.

≡≡≡

The Road to Bombay
⫶⫶⫶
[4 March 1986]

The flight from London to Bombay does not get off to an entirely auspicious start.

The screens are lowered from the aircraft's ceiling, and a crisp English female voice announces a brief video explaining the operation of "the toilet area." There may be people aboard who are not familiar with the way these devices work. If so, she goes on, they may be sure that the devices are well-thought-out and efficient. The video then takes us on a guided tour of an airliner lavatory. Some details are omitted, but we are shown the correct position of the seat for those who use it while sitting down, and the correct position for those who use it while standing, and how to activate the flushing mechanism.

All of this may, if permitted to do so, have a somewhat disquieting effect. If people who can afford the London-to-Bombay airfare know nothing of flush toilets, what should be expected from their less affluent countrymen at home?

As it turns out, on the way into Bombay from the airport there is a certain amount of public urinating, but those who engage in it do turn their backs to the road. Nothing more serious is seen.

What is seen is spitting on a scale that would not be out of place in an American major league baseball game. The immigration formalities at the airport were slightly delayed at one point where an immigration officer left his post, strode past arriving passengers to a wastepaper bin, and let fly a couple of gobs of reddish slop. Scouts for some American teams may want to look him over.

Before you reach this stage, your plane heads into Bombay through a world-class smog. The pilot explains, perhaps half-jokingly, that it is caused "by the cooking pots." Dust and automobile exhaust and industry no doubt make their contribution as well. When you are in it on the ground, the smog makes the eyes sweat and the stomach sick.

The way into Bombay through the smog and incessant horn-blowing that seems unaggressive and considered merely part of the process of driving is depressing. People in vast numbers live by the side of the road, often in mud, in lean-tos and hovels made of corrugated iron, pieces of wood, burlap bags, anything they can find. Some live in sections of cement pipe apparently placed along the road as part of a water project not yet under way. Some have no shelter.

As your car moves in fits and starts through the rush-hour traffic, beggars come to the windows—children, cripples, mothers with sick-looking babies. You try to look straight ahead, but it's hard to do. After a while, the roadside hovels become mixed with apartment buildings, dreary and insubstantial-looking and run-down. Apart from a couple of temples and a few Victorian pubs, there is not a building of interest or charm.

Bombay does, of course, have its modern center, where the hotels and office buildings and apartment houses resemble those of countless other cities. Reaching that center is actually harrowing.

The effect of all this stuns you, not least the families sleeping on the pavement outside your hotel. The hungry children are so ubiquitous you cannot face them: you wind up unable even to take a stroll.

You had, of course, heard about India's unsolvable problem, about the poverty and degradation, about the teeming people. It's different—even inside a chauffeur-driven car—when you are among them, when you're there.

Asian Observations
•••
[21 March 1986]

Incidental intelligence picked up during a swing around some Asian ports:

India is to have its first condominium. A Bombay newspaper carries a big advertisement for it, although the condo is to be in New

Delhi, "minutes away from the city center," on—for those who may be interested—the Gurgaun-Mehranli Road. It has an unusual feature, housing for domestic servants. The accommodations are described as "Manhattan apartments," and although this is not defined in detail, the description is plainly meant to be impressive and may be taken by Manhattanites as a compliment.

India has an economic-moral-ecological dilemma, arising from frogs' legs. It involves what Americans call trade-offs. Exports of frogs' legs bring India foreign exchange and provide thousands of jobs. That's the plus side. The minus side is that the frogs die in agony after being thrown back into the water after their legs are removed, and that reducing the frog population may lead to increased breeding of mosquitoes that carry malaria and filariasis, and of other insects that damage crops. A decision on a ban on exports is due any day.

There is a school of thought, indulged rather than accepted, that Sri Lanka, not usually thought of as one of the biblical lands, was Adam and Eve's Garden of Eden. Drive around it—it's one of the greenest and lushest places on earth—and you can understand it. Sri Lanka, which was its name before it became Ceylon, is said to mean "Splendid Island."

Unlike India, Penang, the island that is the principal resort in and for Malaysia, already has condominiums. One of them proclaims itself—this must have been used somewhere else, if only by coincidence—A Site to Behold.

Singapore, which is after Rotterdam the second-busiest port in the world, is probably also the most hortatory. STRIVE FOR EXCELLENCE, signs say, and MAKE COURTESY OUR WAY OF LIFE, and THERE IS A PART FOR EVERYONE IN TOTAL DEFENSE. It may well also be the cleanest port: A fine is imposed for littering, and there is evidence that this does the job. There is, in addition, a fine for jaywalking. We saw none.

Singapore appears to offer the ultimate in the welfare state, combined with an unchallengeable paternalism. Anyone looking for the last word in urban renewal can find it here. Block after block of old two-story houses, often with a shop below and living quarters above, has been demolished. Chinatown, as it used to be, has all but disappeared. The great majority of the 2,500,000 Singaporeans live in apartment buildings, gigantic and characterless, financed by the government. They are helped to buy their apartments by a government subsidy, which rests in turn on forced savings.

The government also does not like traffic jams or pollution. They are combatted by a heavy duty on automobiles, all of which have to be imported, and by a rule that no car may enter certain intersections at certain times with fewer than four occupants. Enter them anyway and you pay a fine on the spot.

Singapore has under construction what is to be the tallest hotel in the world, seventy-three stories, two higher than the current leader, which is in Atlanta. Perhaps Atlanta won't mind.

Outside the port of Pattaya, in Thailand, on the road to Bangkok, an old Dakota transport plane sits on a hill. It is used as a restaurant, and may be regarded as a lineal descendant of the old trolley diner. It is a reasonable guess that it was placed there to enable foreign tourists to make easy wisecracks about not wanting to be reminded of airline food.

That ends this column. More Asian observations later.

AFTERTHOUGHT

Early in 1987, the further exporting of frogs' legs from India was banned.

≡≡≡
Asian Observations (2)
III
[21 March 1986]

More incidental intelligence picked up at a number of Asian ports:

Bangkok means City of Angels. Tour guide, a former interpreter for the United States Army, as coach reaches outskirts: "Ladies and gentlemen, welcome to Los Angeles."

Famous last words, on a hot and humid day, brought on by a

notice that visitors must remove their shoes before entering a Buddhist temple: "I'll never get them back on."

More famous last words, as visitors are asked to sit on the temple floor while contemplating the statue of the Buddha: "I'll never make it back up." Those who do risk sitting down are asked not to point their feet at the Buddha; the feet are the lowest and least highly regarded part of the body; pointing them at the Buddha is considered disrespectful.

Between Pattaya, the port for Bangkok, and Hong Kong, the ship skirts the coast of Cambodia and Vietnam. Especially off Vietnam, you stare at whatever land is visible: shallow beaches, ranges of hills, offshore islands. There are few signs of habitation, only occasional fishing boats. The emotion you feel is vague, unhappy, wondering. You shake your head. Is this the place? The next morning, the ship's navigator announces that at midnight, we were on the same parallel as Saigon. It seems unreal. Did it happen? You think of the Vietnam memorial in Washington. It happened.

Hong Kong is the most densely populated place on earth: more than 5,000,000 people crowded into 400 square miles. There is no room to spread out, so the buildings go up, endless "tower blocks," as the British call them, vast apartment buildings that may seem to the ungenerous to be hardly more than filing cabinets for human beings but that nonetheless constitute a housing miracle brought off by the colonial administration and some private companies. From most vantage points, Hong Kong is a mass of gray and white tower blocks. In mist and fog, they take on an eerie, disquieting quality. They remind you of a grim castle in which the rooms defy counting, and where a princess is held captive. By the time the prince finds her, he is old and stooped, but his youth is restored by her kiss. This of course is a happy ending, which may be more than should be hoped for. The mountain of apartment windows symbolizes the present, and still more the future in this part of the world, an endless supply of people, spilling over wherever they are able to.

In the midst of all this, who should turn up but George Bush. Not in person, but in a photograph gracing a shopwindow in a particularly elegant hotel, the Peninsula, where, as it happened, the British surrendered the colony to the Japanese on Christmas Day, 1941. "To

Johnny and Tony," the inscription reads, "with thanks and with personal best wishes to you both and to my friend Ascot Chang. Sincerely, George Bush."

In the photograph, Bush is flanked by, presumably, Johnny and Tony, and is, appropriately, in his shirtsleeves, for Ascot Chang also has this message in his window: "Take our word for it. Ascot Chang is Hong Kong's most respected shirtmaker."

At Hong Kong Airport, there was a reminder of the unnerving Indochinese coastline. About three dozen Vietnamese, small men, small women, small children, were gathered on benches near a departure gate. Some were animated; most were quiet and expressionless; all wore paper tags around the neck to show that they were refugees. They were heading for the United States.

How to Help Africa
III
[27 March 1986]

How do you help a starving African farmer?

Give him food, of course.

But how do you help him in the long run, so that someday he will no longer need your food? The answer is, enable him to live as an African, not as an imitation European or American farmer. In other words, in the part of Africa that has been in the grip of famine for the last three years, salvation may lie in going back to old techniques, not ahead to new ones.

This is the argument being put forward by a man greatly experienced in Africa, Brian W. Walker, former head of Britain's Oxfam, now president of the International Institute for Environment and Development. Tribal records in Africa, Walker says, go back three thousand years. Even making allowances for population growth, there is no evidence of anything "remotely comparable to the scale of human death and suffering experienced today as a result of poverty-induced hunger and malnutrition."

Note the word "poverty." Drought precipitated the famine, but it is, Walker says, poverty that is the basic problem. How did it come about? Here is Walker's answer: "The major cost of colonialism, for which Africans are paying today, was the breakdown of pastoralism, nomadism, and settled living. Pastoralists raise livestock for their subsistence. Nomads are roving pastoralists. Hitherto, people had carefully constructed a balance with their environment. This balance was the key not merely to survival, but to food abundance and the evolution of rich civilizations over three millennia."

Colonialism, according to Walker, put an end to that balance. It substituted the market economy and single-crop farming, with that crop often intended to produce cash, not food. It offered high-tech and high-energy farming, requiring a dependable water supply and big investments, neither of them readily available in Africa. The boundary lines the colonial powers imposed did not help, either. They interfered with logical regional groupings and movements. There were also the African governments, many of them corrupt or cruel or naïve, and too eager to follow Western models, and eager as well to spend money for military prestige. Eventually, all of this, coupled with the drought, brought disaster.

Nor is that the end of the catalog. Africa's population in 1980 was 470,000,000. By the year 2000, it is expected to be 850,000,000, and if the trend is not checked, 1,500,000,000 by 2025. That would be a quarter of the world's population. Africa now has ten percent. The pressure on the land, and the environmental degradation, already profound, can be imagined.

What is to be done? Many things, says Walker, all of them based on the fact that more than seventy percent of Africans live in rural areas as subsistence farmers. Development plans have to be acceptable to them, and have to recognize the central role of women, who with children provide much of the labor. The goal would be producing food to eat, without technological innovation, single-crop farming, or much use of pesticides and fertilizers. This means, specifically, no plows, but rather hand hoes. No tractors; draft cattle, and camels, are needed. No crop spraying for weed and pest control—traditional methods, such as the right mix of insects and plants, are better. No big silos with controlled temperatures and humidity, but rather small village storage places. No water if the land is dry, and no fertilizers if it lacks nutrients. Better to find plants that suit the land as it is.

Incentives will be useful, meaning cash benefits and credit, and soap, salt, bicycles, oil, and transistor radios in the village shops. And there should be vegetable gardens, and gardens in the cities, on rooftops, among other places. In short, think small.

This column is only a summary of Walker's argument. That argument can be found in full in a short book published by the Foreign Policy Association and called *Authentic Development in Africa*. Authentic development, says Walker, with the emphasis on authentic. That is the key.

Canadian Coincidence
III
[22 June 1986]

A bit of irony from our Canadian friends (*Un chose ironique de nos amis Canadiens*): They are still arguing about which language, or languages, to use in the province of Quebec when something like a million Canadians cannot read in any language.

The irony arose, during a recent visit, from one of those wonderful coincidences—in Montreal, seven shopowners were fined because they posted in English such messages as "Taste Our Coffee, Compare Our Prices, and Discover Our Quality." At the same time, a campaign was being organized to help the 4,000,000 Canadians who are thought to be functionally illiterate. That is one in every five adult Canadians, with a quarter of them unable to read or write at all.

These figures may come as a surprise. Canada gives the impression of being a calm and rather serious country, where they order these things better. Also, it is without the problems caused by centuries of deliberately maintaining a large group of its people—as the United States did with blacks—in an inferior position. And, though it has substantial immigration, it has not had great waves of newcomers overwhelming the system of education and insisting on being taught in the language of their forefathers.

Nonetheless, the Canadians have the affliction, too, and it sounds familiar. Most of the functional illiterates are school dropouts. Many are unemployed and don't even look for jobs because they know they cannot get one or cannot face the embarrassment of being unable to read training manuals and other instructions. So the Canadians are undertaking to do something about illiteracy, and publishers are putting up some of the seed money.

As for the other half of the coincidence, in Montreal seven businessmen were fined from $50 to $500 for violating the province's law prohibiting signs in English only. One of those clipped was a veterinarian; another the coffee shopowner already mentioned, by name Rajinder Sud; a third a company that had its employment forms in English only.

Another eight companies pleaded not guilty and are to appear in court in August and September. Five more are to be in court on July 14 (*le quatorze juillet,* by golly and *sacre bleu!*), among them a delicatessen charged with advertising "corned beef" and "smoked meat." Smoked meat is what we, or some of us, *quelques uns de nous,* call pastrami.

All of this grows out of a law passed in Quebec in 1977 which requires that commercial signs be in French only. A Quebec court has ruled that this requirement violates the guarantee (*la garantie*) of freedom of expression in the Quebec charter, and there will have to be a ruling next by the Court of Appeals. Complications arise: Can it really be illegal to post a sign in English? If it is and a merchant posts his sign in English and in French, does that make it all right? If smoked meat is impermissible, could pastrami, as a generic term, get by instead of *viande fumé?*

One counts on Canadian good sense to resolve the issue peacefully, though this has at times been a burning issue in Quebec. It would be a shame if the Canadian way of life and the compact between French- and English-speaking Canadians foundered on a pastrami sandwich, on rye.

By the way, the term the French in France use for sandwich is sandwich, which is English and dates back to the eighteenth century. Confusing, *n'est-ce pas?*

Ignore Me
III
[2 March 1987]

Readers of this column should be advised that they are wasting their time. Columnists ought to be smart. I am not. Ignore me.

Consider the evidence: My wife and I were to fly from New York to Canberra, Australia, with the first stop, for a little more than a day, in Phoenix, Arizona. To get us to Kennedy Airport, a car, with driver, was ordered from a service we had used a number of times before. Twice the car had not shown up, but the service had been contrite about it, even sending a postcard bearing an apology and offering a small discount next time around.

On this occasion, the car again did not show up, and after some waiting, we took a taxi. The drive to Kennedy produced a question: Why rely on a service that expected to be so unreliable that it had a printed form to send to inconvenienced customers? No reassuring answer presented itself.

Moral: Don't read my columns. My intelligence doesn't warrant it.

In the taxi, there was no license for the driver attached to the dashboard, and although a "No smoking" sign was posted, the driver was smoking a cigarette. At the airport, he managed to break off the key to the trunk while trying to open it, thereby imprisoning our luggage. After memorizing his license number in case he took off, I was preparing to borrow a tire iron to jimmy open the trunk when the driver somehow contrived to turn the lock with the piece of key still in his hand. We made the plane.

All of this began when I booked a service that had a proven record of failure. Moral: Don't read my columns.

From Phoenix, the original booking to Canberra had been by way of Los Angeles and Sydney. When it became evident that we could leave Phoenix a few hours sooner, I asked the office arranging the trip to work out an earlier departure. It sent us by way of San Francisco. On arriving there, we learned that the flight would pass through Los Angeles on the way to Australia. In fact, it was the same flight. San Francisco was the starting point. By leaving earlier, we had tacked on a three-hour detour.

Moral: Don't read my columns.

The flight was delayed by electrical problems, and the connection in Sydney was missed. The airline misplaced a piece of our luggage —it turned up a day later—and when we did land in Canberra, the airport was being rebuilt. Passengers had to carry their own luggage to the taxi ramp. An airport employee, asked whether there were porters or carts for the luggage, replied, "We don't do that sort of thing here."

The hotel, when we got there, had no record of our reservation and of the fact that it had been paid for in advance. The reservation notice did arrive during our stay, by which time the value of the United States dollar had fallen, and the advance payment no longer covered all it was intended to.

Moral: Don't read my columns.

P.S. Back in New York, a card of apology from the limo service awaited us. It offered a slight discount. If I ever use it, please— please—don't read my columns. Ignore me.

The Merchants of Hong Kong
[2 March 1987]

If the merchants of Hong Kong are off their stride, as much as thirty seconds may go by after you leave the gangplank of your cruise ship before someone sidles up and asks whether you would like the services of a custom tailor. Normally they do it in fifteen.

You ignore the sidler, and those who follow, for you are determined that no shopkeeper will be able to say, "Here comes another of those dumb, gullible Americans." You consider not shopping at all, but on reflection that makes no sense: What, after all, are you in Hong Kong for? So, wandering through the streets, you enter a shop lighthearted and confident. "Let's see what they've got," you tell yourself. The step is fateful. You have entered an uneven contest.

The selling technique of the Hong Kong merchants borders on brainwashing. It resembles the method of the infinitely patient interrogator, who keeps at it day after day until the victim wants to tell him something, comes to feel that he owes him that. The merchant does it by going to tremendous trouble and by talking endlessly. The question is not whether you will buy but what. For buy you must.

Let's say you are thinking about getting a tablecloth and a set of napkins. Out they come from a neat pile. The cloths are wrapped in plastic, which is torn open. Others are dislodged and fall on the floor, making you feel guilty. As cloth after cloth is spread out for you to see, the talk goes on: "Which one you like buy best? Maybe you take both. Yes, that best. Take both." You look at the chaos your visit has brought on, and the expenditure of energy by the shopkeeper and his assistant. Undecided, you look longingly at the door.

Signs in the window have already proclaimed "Sale!" and thirty percent discounts. Now comes "a special price because it Sunday." You are seized by regret for having made the shopkeeper work so hard. Also, you don't want him to think that you are poor. You'll show him Americans still have what it takes. You are, in consequence, the new owner of a tablecloth. Or two. Or—for presents, you tell yourself—more.

Or perhaps the owner of shirts. You have always wanted one tailor-made. Here is your chance. They'll do it overnight. So in you go. It quickly becomes clear that it is foolish not to buy at least three. A set of three is logical when you are buying shirts. The shopkeeper thinks you should buy seven.

"Seven? That's ridiculous. I already have more shirts than I know what to do with."

The shopkeeper explains. The unit price for seven is much lower than it is for three. You can't afford not to buy seven. A man recently came in and bought twenty, and he is a regular who comes back year after year. Now the shopkeeper begins pulling out lengths of material, making certain that some of them fall on the floor and that others are knocked awry. You feel guilty but hesitate. It is time for "a special price." You take off your jacket and let him measure you. Next day you will be the owner of seven new shirts.

What about a suit? He can have it ready tomorrow morning. Only one fitting. Look at the material. Out come the lengths. This time you must save face. No suit.

When you go to collect the shirts, the shopkeeper wants to know what time your ship sails. That evening, you tell him. Still plenty time, he says. Make you suit. Special price. By now, however, you are hardened. You have exchanged jokes with other passengers: "How much money did you save today?" "Did you leave anything for us?" "Here comes the walking trade deficit."

So, still no suit. When the ship leaves the dock, though, you wonder. "Should I have taken a suit? Maybe instead of those shirts? Maybe both? After all, what were you in Hong Kong for?"

Johannesburg
###
[30 October 1987]

Johannesburg, South Africa. It is a name that carries a strong flavor of menace, tension, sadness, oppression.

Actually, your arrival is quite benevolent. The immigration officer, having ascertained that it is your first visit, makes you a present of a set of picture postcards. It is a form of advertising for tourism, to be sure, but still, no other country in your experience has done that.

Outside the airport terminal building, a truckload of soldiers armed with machine pistols stands at a traffic light. Maybe it just happened to be passing through. In any case, you see no more such sights during your four-day stay, though you do see a profusion of gun-toting policemen and security guards, even the guards inside your hotel. As you enter the hotel, a man, large, white, and young, asks for identification. Your driver, a black man, assures him that you are "from overseas" and all right. You are not challenged again.

The United States has imposed economic sanctions on South Africa, but there is much evidence of American influence. One day you pass a Kentucky Fried Chicken training center. Almost the first sight that greets you at the airport is a poster advertising a local magazine. Dolly Parton adorns the magazine's cover, and inside the reader is promised information on how Miss P. "stays trim on seven meals a day." Also spotted are cars bearing "I Love New York" signs, with Johannesburg replacing New York.

Johannesburg's downtown is bright and shiny, full of those buildings that look as though they are made of plastic and glass. Your hotel is interchangeable with big-city hotels all over the world.

If you look for overt signs of hostility between blacks and whites, you don't find any. The hotel head porter, on being asked, does advise against taking a walk at night, except in the hotel's immediate vicinity, and certainly against carrying a wallet: "They won't snatch the wallet. They'll tear the whole pocket off." Still, that might happen anywhere, and in general, the tone of public behavior seems tranquil enough.

This of course tells you nothing about what may be boiling beneath the surface. The local paper carries a front-page notice: "In terms of the State of Emergency regulations, news, pictures, and comment in this newspaper may be restricted." A celebrated South African, not on the record, says that apartheid "is falling to pieces around our ears." He also criticizes "self-righteous Americans, who do not believe there are any decent white South Africans at all," and he says that sanctions will not succeed, because they are intended to intimidate the Afrikaaners who run the government and they will not be intimidated. The outlook: Not armed revolution, because the blacks don't have the arms or the money, but "an evolutionary period, difficult and painful."

Others tell you that the sanctions help principally Japan, which has replaced the United States as South Africa's chief trading partner, and Taiwan, and some European nations. They have also helped some local businessmen, who bought the assets of departing American corporations at knockdown prices, sometimes twenty cents on the dollar. If the blacks really want sanctions, you are also told, all they have to do is walk off the job.

There is a bit of encouragement: Some white businessmen accept that white supremacy cannot last and are making connections with important blacks to create goodwill and understanding that may be helpful when the inevitable convulsions come.

There is also what may be a wise appraisal from another South African, that it is not too late for negotiation, but too early, because both sides still believe they can win.

Live
From
London

∎∎∎

The British Sundays
III
[4 December 1984]

Some of those among us are old enough to remember that World War II song "There'll Always Be an England." It is still sung, and as the world goes these days, England's continued existence is as nearly certain as anything else. I can confirm that, when last I saw it, England was still in place and plainly expecting to stay there.

Also in place was that peculiarly British institution, the really deplorable Sunday newspaper. Some of the British Sundays have hardly changed over decades; they continue to rely on stories with headlines such as "Why sexy Samantha wants to be plump" and "I didn't want to strip—I don't like my body" and "British women—why do they go so far?"

Let us examine these notable examples of journalism. Sexy Samantha is an actress who professes to believe that men like to marry thin women but prefer sleeping with plump ones. The girl who didn't want to strip also was an actress who had to appear in a swimming pool scene. The question about the unrestrained actions of British women was attributed to Barry Manilow, who it seems is in danger of being mobbed by "mums with money to burn and one thing on their minds." So troubled is Manilow by these mums that he is considering punishing them by performing in Britain less often.

The British Sundays inevitably contain advice to the lovelorn, as in "The girls tell what turns them on." The qualities that turn them on are, on examination, disappointing: good teeth, good hair, a nice smell, a smart appearance, a sense of humor, success, power, money, strength, reliability, kindness, compassion, and a twinkle in the eye. It all sounds manageable.

Where possible, the British Sundays like to combine a number of surefire ingredients, notably crime and sex. Thus: "The night I came face-to-face with a burglar in my bedroom" and "Traced: A young mother snatched from 'Svengali' influence of a husband her family hates."

There are, of course, the routine stories: "Riddle of why top lawyer declared daughters illegitimate" and "Girls flee slave gang," "Young lust lures wife away," "Girlie mag shocks residents," and "Tale of sex and drugs at office." There are always animal stories:

227

"Homesick collie jumps ship," about a sheepdog that didn't like leaving the farm in Scotland for a sea voyage to a new owner, though he did make it on the second try. And there are ghost stories, for example that of a medium who stayed in a hotel room occupied by a celebrated comedian before his death. The medium heard him say "Enjoy the bed" when she got up during the night to make some tea. That's another thing. There has to be something in the Sundays about tea.

In spite of all of this, and the young woman who found evidence of former girlfriends in her fiancé's house, said evidence including a forty-two-inch bra, I must confess some disappointment. On previous visits, the stories were better. There was, among others, "Mystery spray from helicopter as women have tea." Mediums and tea, after all, are old stuff; helicopters and tea, relatively new. And there was "Prickly passion put me in a panic." That turned out to have to do with a woman who heard heavy breathing coming from some bushes outside her house. Accompanied by her son, who was carrying a gun, she investigated and found two mating hedgehogs.

Towering above them all was this: "A gipsy's warning comes true for a bandit who wanted to be a poet." A gipsy, a warning, a bandit, a poet. In the context, every word a cliché. The ideal story for the British Sundays.

Dr. Thatcher, I Presume?

[1 February 1985]

Heard the latest from the city of dreaming spires?

No honorary degree for Margaret Thatcher. That's right, the Prime Minister. Oxford said no. Not quite as one man—the vote, by the teaching, research, and administrative staffs, was 738 to 319. Still, no. That makes Mrs. Thatcher the first Oxford-educated prime minister since 1946 not to be granted an honorary degree by the university. Clement Attlee (later Lord Attlee) was given one. Sir Alec Douglas-Home (later Lord Home) was given one. So were Harold MacMillan (later Lord Stockton), Anthony Eden (later Lord Avon), and Harold Wilson (later Lord Wilson). Likewise Edward Heath (later Edward Heath). Not Mrs. Thatcher.

If Mrs. Thatcher needs any consolation, she might consider the proposition that when it comes to honorary degrees, it is more blessed to give than to receive. It may even be, taking into account the rate at which they are shoveled out, that there is more distinction in being turned down for one than in having one conferred on you. Honorary degrees have become routine. In this country, certainly, colleges and universities beat the bushes looking for, as they are unfortunately called, honorees and awardees. Even newspeople get them.

The new doctors are apostrophized thus: "You have opened wide the doors to human understanding by your study of paradoxical counseling techniques related to the functioning of the brain as an input control system." And: "Through your original, bold, comprehensive, measured, and timely recognition of strategies of experiential education, including combined cognitive, affective, and skill objectives, you have earned the thanks and admiration of the nation." And: "Your music, strong and thrusting, with its daring absence of melody and harmony, is the music of a restless, ever-adventuring people. Your alma mater is proud to call you her daughter."

Why was Mrs. Thatcher denied such an apostrophe? Two explanations have been put forward. One was opposition to her policies in general, but that does not hold up. There was opposition to the policies of her predecessors, too. The other was unhappiness over her government's cutbacks in money for education. This is more logical. A petition signed by some three hundred dons (professors) before the vote said that she "had done deep and systematic damage to the whole public education system in Britain, from the provision for the youngest child up to the most advanced research program." The university, the dons said, that is "widely perceived to stand at the pinnacle of British education" should not be giving her "its highest token of appreciation."

That does make some sense. There were other reasons, including, no doubt, some showing off by the dons, not all of whom shun publicity, and some cutting up of a kind not unknown in the academic world. There was also Mrs. Thatcher's unyielding manner, which led to a fairly notable pun. In the early 1950s, a play by Christopher Fry called *The Lady's Not for Burning* was produced on both sides of the Atlantic. Years later, Mrs. Thatcher responded to calls for a change in policy by saying, "This lady's not for turning." One of her supporters at Oxford said that withholding the degree was futile. He added, "This lady is not for spurning." That made it, for him certainly, all worthwhile.

Mrs. Thatcher's reaction to the Oxford vote was typically frosty. A spokesman at Ten Downing Street said that it was gracious of those who had done so to propose the honorary degree, but if the university "does not wish to confer the honor, she is the last person to wish to receive it." So she will not get the honorary doctorate in civil law, and she will have to content herself with the degree in chemistry she earned in 1947. She will probably bear up. That degree was real.

≡

No National Swoon
∎∎∎
[22 May 1985]

Not the least valuable contribution Americans make to the well-being of their friends and allies is that of serving as objects of scorn. So we see a generally serious British newspaper, the *Sunday Telegraph* of London, putting forward an explanation of recent public appearances by Mikhail Gorbachev that rests on the alleged goofiness of Americans.

The new Soviet leader not long ago walked around an industrial suburb of Moscow, seeing the people and permitting himself to be seen. Soviet television was there. A few weeks later, Gorbachev spent three days in Leningrad, again seeing the people and being seen. Again Soviet television was there. Why did Gorbachev make these public appearances? Perhaps, the *Telegraph* surmised, "to appeal to the Soviet people over the heads of the older Brezhnevite politburo members whom he must replace if he is to achieve his desired economic reforms." More likely, the *Telegraph* thought, his principal purpose was "to win the approval of Western public opinion, particularly in the United States." When he visits the United States, the *Telegraph* went on, Gorbachev looks set "to take the impressionable Americans by storm."

Ah, the impressionable Americans! What would our allies do

without the impressionable, volatile, naïve, good-hearted but gullible Americans? But consider: Soon after Gorbachev succeeded Yuri Andropov, he and his wife visited London. Mrs. Gorbachev appeared to be lively, reasonably attractive, and well-dressed. Gorbachev himself was a competent debater and not without charm and humor. The way the British went on—"I can do business with this man," said Prime Minister Thatcher, Britain's Iron Lady, visibly melting—there were fears in the United States that the British might pull out of NATO and leap headlong into the Warsaw Pact. This, we may be certain, accounted for the *Telegraph*'s patronizing comment. The British were embarrassed by their own conduct. How to recover? By suggesting that if they, vastly experienced and intelligent as they acknowledge themselves to be, were so taken with the Gorbachevs, the Americans would lose control completely.

Behind this nonsense, and the competition in impressionability or the lack of it, may be seen a matter of some seriousness. We do risk being excessively cheered by a mere display of normal affability and reasoned argument because we have for so long gone too far in the other direction. A small sensation is created when a Soviet representative appears to be something less than an ogre or a mechanical man, and when his wife uses makeup and wears shoes smaller than gunboats.

The usual remedy lies to hand—a little reality and some sense of history. Of course there is a tremendous difference between Gorbachev and Josef Stalin. Of course the possibility of useful relations may well be brighter with someone of Gorbachev's generation in power. It does come as a relief that Gorbachev and his wife are recognizable human beings who would not be out of place in non-Soviet societies. But our patronizing British friends need not worry. There will not be a national swoon if the Gorbachevs show up in our part of the North American mainland. Marxism-Leninism will not become the creed of the United States Chamber of Commerce. We will not unilaterally disarm.

The fact is the British, with the long devotion of so many of them to the tenets of socialism, are more vulnerable than we are. Remember, Gorbachev went to Britain first. There must have been a reason.

On the Terraces

III

[3 June 1985]

The British satirical magazine *Private Eye* has among its regular cast of imaginary characters a married couple, Sid and Doris Bonkers, devoted soccer fans both, and a soccer—the British call it football—reporter, referred to as "Our Man on the Terraces." The "Bonkers" speaks for itself, or speak for themselves. "Our Man on the Terraces" takes some explanation.

In the great soccer stadiums of Britain, there have traditionally been great expanses in the stands at each end of the field where there are no seats, only terraced cement or concrete on which the fans stand, with iron bars to hold on to. In other words, those in the terraces stand for hours, before, during, and after the game. There is no question of their sitting. The price they pay is, of course, commensurately lower. This sheds some light on last week's horrifying events in Brussels. Soccer is largely a working-class obsession in Britain. Not exclusively, but largely. The terraces are the embodiment of this.

It comes as a surprise to many Americans when the British are uncivil. We know that their crime rates are laughable alongside ours. And the Britons we see—politicians, academics, actors, businesspeople—tend to be educated, well-spoken, urbane. This is also true of the Britons we see on television and in the movies. There have been exceptions—the films *Love on the Dole* and *This Sporting Life* come to mind—but they were exceptions. The underside of British life we do not usually know.

That is understandable. American tourists don't seek out the gray, mean working-class districts of British cities; why should they? The painfully ugly working-class accents of the British, cockney and the rest, can be shrugged off as a bit of local color. So, for many, even some aware of the underside of American life, what happened at the Liverpool-Juventus match came as a shock. It can be explained.

To begin with, rowdyism by soccer fans is, to some extent, a class thing, an act of defiance directed against the establishment, and perhaps made sharper by the existence of a Tory government in Britain, headed, what is more, by a woman, and by the persistence of high unemployment.

There is, in addition, a tradition—something like the idea that even the poorest are entitled to meat on the weekend, "the Sunday joint"—that fans will let off steam at "the football." Letting off steam is not necessarily rioting, but as public manners have declined over the last few decades, violence has come to be seen increasingly as fun. Noise has, too. All of this is encouraged by the violence that is now standard on television and in the movies, and in the battering, pounding, monotonous sound that now passes for music. It is as though there is a right to noise and violence.

Another point: Soccer, wonderful game that it is, is a small game. Compared with some other sports, American football, for example, it is short on spectacle, because it is played with the feet, almost entirely with the feet, and there isn't that much that can be done with them. For long periods, the ball is booted and kneed and headed around the middle of the field, and nothing much happens. It is hard for such a game to sustain the ballyhoo that surrounds it, and often the excitement has to be supplied from the outside. Rowdyism supplies it. At the same time, the players are built up as heroes and extravagantly paid. This must arouse envy among the spectators, especially the young males, who want to show that they are tough and strong and deserve attention, too.

Not that any of this justifies or excuses what happened in Brussels. Nothing can do that.

AFTERTHOUGHT

The horrifying events in Brussels took place during a European Cup Final match between Liverpool and an Italian team, Juventus. In rioting that British fans were accused of starting, 39 people were killed and 454 injured. In September 1987, twenty-five British fans were extradited to Belgium to face trial for manslaughter and assault and battery, with possible prison sentences of up to ten years.

By mid-1988, the trial had not taken place.

I Confess:
I'm Undercoiffed
III
[9 September 1985]

Thanks to a recent visit to London, I have lately been feeling under-dressed. Also inadequately made-up. And underdecorated. And miserably undercoiffed.

To begin with, the only leather in my wardrobe is in the shoes. There is none of that black, heavy metal sort of thing, in jacket and trousers, with its air of menace, sometimes helped along by cartridge belts, and chains, and metallic studs stuck onto belts and sleeves. Of boots, I have none, nor sashes to be worn round the head. Nor a single earring, unlike the theater box office attendant whose skinhead was racily enhanced by a tiny, shiny earring at each lobe, and a small, shiny, pointed one at each top. He looked like a lamp glowing faintly in the dark.

Men's earrings in London are often circular pieces of metal of sizable diameter, dangling challengingly, as if to say, "What's it to you what I'm wearing?" There is, in addition, nose adornment, with bits of rhinestone stuck onto the skin. There may be some significance in whether the glitter is on the right of what the British sometimes call the beezer, or on the left, or on both. Inquiring, however, would only encourage this sort of thing.

London makes one's shortcomings immediately evident. Tattoos, for example. Being tattooed is believed to be a sign of manliness, even though it is increasingly done among women. The appeal of having the crudest kind of art attached to you forever has always escaped me. No doubt this reflects a lack of imagination on my part.

Said lack also applies to hair. I can readily imagine—and even remember—having more of it, but that is all. Yearn for a ponytail, or the flat top that makes the head look like an outsize scrubbing brush, or a streak of green or purple, or a sunburst on top, or the hair that juts forward like a ship's prow? No.

The preoccupation with what once would have been thought outlandish appearances is by no means peculiar to London, but it has been carried furthest there. A young woman approaches. She has a Mohawk, and the ridge of hair remaining atop her cranium is a repellent pink.

She looks more defiant than happy. Here is a young woman all in black, except for a rim of white on the uppers of her shoes. Her net stockings reveal a large expanse of thigh. Her face is dead white, and her hair has been painted—it looks as though it was done with a roller—shellac red. Here is a variation—a girl all in black whose face is white, but with black eyebrows, black lipstick, black-dyed hair that sticks up in spikes.

Here come a young man and a young woman, he in black, she in red. Taken together, they are a color scheme. Here comes another such, with the young man holding a chain clipped around the woman's neck. A young couple at a newsstand buy the magazine *Hair* and the magazine *Hair Flair*. The latter offers "250 new styles."

What do these young people do? You don't see them working anywhere. Would anyone employ them, outside the emporiums that peddle the stuff they wear? Do they consider their natural appearance so dull that extreme camouflage is called for? A young woman has been turned into a conehead. Is this an improvement for her? Another young woman emerges from a hairdressing establishment called The Mad Hackers. Her hair has been made to look like popcorn that didn't quite pop. Does she feel better about herself?

There is a certain amount of whimsy in this, and here and there a bit of originality. For the most part, though, this kind of dressing is a form of class warfare: If you can't beat them, don't join them— shock them, annoy them. Also, of course, it has a sexual content, an element of flashing, of wantonness. The chains, the leather, and the rest carry a message. So, above all, does hair dyed the color of a diseased carrot.

The Birmingham Riots
[16 September 1985]

In trying to understand the September riots in the English city of Birmingham, and the lesser disturbances in Coventry and Liverpool, it helps to bear in mind that perhaps no country has been changed so drastically and in so many ways as Britain, and in so short a time.

The British Empire was the greatest the world has ever seen. It was literally true that the sun never set on the British Empire. When the Empire went, in the years after the Second World War, it went fast. Change had set in before, of course, with countries such as Australia and New Zealand and Canada becoming more and more independent. But the great, traumatic surgery came later, with the setting free of India and Burma, and the colonies in Africa and this hemisphere. Where there were no colonies to go, influence did. President Harry Truman proclaimed the Truman Doctrine in 1946 to protect Greece and Turkey, partly because Britain could no longer meet its traditional responsibilities in Greece. In the same way, the United States moved increasingly into the Near East and the Middle East as British power faded. Nothing spoke more dramatically of Britain's decline than the taking over of the Suez Canal by Egypt.

With the Empire went economic strength. Moreover, World War II drained the British; they have still not recovered. Details are hardly needed. All that is necessary is to look at the value of the pound sterling, roughly a third of what it was when the fighting stopped in 1945.

It comes as a shock to people when their currency is humiliated. There were others. After much travail, Britain entered the European Economic Community, the Common Market. In so doing, it surrendered part of its sovereignty and qualified its "special relationship" with the United States and what remained of its special ties to the nations of the Commonwealth. The resulting position was confused and confusing.

The list goes on. Britain became "metric," that is, it went on the metric system. It changed its currency, so that the pound was decimalized and the shilling disappeared. So did the guinea, which was one pound and one shilling and had a particular place as the measure of currency professionals charged. Also, Britain in the seventies went through what may have been the heaviest inflation in its history. That leaves a mark.

There was more. Britain had been a white nation. It is no longer. The transformation has been remarkably rapid. The British had colonized much of the world. In the fifties and sixties and seventies, the movement was in the other direction and on a very much larger scale, for the British had never depended on numbers in their colonies but on cleverness and firepower and, where necessary, using others. So people from what had been colonies poured in, bringing strains in society that simply did not exist before. People to whom the British used to feel superior are on the ground in Britain today, a reminder of the country's change, an unexpected complication of life, so that, for example, there is now a demand that the principles of Islam be taught in schools with predominantly Muslim student bodies. Indeed, that is happening.

All of this came about at a time when public manners were changing; when acceptance of "place" was much less automatic than it used to be; when ghettos were taking shape in the cities, and with the ghettos and deprivation, resentment. Thus the scattering of attacks by whites on nonwhites. So we see a new Britain, facing some of the difficulties that other countries do, and facing some that are peculiarly her own. Complicating and sharpening all of this is an unemployment rate that steadfastly refuses to go down. It isn't easy to be optimistic about any of it.

God Bless You, Dearie!
[16 July 1986]

By dint of luck and planning—whether good or bad luck and planning is a fair question—here we are in London during the run-up (British expression meaning "period preceding" or "preparations for") the wedding of Prince Andrew and Miss Sarah Ferguson. Check that: Buckingham Palace's preferred terminology is the wedding of His Royal Highness the Prince Andrew and Miss Sarah Ferguson.

Somewhere, in the millions of words spilled out about the presumably happy couple, somebody has complained about the amount of attention being paid to "these quite unremarkable young people." That seems unfair. Whether they are unremarkable is for those who know them best to say, but the Prince Andrew and Miss Sarah are not responsible for the loony goings-on surrounding their wedding. It isn't their doing that Britain retains the institution of monarchy, with all that that implies, and has a frequently fawning, frequently exploitive, and frequently dirty-minded press.

Not that these loony goings-on are confined to Britain. The wedding is not being exactly ignored elsewhere, certainly not in the United States, and perhaps 300,000,000 people are expected to watch it around the world. It is, however, among the British that the preoccupation naturally reaches its peak. Here, for example, is an advertisement taken out by the telephone company that promises "a series of exclusive talks, each lasting two minutes, about various aspects of the wedding," to be changed daily until July 25, which is two days after the ceremony, and including profiles of the principals and plans for the service.

This telephone line must be aimed at people too busy to read the newspapers, which for months have been counting down to the great day and running such features as "The Fergie File," which pose such questions as whether Fergie has lost a few inches here and there because of prenuptial nerves.

There have been events of this kind before, of course, most recently the wedding of the Prince and Princess of Wales, who must have been the most eagerly ogled couple in the world. They may still be. The Andrew-Fergie thing is, however, different. She is not the first daughter of divorced parents to be welcomed to the Royal Family—the Princess of Wales was that—but she is the first with a past sufficient to inspire the headline "Love on the Rebound?" This is thanks to her earlier affairs, including a three-year liaison with an older man named Paddy McNally—"Does Fergie Still Pine for Paddy?"—and thanks also to the Prince Andrew's, especially one with soft-porn film actress Koo Stark—"Does Andy Still Pine for Koo?"

So it was that one of the more delicately phrased newspaper stories a week or so before the wedding dealt with "Andy and Fergie on the Marriage Couch." An expert from a body called the National Marriage Guidance Council offered this opinion: "In many ways, having an experienced woman can be much better than going to bed with a shy, blushing girl."

Thus reassured, the nation can breathe easier. Whether the Royal Family, as an institution, can is another matter. The Prince Andrew and Miss Sarah and their wedding, with the attendant pomp and splendor, will contribute to its normal functions, which include providing spectacle, tourist attractions, and help for Britain's fashion industry, and the opportunity for loyal London women to line the processional route and call out to a royal bride, "Good luck, dearie! God bless you!'' To this may be added supplying titillation, occasional scandal, and faintly prurient interest.

Monarchy, it seems, moves with the times.

AFTERTHOUGHT

After their marriage, the Prince Andrew and Miss Sarah, the latter transmuted into the Duchess of York, continued to draw press attention, but they were overshadowed by stories about difficulties said to be arising in the marriage of the Prince and Princess of Wales. Titillation, occasional scandal, faintly prurient interest—supplying these is, as noted, part of the royal family's obligation. The obligation was met.

It was met also by the Duchess's becoming pregnant, and by stories in the tabloids about the Duchess's father, known as the Galloping Major, and his tastes in commercial sex.

Sam and the Yobs
⫴
[15 August 1986]

A recent trip to London was decidedly fruitful. It yielded the following notable news item:

"Page 3 beauty Sam Fox was attacked by 50 crazed Liverpool football fans who tried to rip off her clothes as she sang to a huge crowd in Germany last night.

"Chartbuster Sam had to be carried to safety by her minders as the Mersey yobs burst through the barriers at Hamburg's stadium.

"The pin-up turned singer was halfway through her second number, 'Touch Me, I Want Your Body,' when the fans stormed across the pitch through lines of photographers.

" 'It was scary—they all tried to grab a bit of me,' said Sam. 'Luckily my minders stopped anyone from actually ripping my clothes off.' ''

After a sigh of relief that Sam's wish to be touched had not been immediately granted, a word of explanation: The item appeared in *The*

Sun, which daily displays the female bosom, undraped, on its third page. Sam has been there. This forthrightness may help to account for the *Sun*'s circulation—4,500,000, Britain's largest.

Allow for the possibility of some exaggeration. Still, the story tells a good deal about the loutishness now so much admired among young Britons, especially the football, which is to say soccer, fans, who are now virtually banned from Europe. "Yob," by the way, is short for "yobbo," a word not much used in the United States. It means lout, or hoodlum. Even in that most British of sports, cricket, players dissatisfied with an umpire's decision, with the television cameras picking it up, scowl and sigh. Not long ago, that would have been unheard of.

The day probably never will come when cricketers, in the manner of American baseball heroes, shove umpires, and kick dirt at them. Still, Britain has changed, and is changing, at an astonishing rate. One reason is that its culture is being overwhelmed by imports from the United States. On a recent Saturday, the four television networks among them offered *The Dukes of Hazzard;* a program about American soap operas that included interviews with cast members from *Dynasty* and *Dallas;* golf from Toledo, Ohio; the western movie *Red River;* a "Blondie" movie from 1940; a Clint Eastwood movie; James Cagney in *Yankee Doodle Dandy;* the Bob Newhart show; *Hill Street Blues;* and the Cagney movie *White Heat.*

That was not enough, so Sunday brought a Dick Van Dyke TV film; a concert in Houston billed as the largest laser show ever staged; the movie *Reflections in a Golden Eye;* more golf from Toledo; the current TV show *Murder, She Wrote;* and another installment in the Cagney Festival, *Each Dawn I Die.* And reaching back into American television's past, *Twilight Zone.*

Of course, these imports themselves do not cause football fans to fight. It isn't that. They do, however, leave less and less of traditional and indigenous Britain, and they do so at a time when the old anchors of empire and respect for authority are gone. All of this is aggravated by the effects of onrushing immigration, by the decline of religion, by high unemployment, and by a wish on the part of many of the young to seem defiant. This wish is expressed in their clothes, their hairstyles, their drugs, and their music, and it is encouraged and exploited by those who profit from it. Encouragement is provided also, no doubt, by the almost daily doses of violence—hooliganism, really—seen on television from Northern Ireland.

So it is that one embodiment of today's Britain—not the only one, by any means, for there is still much courtesy and kindness about, but a prominent one—is the yob.

The Thinking Prince
III
[15 September 1986]

This is a little behindhand, but then I am still somewhat stunned by the idea of being expected to take seriously Britain's Prince of Wales. Nothing personal, you understand, and nothing intended to suggest that he is not welcome on these shores, of which, by the way, he seems rather fond. Still, should we really be asked to accept words of wisdom from Prince Charles?

The Prince was among the speakers at Harvard's 350th anniversary ceremonies this summer, and was his usual friendly and self-deprecating self. He made a few jokes and acknowledged that in Massachusetts, princes are an anachronism.

The pleasantries were acceptable, as such things go, but of course they were only part of the buildup to the Prince's weightier remarks. "To avert disaster," he said, "we have not only to teach men to make things, but to teach them to have complete moral control over the things they make." He also said: "Never has it been more important to recognize the imbalance that has seeped into our lives and deprived us of a sense of meaning, because the emphasis has been too one-sided and has concentrated on the development of the intellect to the detriment of the spirit."

The suspicion arises that the Prince's timetable was out of whack by about nine months. He sounded as though he were delivering a commencement address, or a distillation of commencement addresses. What, it is fair to ask, are his qualifications for lecturing the rest of us? What, except hunger for a bit of royal glamor, could have led Harvard, allegedly our greatest institution of higher learning, to ask him to travel three thousand miles in each direction to unload generalizations such as these? What experiences has he had that make him

242 I MUST SAY

a sage worth listening to? He is, to be sure, a well-known figure, but he was born into that, and born as well into one of the richest families in the world. It might be expected that he would count his blessings and guard his silence, except for pro forma pronouncements on state occasions. Not so. Charles wants to be a moral influence and to be known as a thinker. Harvard, for its own reasons, humored him and fell in with that.

Charles does a good deal of this kind of thing at home, on the ground that when he succeeds his mother on the throne, he does not want to reign over an unjust and unstable society. He gives interviews, hitherto unheard of for someone in his position, and has become a television personality, turning up on chat shows. This sort of conduct may be unwise in a constitutional monarchy, and some of Charles's harsher critics regard him as a meddler in what are essentially political matters, a public busybody looking for something to do, and, on the subject of the spiritual, faintly batty.

That, however, is Britain's worry, and Charles no doubt believes that by functioning as a kind of lay pope, he is helping his country and humanity as a whole. On this side of the water, the question is a different one. Hortatory speeches about the imbalance between the material and the spiritual, or the intellectual and the spiritual, are a dime a dozen. They do not have to be imported.

Charles is thirty-eight years old. Decades of commencement-like addresses from him may lie ahead. Given his example, other members of the Royal Family may join in. They should not be encouraged.

Afterthought to Live
From London
III

The British sometimes accuse Americans of being excessively commercial-minded. Where do you suppose the following advertisement appeared?

Promote your service or product here or in one of our other many locations. It will be read ... and read ... and read ... and read ...

A clue: It was in a London theater, in the men's room. A more specific clue: It was placed by a company called Stallwords. Stallwords added, with some justification, ''Advertising With a Difference.''

Word
Play

Clarity Itself

On March 14, 1982, the *New York Times* printed, on its Op-Ed page, a piece of mine about language for which the *Times* supplied the title "Clarity Itself."

Four days later, the piece was placed in the Congressional Record by Senator David Pryor, Democrat of Arkansas. Turnabout is fair play, so here is a reprint of what appeared in the Congressional Record:

CLARITY ITSELF

Mr. Pryor: Mr. President, last Sunday, Edwin Newman published in the *New York Times* an article on something in the Pentagon called "The Professional Organizational Effectiveness/Development Publication of the United States Army." Mr. Newman is a notable detective of sins against the language. He is eminently qualified to judge the style of documents from the Pentagon. He points out in this article the utter nonsense, the wasted time, and the poor management of this so-called operating model for a new age of leadership.

As a worker in the field of bureaucracies, I see every day the violation of good judgment in the use of English. Why does the Government insist upon the complicated when the simple is at hand? Why does the Pentagon, especially, deal in convolutions when it could easily go straight to the mark? Of all the special areas of Government, the military knows the value of being crisp and to the point. Yet it is probably the most guilty in using jargon and bombast.

Mr. Newman's article is perceptive and accurate, and I recommend it to my colleagues. It is humorous as well. But Mr. Newman makes a serious point, and I hope this will not be lost on his readers. Here it is:

The Pentagon budget is bloated beyond all reason. Congress is looking for places to cut back. This year's struggle over spending, in fact, promises to be one of heroic proportions. Yet the Pentagon sponsors high performance programming that features "a new cognitive model" in the form of "nested frames of reference" intended to be useful as "a general diagnostic framework and as a self-refining road map for leader and organization development."

I know, Mr. President, that the MX, the B-1, chemical weapons, and cost overruns on the Trident are all much larger than the budget for high performance programming. But I agree entirely with Mr. Newman's conclusion: When the time comes to cut the Pentagon budget, this may be the place to start. I ask that his article be printed in the RECORD and read by all concerned with the language—and with the Pentagon budget.

The article referred to is as follows: [From the *New York Times,* Mar. 14, 1982]

CLARITY ITSELF
(By Edwin Newman)

Leaks are in fashion. I've been given one. It is from OE COM-MUNIQUE, which is "The Professional Organizational Effectiveness/ Development Publication of the United States Army." Stamped "Secret" and passed to the Kremlin, it might end the arms race. For anybody reading this document would conclude that America is doomed and that no outside effort will be needed to bring it toppling down.

The article from OE COMMUNIQUE is called "High Performance Programming: An Operating Model for a New Age of Leadership." The authors are LTC Frank Burns and Dr. Linda Nelson, assisted by Robert Klaus and LTC Lee Gregg. LTC (Lieutenant Colonel) Burns, evidently the key author, has been director of a personal growth center, is a certified master practitioner of Neuro-Linguistic Programming, and is 5Z ASI qualified, meaning that he is qualified in Organizational Effectiveness. We are also told what High Performance Programming is. It is "a new cognitive model," in the form of "nested frames of reference," intended "to be useful as a general diagnostic framework and as a self-refining road map for leader and organization development."

At the outset, LTC Burns and the other authors explain their method: "As an exercise in consciously disciplining our own conceptual modeling we have chosen a *set* of interlinked operating presumptions." They go on: "This set of propositions forms an encircling paradigm for our HPP model, and a metastrategy that continues to guide our refinement and use of it."

Let's pause here to follow the wise advice the creators of HPP give their readers: "Clear your receiver processes so that this new information can come in cleanly without getting garbled." Now then, a couple of the interlinked operating presumptions that survived the consciously disciplined conceptual modeling:

"The purpose of any *system* is to produce a valuable future in the larger and lesser systems served."

"High performing systems and leaders choose their values and beliefs and then reinforce them in others through congruent behavior."

Receiver processes still clear? On to the "Preframe": "A model of sufficient elegance to meet the challenges of the future must provide a framework which is capable of transforming the shifting complexities of the present into a coherent pattern. As well as providing a master pattern, such a model must have the generative capacity to install an extensive cognitive program in the reader."

At this point, my cognitive program collapsed, but stern measures got it back into shape to receive the next HPP installment: "We have been programmed to think of performance as the outcome of supervision which is responsive to orders and tasks . . . Although this frame of reference has been useful, if we now want to elicit higher levels of performance (than we currently obtain operating within this frame) we need an enlarged frame of reference that generates a greater range of behavioral options. (This is 'basic Ashby'—whose Law of Requisite Variety should guide our cybernetic designs.)"

Now comes the revelation. The basic Ashby enlarged frame of reference is the proactive, which "generates a greater range of options and shows what we must do to tune up our whole organizations as proactive systems." The proactive thereby "achieves results-oriented performance through values-based leadership practices which link objs-oriented mgmt procedures to individual performance evaluation processes."

I have now worked through ten pages of "High Performance Programming," picking out what may generously be called the highlights. There are nine pages to go, pages laden with paradigm shifts, autocatalytic reactions, and step-function enhancements, and with charts and heavy lines and light lines and broken lines, arrows in various forms and thicknesses, and boxes, shaded and unshaded and with or without words. There is also the linking of the proactive with the responsive, which takes in Holistic Leadership, Evolutionary Management, Capacity Identification, Paradigm Planning, and Metasystems Development, with high performing the result.

So there it is, all fitted into an "outframe" that "is suggested as the next logical enhancement in our perspective."

Is the Army really spending time and money on this nonsense? Yes. OE comes under the Army's Management Directorate, which is under the Chief of Staff. There is an OE Center and School at Fort

Ord, Calif., where lecturers appear by invitation; a seminar on HPP was attended by generals and other high-ranking officers and civilians.

The HPP article was originally published by Delta Force, which is "a futures group that looks at new ways and new things," and which uses meetings, seminars, and papers "to get feedback."

Here is some feedback: Cut the Pentagon budget? I know a place to start.

Business Language
...
[July 1984]

What's that you say? You don't own a car? There's a better way to put it. You, my friend, are transportation-disadvantaged.

And you say you're the sort of person who doesn't like to take chances? That's awfully unimaginative. Use the economists'word for it: You're risk-averse.

Now you're saying you might be wise to stop smoking? Wrong again. Don't stop smoking. Engage in smoking cessation.

Terms like "transportation-disadvantaged" and "risk-averse" have a great attraction for many Americans. They are attractive because they introduce an unnecessary abstruseness, overtones of profundity. But they are used not for that alone. The more difficult and complex you can make your job sound, the more money you are likely to get for doing it, and the more prestige you are likely to have.

This is as true in private industry as it is in government. The last time I was at the Sheraton Hotel in Boston, guests formed a single line while waiting for the cashiers. Sheraton posted a sign describing this as "our single line concept." In the same spirit, a loose-leaf appointment book has become a "desk-top visual system," being behind schedule has become "negative slack," and too small "suboptimal in scale." In some corporations, subcontracting is now "outsourcing." There are buildings (I believe this began in Canada) where elevators are called high-speed vertical transportation units.

Sometimes the language used is so unnecessarily elaborate that those who use it lose track of what they are saying. Here is the Minnesota Association of Cable Television Administrators explaining why the Association was formed. It was formed "to facilitate the general lack of communication among municipalities in the state of Minnesota regarding cable television." To facilitate the general lack of communication—there's a worthy cause.

Businessmen and businesswomen will actually take courses in "leadershipping," and go to lectures to learn how to "establish long-term changes in culture and technology through a transition-parallel structure utilizing an 'open-systems perspective,' " and to hear about "decision-making processes based on synergistic convergence." Some have even undertaken to learn about "eyeball-to-eyeball interface on a global scale."

This mumbo jumbo is put forward with utter seriousness, much of it to impress, to intimidate, to make what is being done seem impenetrable and vastly technical.

In the world of transition-parallel structures and the desk-top visual system, executives being fired or dismissed are only rarely fired or dismissed. They are, instead, outplaced, or terminated. To do this, their companies may call in outplacement experts or termination assistants, or even dehiring specialists. They bring forth a "choice matrix," which is a list of the things the executive would like in a new job, followed by a "discharge scenario" in which he will be found another job. But it won't be called that. It will go under the name of executive retrieval, or management recycling. And during this time, the dehiree will not be out of work. He will be going through an orderly transition between career stages.

Let's say the problem faced by the executive—a female this time—is less serious. She has not been dehired, but she's not getting anywhere. No promotions. She is then said to have reached a plateau. Columbia University maintains a Center for Research in Career Development, so it took it upon itself a while ago to define "plateau." It is "the point in an organizational career where the individual is unlikely to experience hierarchical mobility."

Of course, the hierarchically immobile can always quit and take their chances, but usually they don't. They're not the type. They're risk-averse.

Destiny! Behave Yourself!
▮▮▮
[July 1984]

Controlled your own destiny lately? A good many people would like you to. One of the latest recruits to the ranks of those who believe that destiny should be brought to heel is the marathon runner Alberto Salazar. In an article in the *New York Times,* Salazar wrote, somewhat inexplicably, that runners "should be allowed to shape their destiny with their own hands."

Another recent advocate of destiny-control is Henry Cisneros, the mayor of San Antonio and a comer among the younger Democrats. "I'm not so much an apostle of high-tech," Cisneros told an interviewer, "as I am an apostle of cities being directly involved in economic development—becoming masters of their own destinies."

In the destiny-controlling competition that is a feature of American oratory, Cisneros was by no means breaking new ground. We have it on the authority of the Department of Housing and Urban Development that "cities can learn to become masters of their own destinies." Perhaps Cisneros heard that. Or perhaps he took his cue from President Reagan, who at various times has wanted the American people, Lebanon, and the people of Afghanistan to decide their own destiny. Last summer, he declared himself to be "working to improve the destiny of all Americans."

There is a small difficulty here. Nobody, not even presidents of the United States, can determine, decide, or improve his destiny or anyone else's. Destiny is, by definition, inevitable and ineluctable, an invincible necessity. That is what the word means. It is also, it appears, an impenetrable mystery to any number of well-known people. Mr. Reagan may be the leading proponent of destiny-control of our time, but he is not without rivals. During the Democratic primaries, when ringing declarations were in order, Senator Gary Hart thought that "people have a sense that we are losing control of our own destiny." Senator John Glenn wanted this to be "a nation that controls its future destiny." Jesse Jackson proposed to "throw down the gauntlet of destiny."

Nor is it only politicians who are confused. *Forbes* magazine, in advertisements, promised to "help you shape your own destiny." Lee Iacocca of Chrysler thought it was "time the leadership in this country took charge of our economic destiny." The *Los Angeles Times* head-lined: "Blast victim regrets not being allowed to control destiny." Heavyweight thinkers from the News Study Group at MIT wrote in *TV Guide* that social psychologists believe that what we see on television news programs "makes us doubt that we are in control of our destinies."

In no field is destiny more often alleged to be controllable than sports, especially, for some reason, football. "Keep in mind that Seattle is still the master of their own destiny," said ABC's Frank Gifford. "We control our destiny," said New York Giants linebacker Harry Carson. One magical day, a sports broadcaster saw the possibility that the New York Jets would "recontrol their own destiny." Who was it? Of course. Howard Cosell.

"This generation of Americans has a rendezvous with destiny." Franklin Roosevelt said that on June 27, 1936, while accepting renomination. It sounded good, even inspiring, but it was meaningless. Everyone has a rendezvous with destiny. We don't know what that destiny is. It is, moreover, preordained and immutable. That's the catch. That's why we can't control it.

AFTERTHOUGHT

Late in 1987, the mayor of San Diego, Maureen O'Connor, found herself troubled by the amount of building going on there, and the growing population. She wanted to impose some limits. She did not, however, yearn to control San Diego's destiny, only its "growth destiny."

Plain English
[July 1984]

Read the following:
Sorry. *Please* read the following:
"In the event of default in the payment of this or any other

Obligation or the performance or observance of any term or covenant contained herein or in any note or other contract or agreement evidencing or relating to any Obligation or any Collateral on the Borrower's part to be performed or observed; or the undersigned Borrower shall die . . ."

Keep at it.

". . . or any of the undersigned become insolvent or make an assignment for the benefit of creditors; or a petition shall be filed by or against any of the undersigned under any provision of the Bankruptcy Act; or any money, securities or . . ."

Don't quit. You're almost there.

". . . properties of the undersigned now or hereafter on deposit with or in the possession or under the control of the Bank shall be attached or become subject to distraint procedures or any order or process of any court; or the Bank shall deem itself to be insecure . . ."

That's enough. You've made it. The length of what you read, by the way, was 147 words. They specified the circumstances in which a loan granted by Citibank would be in default.

Now, please read this:

"I'll be in default:

"1. If I don't pay an installment on time; or

"2. If any other creditor tries by legal process to take any money of mine in your possession."

That was twenty-eight words, drawn from Citibank's simplified promissory note, the "after" to the "before" above. The meaning is the same.

The example is drawn from a book called *How Plain English Works for Business,* put out by the Department of Commerce. It contains twelve case studies of how direct, comprehensible English paid off for a variety of corporations in their dealings with their customers. Among them were Pfizer, J.C. Penney, Shell, Target Stores, Roche Laboratories, and Home Owners Warranty, and three insurance companies—Aetna, St. Paul, and Sentry. There was no magic formula, and it wasn't always easy. But they all found it worthwhile. So, no doubt, did their customers.

The change cannot always be so drastic, and the purpose is not necessarily to make the passage shorter, but rather to make it clearer. In an insurance policy, "However, unintentional errors or omissions on the part of the Insured shall not operate to prejudice the rights of the Insured under this Policy and its Insuring Agreements" became

"Of course, everyone makes mistakes. Unintentional errors or omissions won't affect your rights under this policy."

Perhaps I should declare an interest here. I was among the participants in a meeting last year, a meeting called by Secretary of Commerce, Malcolm Baldrige, that helped to shape the plain English campaign. We did well.

AFTERTHOUGHT

It was a sad day for English when Secretary Baldrige died in a rodeo accident in 1987. He had taken the fight for the language into the front lines—Washington.

The Gubment and the Fanger
[30 November 1984]

Some people think that one thing wrong with the American system is that the feddle gubment is forever putting its fanger where it doesn't belong. Where may those people be found? In the American south, of course. There are also people in other parts of the country who believe that Washington is excessively obtrusive, but they don't put it in quite the same way. "Feddle gubment" and "fanger"—there are five fangers on each hand; even the gubment can't change that—are strictly southern. They are also, when genuine and not affected, delightful.

It is, for this reason, faintly distressing to hear of the activities of Beverly Inman-Ebel. Ms. Inman-Ebel, an Ohioan who has lived in Tennessee for some years, has been teaching a course, at a college in Chattanooga, called Southern Success Without a Southern Accent. Obviously there is a demand for the course, or it would not be offered. It is equally obvious that southerners may be held back by their accents, when those accents are extreme, because they have, over the years, been made into a comic turn. The blathering southern senator has been a figure of fun. It is also true that Ms. Inman-Ebel does not want her students to lose their accents permanently. She is only trying to help them get along in the world. Their viewpoint, and hers, is understandable.

Still, anything that even unintentionally jeopardizes feddle gubment and fanger does risk bleaching some of the color out of American English. Take an example: ast, which is ask. And the past tense of ask, which is also ast, as in "He ast for it and he got it." He may well, by the way—as we learn from a little book called *The Southern Legislative Dictionary,* by Allin and Fisher—have done the asting while sitting at his dest, maybe during a debate on proprashuns, before he became tarred.

Tarred, which stands in for tired, also brings to mind bard, as in "He bard a dollar." And har and far—"She has the authority to har and far"—which are necessary in any bidness. There is quite a trade in books about southern speech. "Bidness," which may be recognized as "business," was cited in *How to Speak Southern,* by Mitchell and Rawls.

In any southern lexicon, "cheer" will be found. It may mean that somebody is shouting "Hurray." It will more often be used to designate a piece of furniture, with one seat, as in easy cheer. Where is that piece of furniture? Rat cheer, that is, right here.

It goes almost without saying that not all southerners speak this way. Far from it. The higher up the social ladder one goes, the less is this kind of thing likely to be heard. And scholars no doubt can explain how these pronunciations came to be, why "freezing" comes out "phrasin'" and "heinous" comes out "hanius," and "rench" replaces "rinse." (She renched her hair is much less disturbing than it sounds.) The explanation I prefer is that these pronunciations—and this is mountain speech—not southern—crope up on us.

Speaking for myself, or sef, I'd hate to see regional accents in the United States disappear. They add to the variety of our lives; they do it with no strangs attached; and they do it, in that happy phrase, rat cheer.

Menu Language
###
[17 December 1984]

The festive season is on us. (There's a scoop!) You may want to celebrate by having a festive meal at a festive restaurant. If you do, you will probably run into that curious feature of American life, menu language. One aspect of menu language is misspellings. Another is a mixing of English and other languages, usually French and Italian, in the interest of creating a "continentale" impression. All of the examples that follow are authentic, meaning that they appeared—before my very eyes—on the menus of restaurants of some pretension.

We begin, then, with soup d'jour, said soup being, perhaps, cream of brocolli. No soup? An appetizer? How about peal and eat shrimp?—which obviously rings the bell with some diners and may be had on the pre-fix luncheon or à la carte? If you'd like something more adventurous, Monsieur et Madame, there are escargots served in barquette. Here, now, is a philosophical question: If they are "served in," why can't they just be snails served in a pastry boat? Why the escargots and the barquette? For that matter, why do so many menus list potato du jour? And why should there be medaillons de veau à la cream? How is it decided where the French falls and where the English? And what is the explanation of that favorite American menu word, almondine? In French, it's amandine. In English, it's with almonds, which seems perfectly honorable.

But I'm getting ahead of myself. We haven't yet made it through the London broil du bordelaise, which if it means anything means the London broil of the woman of Bordeaux and is ungrammatical in French, as well. Or Signor and Signora might prefer escalope du veal scallopini. Escalope is French, veal is English, and scallopini is Italian, and escalope and scallopini mean the same thing, so this notable concoction is a scallop of veal scallops, a dish much favored among connoisseurs of the veal scallop in scalloped form.

If, Sir, your taste was formed in England, you may want to try the petite wellington du boeuf, which is apparently either a small boot made of beef or a piece of beef that tastes like a boot. An alternative would be roast beef served with au jus, a growing favorite in the United States, where, on this precedent, it may soon be possible to get pie served with à la mode.

Back to the entrées. Perhaps Monsieur would like the deviled rack of spring lamb bouguetiere, which comes with a bouguet of fresh vegetables, or chateaubriand pour doux, which isn't one of your fast foods; it takes time to prepare and can't be served un, doux, trois. Finally, Signora, we have serloin tips with sauce bernaise, sole farce, fruits der mer, and as side dishes, kish lorraine and spinash pie.

All of this is fairly heavy to digest, so you may want a small salad, say the covenant garden salad, followed by cantalope or royal potporie of fruit. And there are specialties of the house: grand mariner souffle, which is for the seagoing; an Irish creation called lemon moran pie; and ice cream log assorti. Or something lighter: sherbert.

That is the end of the meal, Monsieur et Madame, Signor e Signora.

As the old saying has it, Shotgun à son gout.

AFTERTHOUGHT

There is no end to the unintended delights of pretentious menu language. I will add only one, spotted at a Dublin hotel at Christmastime: Gateau de Yule.

Hurtling the Obstacles
[29 April 1985]

Last Friday was a beautiful day in New York. The sky was blue; the sun shone down, but gently; the temperature was about 70 degrees and humidity was low. People meandered along, and the city seemed positively benevolent. To top it off, a grocery had posted a sign saying that it sold barbecued chicken. That's right: barbecued. Not the almost unavoidable barbequed, which if it were spoken aloud would come out barbecked. The correct spelling: barbecued.

Oh joy, oh rapture unforeseen. It seemed too good to be true. It was. At the next corner, a number of young women, acting on behalf of a company that sells chocolate and evidently wants to ingratiate

itself with the public, were handing out lapel buttons. The buttons bore
a reminder that daylight saving time would soon be on us and so, come
Saturday night, clocks should be put ahead. The young women un-
loosed a brief spiel as they handed out the buttons to passersby not
too preoccupied to take them. "Don't forget daylight savings time,"
they said.

Daylight savings. Are we savings daylight when we advance our
clocks an hour, or are we saving it? Why, in the same way, do shops
offer "a 10 percent savings," and "a savings to you of . . ."? Whence,
in this context, "savings"? Probably from the savings banks. They
are perfectly right to call themselves that, but their term is wrongly
applied elsewhere. The incorrect use is now heard more often than the
correct one.

Ah, well, daylight savings time started a train of thought. Barbequed chicken, even with the clocks an hour ahead, might find itself
on the menu with san pareil pâté, named for the well-known Spanish
saint, San Pareil, and—yes, I have seen all of this—blueberry pie
baked on the premise. What premise? Presumably the premise that it
would be eaten. Where was the premise to be found? Possibly in a
duel entrance kitchen. Most people would be tempted to use another
entrance. All of this at a restaurant that prides itself on its unobstructive
service.

Mistakes, it might be said—it has been said—exude out of some
of us. One tries to take the mistakes in stride, but occasionally one is
put to route. I remember being put to route by a sign on a used-car
lot: "No car on the lot over $450 and up." I am also put to route by
the instruction given as one's airliner nears its destination: "Please
remain seated for the duration of the flight." By the time this announcement is made, perhaps ten minutes from the airport, it is too
late for anyone to remain seated for the duration of the flight. The
duration of the flight begins with the takeoff; it extends from the
beginning of the flight to its end. Besides, what's wrong with the word
"rest"? Or if that isn't grand enough, "remainder"?

Sometimes I am not put to route. I take the blunt of the punishment
but manage to hurtle the obstacles and come through without irreputable
damage, though scathed. I carry on in hope of seeing things get better,
but hold my optimism in obeyance. Because that's how the world is
these days, prone with potential error. So don't get carried away and
don't let your mind get boggled down. Face reality—including daylight
savings.

Hopefully Incredible
[16 September 1985]

It is time to bid a sad farewell to the word "incredible." "Incredible" has been teetering on the brink of uselessness for years, and now it has been pushed over, no doubt inadvertently, by Democratic Representative James Florio of New Jersey. Florio was speaking about a report on Environmental Protection Agency recommendations for the dumping of toxic wastes in his state. He called the report "incredible, if true."

"Incredible, if true." Incomparable of its kind, that. "Incredible" means not believable. Over the years, it has been so loosely used— "an incredible performance," "incredible virtuosity," "an incredible adventure"—to mean fascinating, or impressive, that it has lost all value. It can be placed on the shelf with, among others, "fabulous" and "fantastic." "Incredible, if true" was the clincher.

If it wasn't, "incredibly unbelievable" was. Al Michaels unloaded that during the World Series. Is something that is unbelievably unbelievable true?

It is time also to write off "hopefully." Actually, it is long past time. "Hopefully" kissed usefulness good-bye long years ago. It has not been used correctly, as in these examples, in decades: They entered the contest hopefully but were soon disappointed; and "May I see you again soon?" he asked hopefully as she paused inside the door. "Hopefully," in other words, used to mean in a hopeful manner. Instead we have the ritual incantations: "Hopefully, the operation will be a success," "Hopefully, they'll be there," "It will turn out hopefully all right," and "We are dialoguing, hopefully meaningfully."

It had seemed that no further variations were possible, but that reckoned without Republican Representative Dick Cheney of Wyoming. Speaking of President Reagan's Strategic Defense Initiative, Cheney said that he was in favor of defensive measures that "hopefully, if possible" would stop enemy weapons before they could hit us. "Hopefully, if possible." The phrase is empty. Incredibly empty, someone might call it. Representative Cheney is to be regarded with awe, which makes him awesome, another word that is making its departure from the ranks of the useful. This is so especially in the world of sports, where "awesome" is used to describe the ordinarily talented, the routinely competent. A shortstop who can go two steps to his right is awesome. "Awesome" now means pretty good, and, in another of the annoying usages of the day, we might as well admit to it.

Admit to. What happened to admit? Admitting a mistake or an indiscretion is passé; one now admits to it. He admitted having forced his way in? Oh, no. He admitted to having forced his way in. She admitted making the illegal payment? No again. She admitted to making the illegal payment. Why the change? There is no advantage in it. Quite the opposite. "Admit to" should be used in this way: He was admitted to the patient's room. Or, The engagement signaled her admission to the select company of great violinists. "Admit to" means let in—or it did. For our times, however, with their love of unnecessary syllables, "admit," standing alone, seemed too lean, too simple, too spare. So the incorrect use crowds out the correct one.

This column sounds a good deal like a lecture, a lecture delivered from a podium, but not *at* a podium. A podium is stood on, not at. It is a platform. The conductor of an orchestra usually stands on one. You do not place your notes on the podium, unless you are extraordinarily farsighted, or intend to read them on your hands and knees. The notes go on a lectern, which is the stand at which the speaker posts himself or herself, and which may have on it a microphone and a reading light.

It is too late to save "incredible," "hopefully," "awesome," and probably "admit." Can "lectern" be preserved? It never did anyone any harm.

Please?

Striking a Good Chord
▪▪▪
[16 September 1985]

The legislator on his feet was saying that we weren't out of the woods yet but we had reached that watershed point where it was possible to see light at the end of the tunnel. It had not been easy, he went on, but we had succeeded because we had left no stone unturned in looking at both sides of the issue.

Immediately there was an objection from the other side of the floor: "I believe in identifying what you're doing and then putting it in small chunks. After that, we can set week-to-week goals."

This argument, persuasive perhaps on the surface, brought no agreement. As a result, its advocate was displeased. "The perception of what we are doing here," he declared, "will be heard around the world. If it backfires, someone else will be on the frying pan."

It had been a vigorous debate, spawned by a top-echelon grass-roots effort to find a solution to the nagging problem of preserving the American system of free enterprise. The opening speaker had been tentative. "I don't know," he had said. "I would never question a gift horse in the mouth, but I think the ball is in both courts."

Not everyone accepted that. "Your point of view," said an ageless forty-eight-year-old member, "is very nil. You are walking a double-edged sword."

Soon other voices were heard. "We are in danger," one of them said. "We face a vicious snowball of regulation gathering momentum in its downward climb. This is no time for half measures. It may be necessary to blow it out of the water."

At least one of those present agreed with this analysis. "I'm impartial," he announced. "I don't have anything to grind. But some of the chords the previous speaker struck were good. I hope he'll be able to carry them out."

Now rose a veteran member, who had recently been the subject of an investigation and who had been cleared. "As you know," he said, "I have been exonerated. My light is definitely out from under that bushel basket." Interrupted by applause and cheers, he smiled gratefully and continued: "I have one observation to make. We must act. Tomorrow may be too late. Because the free enterprise system is too important to be left to the voluntary action of the marketplace."

In the end, he carried the day. One of his colleagues paid him a high compliment. "I do not go with you on every ironclad jot and tittle," he said, "but I respect you. I value your opinion. The reason I do is that for a long time, you were on the cutting edge of political ferment. Not many of us can say that."

There were a few dissents. One of the dissenters suggested that the veteran, exonerated though he had been, was looking for a scape-goat on whom to hang the dirty linen while letting others off the hook.

Another objected that the veteran was back to his old overbearing ways. "You were never," he said, "one to eat humble crow."

Things were threatening to become nasty when a kindly female member rose to speak. "As I listened," she said, "I must confess that I fell into a lively reverie with myself. My mind wandered to the great outdoors, where the flora and fauna are in full bloom. Then I could not help noticing that so many of you were firing the first shot. How much better it would be if, instead of these painful interjections, we could work individually together. What we need is appropriate considerations on both sides."

It was the tone that was needed. Recalled to its customary good humor, the legislature adjourned.

Stop! You're Chilling Me

[15 November 1985]

If winter comes, can the chilling effect be far behind?

The answer is no, it can't. The fact is, it isn't behind at all; it's out ahead. The chilling effect is everywhere, and winter has nothing to do with it.

The chilling effect should not be confused with the windchill factor. The windchill factor was dreamed up as a way of telling us that it is colder than the thermometer indicates it should be, and also to make weather forecasts take longer.

The chilling effect is something else. It comes about when the first party does something that discourages the second party from doing something the second party believes he or she has a right to do. The person thus put upon cites the chilling effect of what the first party has done, the implication being that said effect is improper, undesirable, and unconstitutional.

Lawyers love the phrase, and so there are times when an impressively large part of the population of the United States is complaining of having been singled out for chilling effect. Here are some recent professed chillees:

Public debate on national security matters. The National News Council spotted the chill coming from the conviction under the espionage laws of a government employee who gave classified photographs to a British publication.

The incentive to lawyers to bring difficult cases. A lawyer thought that incentive would be chilled by the suggestion that attorneys working on contingent fees pay the defendants' legal costs when they, the lawyers, lose the case.

The social activism of church congregations. The chiller, according to the mayor of Tuskegee, Alabama, Johnny L. Ford, was the federal prosecution, for income tax evasion, of the Reverend Sun Myung Moon.

The free exercise of religion. A jury verdict in Portland, Oregon, assessing punitive damages of $39,000,000 against the founder of Scientology and two of its church corporations was identified as the chiller. It must be admitted that $39,000,000 in the process of flying away would create a noticeable draft.

International banking. The chiller here, according to Representative Doug Barnard, Jr., Democrat of Georgia, was changes proposed in the taxing of banks.

Representative George Miller, Democrat of California. He canceled a visit to El Salvador after being told that he was being "investigated" by the Salvadoran extreme right. "I've had my free speech chilled," said Representative Miller.

Broadcast journalism. A report by the Federal Communications Commission found the chiller to be the Fairness Doctrine.

Corporate takeovers in New York State. Chiller: Proposed legislation to make them more difficult. Objectors: Lawyers and investment bankers specializing in takeovers.

Not all the causes involved are so weighty. Other chillees:

The Grand Ole Opry in Nashville. The manager of the Municipal Auditorium in Nashville foresaw the chill before it had taken shape. It came, he said, from a local ordinance that would limit amplified music to eighty-five decibels. (That is five decibels below the "annoyance" level. Discomfort comes at 120, and above that, pain and the risk of impaired hearing.)

First Amendment rights. The United States Circuit Court of Appeals for New York, Connecticut, and Vermont ruled that they were chilled by an award of $10,000,000 to the author Jackie Collins because a magazine printed a photograph of a nude woman it said was Jackie

Collins. (It wasn't.) At that, the original award by a jury, reduced by a lower-court judge, was $40,000,000. The Appeals Court said that Miss Collins was a public figure—apparently no pun was intended—and would have to prove malice.

The chilling effect is now so well established that a rival to it has appeared. The Authors League has come up with the palling effect, which it says censorship brings about. Soon there will be those among us suffering from pall and chill at the same time.

English, by Accident and Dezign
[19 May 1986]

Time for a stroll around the neighborhood, to see how it and the English language are making out.

The neighborhood has gained distinction. It has a new dining establishment, which a hand-lettered sign in the window identifies as a Japanese Restrunt. (Vision of an exceptionally small Japanese taking a nap.)

"Restaurant" is a French word in origin. French itself isn't doing very well. Anyone who is French might walk through the neighborhood wincing. A restaurant posts a sign on the sidewalk that lists some of the dishes featured inside. One is sole meniur. There are many dining places in the area. They offer, among other things, Br. Tuna w/anchovie butter. Also Br. Salmon w/buerre sauce. And Sea trout almondine. (This is a persisting mystery. Almonds are almonds. In French, they are *amandes,* wherefore the cooking term *amandine.* What is almondine?)

Then there are, at non-French establishments, Mahattan Chowder, which is naturally much favored on the island of Mahattan, and sandwich's, which evidently is an abbreviation of sandwiches, employed to save space. (The apostrophe has become an impenetrable mystery to much of the population. Shall we offer it honorable withdrawal and retirement?) At what is presumably an Italian place, you may drink expresso, and at another, order chicken rollantine. It is possible to theorize about what rollantine started out as—rollatini, perhaps—but that is only a theory.

Many people have the impression that foreign cuisine in New York is expensive. Not to worry. There is a restaurant that offers a prix fixed lunch and a prix fixed dinner. The fixed prix at least warns you what you're letting yourself in for.

Leave food behind. Someone on your mind to whom flowers should be sent? Just the thing is available: orchid crosages. Looking for an apartment? Why not try the new condominium on East Forty-Eighth Street? Fourty-Eighth Street is just ten blocks south of Fivety-Eighth Street.

If you do decide to move and take an apartment, you will need professional help. As luck would have it, a van goes by bearing the sign: Teddy Mover's. Ignore the apostrophe. Is this a company that transports only teddy bears? One has heard of the increasing specialization in our economy, but that seems unlikely to yield much of a living. Maybe it would be better to sign up with—another van—Bonified Delivery Systems, who on the face of it are movers who have had bones emplaced in them, in the belief, not yet widely held, that this makes them better movers.

You will of course want help in decorating your new apartment. Still another van goes by, belonging to a company that specializes in dezign. Latest thing, dezign. Looking for bargains? Pick them up at a shop that is "Closeing Our Doors." Finally, there is a shop that calls itself La-Coccette Boutique. Boutique is French, but what is La-Coccette? Phonetic French, perhaps. Note the hyphen. That may be a mistake. The proprietor may have had an apostrophe in mind.

Take it for all in all, though, it's a good neighborhood for shopping, especially for food. At a supermarket, you may, if you wish, buy Ex. Lg. Naval Oranges, possibly just in from sea duty. As for bread, it may be had in many varieties, including a loaf known, inscrutably, as Bono Italie. That may bring to mind the legal term Pro Bono Publique. Or our national motto: E Pluribus One.

AFTERTHOUGHT

A more recent stroll around the neighborhood showed no lessening in the number of Br. dishes to be had. One of them was Br. Norweigan Salmon. Briskit, presumably of beef, turned up, and an establishment enthusiastic about its Hot Meatball Heroes figuratively smacked its lips and rubbed its stomach with a hearty "Yam Yam!" A rival to expresso ventured out: esspresso, as did a French bakery calling itself La Boulangé, which means, if it means anything, the baked (feminine gender).

On the esthetic side, a florist offered Dry & Treeted Eucalyptus.

Springtime in New York
[19 May 1986]

A New York springtime conversation:
 So, how ya doin'?
 Not bad, not bad. How you doin'?
 Not bad. I'm okay.
 So what's witchoo? Anything new?
 Nothin' new. What's witchoo?
 Nothin', really. Nothin' new.
 You all right?
 Yeah, I'm all right.
 So why do I hear you're all the time layin'?
 Who's all the time layin'?
 You. I hearn you're all the time layin'. You all right?
 Where'd you hear I'm all the time layin'?
 From Rudy. He says you're all the—
 I hearn ya. I hearn ya the first time. That Rudy. He needs his head examined. He's a regular maniac depressive. Sometimes I think he should be locked up, lock, sock, and barrel.
 A'right a'ready. Let's talk about something else.
 What else?
 Something important. Whaddya think of them Mets? Who's gonna stop 'em? If this was football, they'd make it into the Superior Bowl for sure.
 That's important?
 Okay. So what's important to you? That Cortisone Aquino, maybe?
 Yeah, she's important. The guy I don't get is this Marcos. All that money. He must have been renumerated in a big way.

They should ought to get that money. They're in a turmoil over there.

Well, it's not like it's all cut and dry. They got problems.

You see Joe lately?

No. Not as of yet, anyways. What about Lou? You see him?

Yeah, the other day. He was like always. Full of anticdotes.

A good guy.

Right. He never leaves you down.

So, what about this weather? Hot enough for you?

I'll say. I thought it would cool off when the rain left up, but here it is, ten A.M. in the morning and it's so hot I'm sweatin'. That was some rain. Get caught in that and you might drown to death. I'm not kiddin'.

You workin' hard?

Oh sure.

You got a vacation comin' up?

Hopefully.

I asked you got a vacation comin' up?

Yeah. Hopefully.

You can't answer a simple question? What's this "hopefully"?

I hearn it on television.

What's it mean?

I don't know. It sounds good. Hopefully this, hopefully that. Everybody says it.

Okay. Forget it.

Well, I'm glad we bunked into each other. Like old times. Give my regards at home.

Same here. Good seein' you.

Nothin' else new?

I guess not. What about you?

Nothin', really.

See you soon.

Way to go.

I Mean, Like, Y'know?

III

[9 June 1986]

Conversation between two vivacious young Americans, slightly exaggerated—but only slightly:

Y'know?

Oh sure.

Well, good. I didn't want you to be, like, left out, y'know?

I told you. I'm with you. So, you were going to tell me what, y'know, happened back in the station.

Yeah. Well, it was a, like, shock, y'know? I mean I'm there, getting ready, okay? And then this. It was like this was a unisex place, y'know?

Okay. But what happened?

Well, there I was, okay? And this guy comes in, okay? And he sees me and I see him and we're both like standing there, okay? Finally he gets the idea and leaves.

But what was he doing in the, y'know, ladies' room?

There wasn't any sign on the door. I don't blame him. It was like I said, like unisex, you know what I mean?

Okay. I empathize.

I can't help asking you. Your verbal skills. I mean they're outstanding, y'know? Like where did you get them?

They trained us. We had, like, five hours a week, okay? I mean, you're up there in front of everybody. Y'know, you have to deliver. It's like if you don't, you're out, y'know?

That can be rough. I mean it's, like, put up or shut up. I'm not so into that. Maybe it's my background, the religion and all that. I'm not so, like, competitive. Y'know?

Well, that goes without saying. I mean we studied that. Family Structure and Societal Values. I was really into that course. It was like I could hardly wait for the lectures. On the religious impulse and all that.

So, to get back to what we were talking about before, it's all, like, turning out all right?

Oh yeah. I can't say it's, like, ideal. But y'know, the future looks pretty good. Maybe I'll teach. Or go into, like, school administration.

When do you think you'll, y'know, make up your mind?

269

There's no hurry. They're, like, easy. It would be different if they were pushing me. Y'know?

I know I said it before, but I really admire your verbal skills. I mean, that's what it's all about, isn't it? Communicating. I mean, I worry about going for a job. I interview well. But then they want to know did you ever, like, run anything, and what are your, y'know, interests.

Wouldn't it be nice to just sail in and they'd, like, say "You're hired." Not all this stuff they put you through.

That would be too good of a good thing. That'll never happen. No way.

Then they hold, like, seminars before you go. I mean, I'm grateful to the university for all the help, but sometimes I think enough's enough, y'know? I mean, you can do the job or you can't.

Sometimes I think it isn't what you know but who you know, y'know?

Well, here's my stop. Gotta go. It was great seeing you. Only I can't believe the time went so fast.

It's like my boyfriend says. That's what good conversation does. So stay in touch. I'd like to hear from you. Y'know?

Strawberries With Like Cream
▪▪▪
[30 June 1986]

Not long ago, I wrote, more in sorrow than in anger, about conversation as it is currently practiced by large numbers of young Americans. The column was called, for reasons all too obvious, "I Mean, Like, Y'-know." Occasionally, I conceded, some information is communicated, and once in a while—the law of averages may be at work here—opinions are clearly expressed. "Like," "I mean," and "y'know" are, however, the words predominantly employed. Eliminate them and some conversations might shrink by fifty percent.

As one unwilling to go about with earplugs, or with earphones more or less permanently festooning his head, I now find that these habits of American speech are leading to new dishes. Gourmets may not find them different from what has gone before, and they are not listed on menus, but they are being consumed.

There is, for example, veal stuffed with like dried mushrooms. Other new concoctions include minestrone with like Parmesan cheese, steak with like French fried onions, carrots and like peas, and strawberries with like cream. Among drinks, a popular one is whisky with like soda.

"Like," misuse, is becoming as widespread and annoying an affliction as "y'know." In fact, they often go together, so that the above dishes are sometimes rendered as veal stuffed with y'know like dried mushrooms, and strawberries with like y'know cream.

What has brought on the "like" epidemic (or to say the same thing but to put it differently, what has like brought on the like y'know like epidemic) is a mystery. Used in this fashion, a fashion that began in the 1950s and 1960s and has suddenly picked up steam decades later, "like" is flatly wrong. It is being used where "about" should be, or "perhaps" or "maybe" or "roughly" or "approximately" or "at least" or "at most." The fact that it is wrong will not keep it from spreading; if anything, the fact that it is wrong adds to the pleasure of some of those who know better but use it anyway, probably (or like) to show that they are not snobs and elitists but have the common touch.

Whenever something such as the like epidemic comes along, there are those who recommend calm and patience and suffering in silence. It will, they say, pass; these things usually do. Maybe they do, or like maybe they do, but recent evidence is not very heartening. "Y'know" has not passed; it is still with us all the time and everywhere, lengthening conversations, adding to their monotony, relieving people of the plain duty, and the satisfaction, of getting to the point, being specific, and thinking things through. The unnecessary "I mean" is also still with us, not quite as prevalent as "y'know" but often pairing with it in the "I mean, y'know" construction and still standing like tall on its own.

To get back to food, a recent trip to California, where the future often arrives first, revealed a waitress not writing down the orders or committing them to memory, but punching buttons on a hand-held electronic device, which made a record of the orders and, so the waitress said, transmitted them to the restaurant kitchen. Presumably there were buttons, or combinations of buttons, to punch for fried like clams, fettucini with like ricotta and ground walnuts, and smoked trout with like horseradish sauce.

I did say that none of these had as yet turned up in print on menus. Give them time.

Y'know?
III
[12 January 1987]

Last Sunday was a big day for pro football, with the semifinal games, Giants vs. Redskins, Broncos vs. Browns, the winners to meet in the Super Bowl two weeks later. For the English language, it was not so big. The language could have been pardoned for calling some injury time-outs.

The mighty *New York Times* began the day by devoting many pages to pregame dope stories, and made some familiar mistakes. "Redskins Battling Destiny," a headline announced. The lead on the story began "No need to belabor the obvious," and went on from there.

It's true of course. There is no need to belabor the obvious. There isn't even any need to labor the obvious, which means to go on unnecessarily about something, to make heavy going of it. To belabor something is to hit it. As for battling destiny—it was bad enough that the Redskins had to battle the Giants—they couldn't have, for the very good reason that none of us knows, or can know, what our destiny is. Even if we could, battling it would be a waste of time, because destiny is preordained and inevitable, beyond man's control. That is what it means.

With that as curtain-raiser, on to the broadcasts. The first of these, Cleveland against Denver, was a letdown. Dick Enberg and Merlin Olsen of NBC speak good English. There were some errors: Enberg uses "culminate" for "climax"; Olsen says "different than" instead of "different from" and "try and" instead of "try to." On the whole, though, they maintained a high standard, and they did that for more than three hours.

Occasionally, Bob Griese, evidently an "analyst," popped in to offer such analytic insights as "They've got to do something to create the momentum back to themselves," and to unload a few "Y'know"s.

Griese's "Y'know" contribution, however, was as nothing alongside that of John Madden, who joined Pat Summerall on the CBS broadcast of the New York–Washington game. Madden said "Y'-know" fifty-six times, and in case anyone felt cheated, he dropped in three more during the postgame show, where he was backed up by Irv Cross, who in a cameo appearance dropped in four.

Madden also said "I tell ya" or "I tell ya one thing" nineteen times, not counting an occasion when he said "I tell ya, y'know." He emitted numerous "Sees" and a sprinkling of "I mean"'s, some of the latter joined to "Y'know," as in "I mean, y'know." Then there was the misuse of "like" as in "for like seven years"; there was a "could have ran"; and there was "the ball moves good." So many g's were dropped at the end of *ing* words that it seemed Madden must believe that pronouncing a g would cost him his job.

Madden knows football, as indeed he should, thanks to his years as a player and a coach. He is an ebullient character who at times even seems to have a sense of humor. Nobody would want him to lose those qualities. It ought, nevertheless, to be possible for him to keep them while speaking better English. He is, in the jargon of the time, a role model, and he has an obligation to those who listen to him to set a decent standard of grammar. Besides, is there a more boring phrase in the language than "Y'know"?

Another question: Doesn't anyone in authority at the network listen to these broadcasts and feel embarrassed? Or do those in authority think that trying to change things by offering Madden a little instruction would amount to battling their destiny?

The Nucular Age
■■■
[26 May 1987]

Nucular weaponry. That's what a responsible citizen ought to be worrying about these days. Nuclear weapons are troublesome, too, but negotiations to control them are in progress in Geneva, with some hope of success. About nucular weapons—that's pronounced nookyular—there are no negotiations. They are simply being ignored.

This can be dangerous. Suppose there is success in Geneva. The treaty is signed, perhaps with Mikhail Gorbachev coming to the United States for the ceremony. Goodwill is in the air. There is talk of agreement in other areas. Then, in accordance with the treaty, Soviet inspectors go to American bases, just as ours go to theirs, to see whether the designated weapons have been removed or destroyed. They find that they have not. The officers in command explain that the bases hold nucular weapons and always have, and it is the understanding of these officers that nucular weapons are not covered. The President never mentioned them. Neither did Gorbachev. The Soviet inspectors report back to Moscow and the treaty collapses.

All right, enough playfulness. What is it about the word "nuclear"? President Eisenhower couldn't say it. There used to be a secretary of energy—his name has faded from memory—who couldn't say it, which was not much of a recommendation for his job, and a deputy secretary of defense. Walter Mondale couldn't say it. Neither could Jimmy Carter, though he made it not nucular but nukeear. It would be interesting to know whether, at meetings of the Carter cabinet, after the president said nukeear and the vice president nucular, lesser individuals had the nerve to get it right.

The weapons are nucular also to Richard Burt, the United States ambassador to West Germany. And to Les Aspin, current chairman of the House Armed Services Committee. That is a bit disconcerting. Can Aspin grapple with issues raised by nuclear weapons if he cannot pronounce them? How do members of his committee keep their minds on their work if, as some of us do, they wait for, and wince at, each mispronunciation?

Those who make it nucular must hear themselves saying it and must hear others who don't. How do they account for the difference? Do they think the others are wrong, and are they too polite to correct them? Evidently they never look up the word in a dictionary. Maybe the word "muscular" leads them astray, or "circular" or "molecular." Only a fiend would distribute a circular written by a molecular biologist and recommending a muscular nuclear policy.

It is embarrassing to hear Russians and other foreigners snapping off the word as it should be when so many Americans cannot manage it. (General Bernard Rogers, the departing NATO commander in Europe, makes it nookalar.) Perhaps strong measures are needed, along the lines of the punishment imposed by a federal judge in Denver when a couple of lawyers filed a request for a "subpeona." It's subpoena, Judge Sherman Finesilver told them, and if you cannot spell it, don't ask for one.

Apply this approach and anyone who could not say "nuclear" would be barred from having anything to say about such weapons or arms control generally. That would, of course, be straightforward and inexpensive, and therefore out of the question. The temper of the times probably would call for offering those who make it nucular psychiatric counseling, so as to avoid damage to their self-esteem.

If that is the price, so be it. Life in the nucular age is becoming intolerable.

My Friends ...
III
[1 June 1987]

Transcript of an imaginary speech for the Constitutional bicentennial season, by an imaginary politician, with some of the mistakes supplied by an imaginary newspaper:

My friends, this is a time for thinking about our forebearers, and remembering our forebearer's creed that a country can be only as great as the people and ideas from which it is borne. Keeping that in mind as we study and celebrate our Constitution will have a salutory effect on us all.

There is a danger that we will fetishize the Constitution. Hopefully, we will bewear of that. Thankfully, that danger is understood by many among us. Regretfully, it is not understood by all.

What are the problems that now impact us? Let's make a full breast of things. We all know that the events that predominate the news are not always happy ones. This is, however, no reason to raise a ruckess just for ruckess' sake. What we have to do is pick up the pieces as best as possible. Let's not tamper with fire.

First, the economy. Everybody hues and cries when it impacts their pocketbook, and it's true, let's admit it, the United States has had a setback in terms of the totality of its economy. What should be done? Our economy needs reincentivation. Nothing less than a bonified effort to reincentivate it will do.

So much for the economy. Now, what about our youth? We know that crime and violence and drug use run rampart among them. I won't pull any punches. We must face the issue four-squarely and head-on. Let me quote here from somebody who speaks from an indepth of knowledge and who is a font of information on this subject but who writes under a norm de plume I would rather not divulge. What we must do, this learned person said, and after much study, ladies and gentlemen, after much study, what we must do, he said, is reorient the criminogenic attitudes of our youth and precipitate behavior modification among them, so as to restructure the parameters of their lives. I agree entirely. It cannot be said any more plainly than that.

I see some of you shaking your heads. I expected that. Some of our people, good Americans all, believe that old-fashioned punishment is the way. My friends, there is in this corner, no support for these portentious recommendations, no identity with that concept. I say that those who follow that advocacy suffer from peripheal vision. Theirs is a philosophy I do not ascribe to.

What we need, I am convinced, is a fair and plaudible effort that will perculate among our youth and help eleviate their condition. And let us not forget affection. The young need affection. Nothing is sadder than unrequieted love.

And let me just say this: Those of us with the wherewithall should benefact civic and educational causes. If you are one of those eligable under that definition, don't be under any allusions that it can be done without you. Give it your full and unequivocable support.

Well, there we are. For the good of our country, a number of things must confluence together. I am not indulging in fantacies when I say I think they can. There is a potential possibility here that must be turned into reality. And when we do these things, we will find that they are also promotive of peace.

We are not there as of yet, but let it be said that Americans in 1987 passed a mild stone in our history. I will do my part with every fibre of my energy. I hope that you will, too.

Thank you very much.

Us, the People
III
[22 June 1987]

The bicentennial of the Constitution of the United States is a happy time. We have much to celebrate. The Constitution, faults and all, is a miracle.

May one, then, be pardoned for hoping that the celebration itself will bring forth an additional blessing? It would be a fairly modest blessing, taking the form of an end to such sales pitches as (Was this the first of them?) "Us Tareyton smokers would rather fight than switch" and, more recently, "Us Palmolive suds don't know the meaning of the word quit." (They don't know the meaning of the word "grammar," either.) In other words, no more commercials with "us" where "we" should be.

How might this deliverance come upon us? What has this to do with the bicentennial? In the preamble to the Constitution, "Us, the people of the United States" do not set out to "form a more perfect union, establish justice, insure domestic tranquility," and all the rest. "We, the people of the United States" do. The phrase is being heard over and over again. Maybe the "we" part of it will sink in.

This may sound insanely optimistic. No more "Even us big shots like Budget Rent-A-Car's low prices"? No more "Us bullshavers have become Bic shavers"? Never again "Us guys at Miller Lite"? Wouldn't these companies risk immediate bankruptcy if, instead of being friendly, lovable, and down-to-earth by misusing "us" they went standoffish and grammatical by correctly saying "we"?

No, bankruptcy would not set in. The Constitution has lasted two centuries with "we" where "we" should be. So has the nation. The advertising geniuses so devoted to us (and to "You did good" rather than "You did well," and who consider "Like I said" a compulsory replacement for "As I said") might take that as evidence.

There is in advertising—this should have been seen coming—a process known as charismatizing the product, and apparently a product is considered well on the way to charismatization when, as in the case of Zest soap, it is said to lather up "pretty good," or when "ain't" can be worked into the slogan, as in Dr. Scholl's "Ain't nothing going to get me down." In the same way, using "don't" where "doesn't" is called for is evidently thought to be worth millions on the bottom line. So is dropping the letter *g*, so that any company would want to make good things for livin' rather than for living, and it would be considered commercially suicidal to sell flour for high-rising rather than high-risin' cake. Maybe a study has revealed that people who pronounce their *g*'s don't have much disposable income, or if they do, don't dispose of it.

It would also be considered foolhardy to begin an automobile commercial with "My buddies and I" instead of "Me and my buddies." "I" has plainly been identified as depressing to spirits and sales. Jordache had a young woman say that she hated her mother. Why? "She's so much prettier than me." *Fortune* magazine—that's right, *Fortune* magazine—followed the same path: "He was my friend and successor. Until he decided he was smarter than me." Maybe he was. At any rate, maybe he spoke better English.

Which brings us back to the founding fathers. The Constitution is a model of good English, clear, direct, and economical. James Madison, Alexander Hamilton, Gouverneur Morris, and the others who fathered it at Philadelphia two hundred summers ago did not think it necessary to spatter it with mistakes so as to appeal to, and insult, the common man.

We, the people of the United States, have many reasons to be grateful to them. In case any advertising agencies are listening, let's repeat that: We, the people.

Gettin' Rich by Droppin' the *G*
[6 November 1987]

It has been estimated, by people who spend their time estimating this sort of thing, that American boys and girls, on reaching the age of eighteen, have seen, on the average, 350,000 television commercials. Whatever the number may be—and the feeling sometimes takes hold that we see that many in a day—too many are ungrammatical, usually deliberately so. When a national effort is under way to raise standards of education, the country is not helped by the glorification of semiliteracy.

It is, for example, an article of faith among some advertisers that dropping the *g* on words ending in *ing* is the sure path to riches. Where *g*'s are not dropped, profit-making is often thought to rest on double negatives, on the use of "ain't," on never saying "I" where "me" can be worked in. In the same way, "as" rather than "like," and "well" rather than "good," are thought to lead in no time at all to the bankruptcy courts.

Over the years, with the same devotion to duty that once led me to listen to John Madden for an entire NFL playoff game to count his "Y'know"'s (fifty-six), I have made a list of some of the more offensive misuses of English in advertising on the air and in print. The misuses are not interesting, just obvious, and childish. A tiny sample:

"Ain't nothing like the real thing," proclaims a hamburger chain. "Me and my buddies," says a retired football player as he begins an automobile commercial. ("My buddies and I" would be considered by advertisers and their agencies to be fatally "elitist.") "Works in as quick as twenty-two minutes," says a product that eases stomach upset.

"Get major credit cards easy," so we are urged. "That works good," says a mouthwash. "You won't believe how great it holds your dentures," says something that holds dentures great. "There ain't nothing like it nowhere," says a car dealer. "I don't have to give up taste or freshness, or nothin'," simpers a model for a breath deodorant. Another model explains why she chooses a particular brand of underwear: "Makes me look like I'm not wearin' nothin'."

"It looks as good as it performs," boasts a motorcycle. "Tastes as good as it works," says a mouthwash that works good. "Frank, me, and the kids want a reliable laxative," declares a housewife.

Is it believable that "Ain't no" will sell more hamburgers than "There is no"? Or that a shampoo will earn higher profits because it claims to be for "bouncin' and behavin' hair," or an appliance manufacturer because it makes "good things for livin'"? And even if they will, which seems doubtful, should these companies be promoting sloppiness and semiliteracy?

There is, moreover, no need for intentional mistakes. There are enough of the other kind. A hotel claimed to be "among the two or three very best hotels in the country between either coast." Given the choice, which coast would you rather be between? In that hotel, it might have been appropriate to use the toothpaste that "cleans beautifully in between each tooth." Unless you preferred the one that "gives like a shine" to your teeth.

A brokerage house promises to build up clients' investments: "Nobody can help you do that better than us." Here is a message from a computer manufacturer: "If the following pages can't convince you what to do with a home computer, maybe you belong in another age." Convince you what to do. Who writes this stuff? Who passes it?

My favorite? It's grammatical but otherwise irresistible: "I never buy any product out on the market that wouldn't shrink hemorrhoidal tissues." What does he eat?

So Goes London
[23 November 1984]

It is widely thought in the United States that the English language, though in evident decline in this country, is in sound condition in Britain. The British, the fond belief has it, have a proper respect for English; they will keep it sound and whole.

This is, a couple of recent visits to London convinced me, wrong, grossly wrong. One of Britain's premier newspapers, *The Daily Telegraph,* reported of a New York literary agent that her efforts to sell the reminiscences of a former maid in the Royal Household had been "successfully foiled." That kind of foiling is generally preferred to the unsuccessful kind. In an obituary of Hans Leip, composer of "Lili Marlene," the *Telegraph* had this: "Standing guard one night under a lamppost, the first three verses came to the author." Maybe the verses were looking for a way out of guard duty.

Participles dangle with some frequency in Britain. "Being June," the BBC's breakfast television show noted, "a million people are on holiday." "Being prime minister," the BBC said about a possible call by Margaret Thatcher on the Queen, "no visit was necessary."

The BBC used to be a stronghold of good English. Now its

correspondents and announcers refer to "these sort of difficulties," and speak of someone who was "looking back in a questionable way." ("Questioning" was intended.) My favorite was the "overcast skies that promised but thankfully did not deliver rain." Overcast skies in a thankful mood after breaking their own promise would be something to see.

Independent Television News is no better. "His mother, as weak as him . . ." ITN said in a report on hunger in Ethiopia. "What is the haggling likely to comprise of?" an ITN correspondent asked another. A third ITN man described a defendant's expression "as each of the charges were read out." Other ITN people misused "refute," said "providing" where "provided" was required, had purse strings snapping shut, and managed to mispronounce such well-known names as Placido Domingo and the Bekaa in Bekaa Valley. One ITN newsreader told us about a self-confessed idler, only to be outdone by the *Telegraph*, which came up with self-confessed fools and a self-confessed art faker. All of these, one supposes, offered their confessions in the absence of someone else to do it for them.

Some of the mistakes make an American feel at home. The *Times* of London, giving the plot of a television drama, explained that a young man had been "pressurized into joining the National Front." The *Evening Standard* had Joan Crawford playing a "flaper" in the movie *Dancing Daughters*. Flapers, it will be recalled, were common in the 1920s. By the time the thirties rolled around, flaping had ceased to be a fad, or even fadish.

The apostrophe is as mysterious to the British as it is to Americans. When Arthur Scargill was on the screen, ITN's *News at Ten* supered "Miner's President." Scargill evidently was president of one miner, although he had 120,000 of them on strike at the time. An advertisement for the movie *Bronx Warriors* proclaimed: "The lucky one's were the first to die." Equally mysterious is the convention that plural verbs go with plural nouns: "Among the huge crowd at the University of Southern California's swimming pool," one read at the time of the Olympics, "was Sarah's parents and grandparents." There was also this: "One of the twenty-four in hospital were serious."

Perhaps the explanation is that the British want to sound like Americans. During the last general election, a BBC newsman told his audience why a particular constituency was being so closely examined. "The way Peoria goes," he said, "so goes the election, as they say in America."

Not quite. We put it differently: "As Peoria goes, so goes London."

Usaw and Sogat
⚏
[11 March 1985]

"Baswa, anyone? Nupe? Cohse?"

"No, thanks. I'd prefer Acas."

Or try it this way:

"So, Usdaw, you thought it would go on forever, did you? Well, it won't. It's over. That goes for you, too, Sogat. And you, Aut. There does come a time."

The above are imaginary but by no means unimaginable exchanges that, if they did take place, would take place in Britain. The British have become increasingly initial- and acronym-happy. Listening to a newscast, visitors need a translator. The names sound like those of robots in space movies. How can you know that BASWA stands for British Association of Social Workers, that NUPE is the National Union of Public Employees, COHSE the Confederation of Health Service Employees? ACAS is the Arbitration, Conciliation, and Advisory Service, which may be called in when BASWA is being intransigent, or COHSE is, or perhaps, on the other side of industry, SSEB is (that's the South of Scotland Electricity Board). Or BNOC, as in:

"Bnoc, bnoc."

"Who's there?"

"The British National Oil Corporation."

Some of the creations have a certain charm. USDAW is the Union of Shop, Distributive, and Allied Workers. SOGAT is the Society of Graphical and Allied Trades. AUT is the Association of University Teachers. There is also NEDO, the National Economic Development Organization, known inevitably as Neddy. And there is the National Union of Teachers, which, when it is being militant, gives rise to such headlines as NUT STRIKE ACTION.

Not all fall trippingly from the lips, or would if actually spoken aloud: DHSS, for the Department of Health and Social Services; CEGB, the Central Electricity Generating Board; and FLCBE, the Federation of London Clearing Bank Employers. Also ASTMS, the Association of Scientific, Technical, and Management Staffs. A special case is the NGA, National Graphical Union, which so often interrupts production of newspapers, one in particular, that it is known to some as No

Guardian Again. This condition may not be pleasing to the National Union of Journalists, NUJ, not pronounced Nudge.

Life today would be impossible without initials and acronyms, because it is so highly organized. If we used full names, we would not have time for anything else. The British case of initialitis is unusually severe, because their great population density makes organization harder to avoid, because of a tendency to formality, and because for them, life without membership in a pressure group seems to be unthinkable.

One result is great acronymic variety—BIFU, EETPU, QUANGO, ASLEF, NACODS, NAHT, AMMA, NACAB. It doesn't matter, but these stand for Banking, Insurance, and Finance Union; Electrical, Electronic, Telecommunications, and Plumbing Union; Quasi Autonomous National Government Organization; Association of Locomotive Engineers and Firemen; National Association—you don't have to believe this—of Colliery, Overmen, Deputies, and Shotfirers; National Association of Head Teachers; Assistant Masters and Mistresses Association; National Association of Citizens Advice Bureaus.

There are also GLEB and NATSOPA. The former is the Greater Something or Other Enterprise Board, and the latter is the National Society of Some Kind of Operatives. I believe they print.

In any case, it is time to stop. Or STOPP. That's the Society of Teachers Opposed to Physical Punishment.

Hopefully Fresh While Referbishing
[8 July 1985]

"You say you've just come back from London? I'm sure you heard good English there. They don't ruin the language the way we do. I just love to listen to the English. They use the language so well."

Do they, indeed? Where do you suppose this was said:

"England, still striving every nerve . . ."

And this:

"Everton are still hoping to revenge their defeat."

And this:

"Passengers misfortunate enough to take the train . . ."

And this:

"A phenomena."

The answer is on the BBC, the venerable Beeb, which also, in a report from New York, supered "Vetinary surgeon," and during the Beirut hostage affair had Americans breathing not merely fire but fire and brimstone. Last summer, when the Beeb covered the renomination of President Reagan and Vice President Bush, one of its newsreaders referred to "the annual Republican convention." It only feels that way.

Maybe the BBC makes that sort of mistake to fight off its competitor, Independent Television News, which supered: "Katherine Ortega, U.S. Treasury Secretary." Ms. Ortega is the Treasurer of the United States. Not quite the same thing. But back to English. During the miners' strike, which it insisted on supering as "Miner's Dispute," ITN brought forth the comment, about attempts to end the strike, that "Neither look enormously promising." True enough, neither were the answer. When three miners who had been working were talked into quitting, ITN put it this way: "Three miners were persuaded off the coach."

Then there are fate and destiny. An ITN commentator said, "The Syrians have become the arbiters of Lebanon's fate." If it is fate, nobody can be its arbiter. The Beeb tried a compromise: "His destiny," said one of its sports broadcasters, "is in the lap of the gods as well as himself."

The notion has to be laid to rest that the language is in good hands in England. It isn't, and the ailment is becoming as widespread there as it is here. "See how one (sweater) shrunk," said a television commercial for Dreft. "A further selection of umbrellas are available on the lower floor," proclaimed Simpson's of Piccadilly. "Additional discount available during period of referbishment," a men's store in Knightsbridge announced. "It would be nice to know that me and my loved ones are covered," said a commercial for Standard Assurance. "Rose's at various prices" were offered by a florist, and another shop was selling cast iron barberque grills.

Some of what you hear makes you wonder why you ever left home. The *Daily Telegraph* described someone as "a self-professed homosexual.'' Evidently the man couldn't get anyone else to profess for him. ''We have the picture back, thankfully, and the horses come out hopefully fresh,'' said a BBC commentator on show jumping. As it thankfully turned out, some of the horses were hopefully fresh and some were hopefully tired.

Here and there, originality creeps in. The deputy head of the National Teachers Union said that, if certain things had come to pass, ''I predict there would have been a strike.'' A risky business, predicting the past. For the most part, though, it is imitation American English one hears: no way, way out, meet up with, address the issues, ongoing, lost out, guidelines, track record, ground rules, get our act together, are you into this, cop-out, funding, commitment, spell out, interface, clout, input, scenario, confrontational approach, laid back, point in time.

We cannot depend on the British, folks. We are going to have to save the language ourselves.

Index